Teacher's Annotated Edition

Grade **3**

Scott Foresman

The Grammar & Writing Book

ISBN: 0–328–20486–2

2 3 4 5 6 7 8 9 10 V000 12 11 10 09 08 07 06

PEARSON

Scott
Foresman

Editorial Offices: Glenview, Illinois • Parsippany, New Jersey • New York, New York
Sales Offices: Boston, Massachusetts • Duluth, Georgia • Glenview, Illinois
Coppell, Texas • Sacramento, California • Mesa, Arizona

Table of Contents

Overview

The Grammar and Writing Book is designed to support and enhance the grammar and writing strand in *Reading Street*. The book includes weekly grammar and writing lessons, a Writer's Guide, writing-for-tests lessons, and a Grammar Patrol handbook.

Writer's Guide

- The Writer's Guide gives students strategies and models for effective writing.

- There is a lesson for each of the following writing traits: Focus/Ideas, Organization/Paragraphs, Voice, Word Choice, Sentences, and Conventions.

- Each lesson has leveled exercises to reinforce the skill.

- There are rubrics for each of the four major modes of writing: Narrative, Descriptive, Persuasive, and Expository.

- 4-, 3-, 2-, and 1-point models for each mode are provided with customized rubrics.

Weekly Grammar and Writing Lessons

PAGE 1	PAGE 2	PAGE 3	PAGE 4	PAGE 5	PAGE 6
Grammar Instruction and Leveled Exercise A	**Grammar** Leveled Exercises B and C	**Grammar** Test Preparation	**Grammar** Review	**Writer's Craft**	**Writing Model**

- Thirty 6-page lessons correspond to the grammar and writing lessons in the Teacher's Edition of *Reading Street*.

- Leveled exercises reflect the topics and themes in the corresponding reading lessons.

- Review and assessment are provided in the standardized test format.

- The writing pages provide support for the end-of-unit process writing lesson in the Teacher's Edition of *Reading Street*. Leveled exercises culminate in a brief writing assignment that relates to the end-of-unit product. For Grade 3, the writing products are as follows:

Unit 1—Personal Narrative
Unit 2—How-to Report
Unit 3—Compare and Contrast Essay
Unit 4—Story
Unit 5—Persuasive Letter
Unit 6—Research Report

Writing for Tests

- Lessons teach test-taking strategies for developing skills such as understanding a prompt, finding a topic, organizing ideas, developing and elaborating ideas, and writing a strong beginning and ending.

- Lessons support the end-of-unit process writing lessons in the Teacher's Edition of *Reading Street*.

- Five prompts duplicate the prompts in the end-of-unit process writing lesson.

- A student model illustrates an exemplary piece of writing.

- Following the model is an explanation of why it merits a top score.

Grammar Patrol

- This handbook includes sections on grammar, capitalization, punctuation, spelling, and handwriting.

Instructional Planner

	Day 1	Day 2
2-3 minutes **Daily Fix-Its**	Use the Daily Fix-Its on pp. TR1–TR10 or the Daily Fix-It Transparencies.	Use the Daily Fix-Its on pp. TR1–TR10 or the Daily Fix-It Transparencies.
15-20 minutes **Grammar and Writing**	Introduce the Grammar Skill. • Guided Practice • Leveled, Independent Practice	Test Preparation • Grammar Practice • Standardized Test Format

The Grammar and Writing Book and *The Grammar and Writing Book Teacher's Annotated Edition* provide many other resources for language arts instruction.

Additional Grammar Practice
Extra Practice for Differentiated Instruction, pp. TR11–TR16

Day 3	Day 4	Day 5
Use the Daily Fix-Its on pp. TR1–TR10 or the Daily Fix-It Transparencies.	Use the Daily Fix-Its on pp. TR1–TR10 or the Daily Fix-It Transparencies.	Use the Daily Fix-Its on pp. TR1–TR10 or the Daily Fix-It Transparencies.
Review the Grammar Skill.	Writer's Craft Lesson • Improve Writing Skills	Examine a Writing Model. • Key features of different types of writing

Additional Writing Resources in the Student Book
- Writing Traits in the Writer's Guide, pp. 2–25
- Rubrics and Models for Narrative, Descriptive, Persuasive, and Expository Writing, pp. 26–45
- Evaluate Your Writing, pp. 46–48
- Writing for Tests, pp. 231–243

Additional Writing Resources in the Teacher's Annotated Edition
- Writing Traits and Writing Features, pp. ix–x
- Strategies and Activities, pp. TR17–TR19
- Prompts for Each Writing Mode, pp. TR20–TR21
- Alternative Rubrics, pp. TR22–TR25
- Self-Evaluation Guides, pp. TR26–TR27

Writing Traits

Traits

- Focus/Ideas
- Organization/ Paragraphs
- Voice
- Word Choice
- Sentences
- Conventions

- **Focus/Ideas** refers to the main purpose for writing and the details that make the subject clear and interesting. It includes development of ideas through support and elaboration.

- **Organization/Paragraphs** refers to the overall structure that guides readers through a piece of writing. Within that structure, transitions show how ideas, sentences, and paragraphs are connected.

- **Voice** shows the writer's unique personality and establishes a connection between writer and reader. Voice, which contributes to style, should be suited to the audience and the purpose for writing.

- **Word Choice** is the use of precise, vivid words to communicate effectively and naturally. It helps create style through the use of specific nouns, lively verbs and adjectives, and accurate, well-placed modifiers.

- **Sentences** covers strong, well-built sentences that vary in length and type. Skillfully written sentences have pleasing rhythms and flow fluently.

- **Conventions** refers to mechanical correctness and includes grammar, usage, spelling, punctuation, capitalization, and paragraphing.

Writing Features

The features below combine to make a writing task successful. The diagram to the left shows how 6-trait writing used in *Scott Foresman Reading Street* correlates to these features.

Traits

Focus/Ideas

Organization/ Paragraphs

Voice

Word Choice

Sentences

Conventions

Focus is the topic/subject of a piece of writing in response to a prompt. It is determined by the purpose, audience, and context of a written work. Writers must establish a focus that responds to each writing task. The topic/subject should be clear, although it need not be stated explicitly.

Organization/Paragraphs is the movement and relatedness of ideas. In a well-organized composition, ideas are complete and developed. There is a consistency of purpose shown in features that contribute toward a beginning, middle, and end. The progression of ideas is clear and smooth, often with connectors that show relationships. There are no gaps that leave readers confused.

Support and Elaboration is the use of specific details that develop the topic/subject and make it clear to readers. Key concepts are related ideas and sufficient supporting details. This means that supporting details must be related to the subject matter and sufficiently developed to present it fully. Effective elaboration excludes details that are off the topic, vague, underdeveloped, or repetitive.

Style is the effective use of language as seen through word choice and sentence fluency. Such language is compatible with the purpose, audience, and context of the writing task. Precise words, along with their arrangement and sound, contribute to an effective style. A variety of sentence types and lengths adds interest and rhythms to writing and helps convey ideas.

Conventions covers correct grammar, usage, mechanics, and sentence formation. Good writers show reasonable control over specific areas such as agreement, tense, case, capitalization, punctuation, and spelling, and write in complete sentences.

Writer's Guide

Focus/Ideas

Students sometimes choose a topic that is too large. (*Endangered animals, My dog Tippy, What I did over spring vacation*) Another pitfall is choosing a topic that doesn't "go anywhere." Occasionally we have a workshop on refining topics. We focus on things such as determining an audience, writing good openers, and developing an attitude toward a subject. We practice narrowing a topic:

> *Natural Resources > Conservation > Saving Water*

Once students feel comfortable with their subjects, they tend to write with more assurance.

Focus/Ideas

Good writers **focus** on a **main idea** and develop this idea with strong, supporting details. In addition, they know their purpose for writing. This purpose may be to persuade, to inform, to describe, or just to entertain. Your purpose is important because it helps you focus your main idea.

A note to a friend could have this main idea and purpose:

Main Idea Convince a friend to see your new kitten

Purpose To persuade your friend

Details give information about your main idea. Lively and interesting words make word pictures for your reader. Be sure to use only details that focus on your main idea.

- Come to see me. My kitten is fun. (no details or focus)
- Come to see my new fluffy kitten. She loves to purr and leap. (has main idea, focus, and details)

Strategies for Focus and Ideas

- Choose a topic you know well or would like to learn about. Then decide on a main idea about that topic.
- Think about your purpose for writing. An adventure story would entertain. A how-to report would inform readers.
- Look at each sentence. If it does not clearly focus on your main idea, drop it or revise it.

A Match the number of each sentence with the purpose that it fits best.

    A Describe   **B** Persuade   **C** Entertain   **D** Inform

C **1.** My dog Sandy did something funny yesterday.

B **2.** Everyone should help clean up the park on Sunday.

D **3.** The rainforest has more kinds of trees than any forest.

A **4.** The shell was pearly white with ruffled edges.

B Some sentences below do not focus on the topic of the rodeo. Write the letters of those sentences. C, F

    A Two white horses danced across the ring.

    B A cowboy showed how to use a lariat.

    C Once I saw a white horse in a wheat field.

    D A rider held on tight as a wild horse bucked.

    E Cowboy clowns pretended to be afraid of a pony.

    F My grandfather used to ride horses in Wyoming.

C Choose one of the main idea sentences below. Then write three sentences about the topic. Remember to use details that focus on the main idea.

- I love playing outdoors in winter.
- Cats (or dogs or hamsters) make the best pets.
- Here are three things you can do to stay healthy.

Possible answer on page TR33

Improving Focus/Ideas

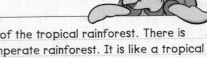

Original

> Everyone has heard of the tropical rainforest. There is another kind. It is a temperate rainforest. It is like a tropical rainforest with plant life and rain, but the weather is cool.
>
> Temperate rainforests are in Oregon and Washington. Seattle is the biggest city in Washington. Unlike the climate in the tropics, it does not rain all year in this area. The summer is dry and cool, but fog comes in with moisture.
>
> Huge trees grow in the temperate rainforest. Some are evergreens. These trees grow where I live too. Rain and fog help the trees.
>
> Everyone should visit the temperate rainforest.

Revising Tips

Use a strong, focused main idea statement. (Revise first paragraph to lead to this main idea sentence: Temperate rainforests have their own locations, climates, and plants.)

Use only details that focus on your main idea. (Take out *Seattle is the biggest city in Washington.*)

Use interesting words to create lively details. *(exotic birds and plants, fog rolls in, towering redwood)*

Be specific. (Tell what kind of evergreens in the third paragraph.)

Keep your purpose in mind. (Change the last sentence to reflect the informative nature of this essay.)

Improved

When you hear the word rainforest, do you think of warm temperatures and exotic birds and plants? The temperate rainforest is quite different from this. Temperate rainforests have their own locations, climates, and plants.

Temperate rainforests are found near the Pacific coast in Oregon and Washington. Unlike in tropical rainforests, it does not rain all year in this area. There is a long rainy season, but summer is dry and cool. Fog rolls in then, and brings moisture from the ocean.

Some of the hugest trees in the world grow in the temperate rainforest. These include evergreens such as the Sitka spruce and the towering redwood. Frequent rain or fog gives the rainforest trees the moisture they need to grow.

The temperate rainforest is a wet, green, beautiful corner of the world.

Writer's Corner

Use your main idea sentence like a camera lens to focus your paper. If any detail does not make the main idea clearer, remove it.

TEACHER TALK

Organization

I often use graphic organizers to keep students on track, especially when doing research projects. I create my own graphic organizers using software programs. They're flexible and easy to use. I also remind students that if they don't have an actual graphic organizer handy, they can generate their own basic organizers. For example, they can make a t-chart or two-column lists to arrange ideas for a compare/contrast essay. They can draw a web for a descriptive piece with the topic at the center and list details on lines that radiate from the topic. For a story, they can generate their own beginning-middle-end boxes and additional lines for characters, setting, and plot.

A careful writer tells about events and details in order. Your **organization** builds a frame to hold your writing. The frame keeps your ideas in place.

Here are some ways to organize your writing.

- a story with a beginning, middle, and end
- a comparison-contrast
- a description from top to bottom
- a how-to explanation

Before you write your first word, think about how you will build your writing. For example, if you want to tell what happened at a school meeting, you would write a report. If you want to explain how to ride a scooter, you would write a how-to explanation.

Once you decide on your frame, choose the details you want to include. You will also have to think about how to arrange your details from beginning to end.

Strategies for Organizing Ideas

- Use a chart, story map, or web to plan out your ideas.
- Begin with the most important detail or save it for last.
- Tell events in the order they happened.
- Use order words such as *first, later,* and *last.*
- Put details that are alike in the same paragraph.

A Write the letter of the kind of organization that works best for each topic.

C **1.** How soccer and football are alike and different

B **2.** Instructions for making a kite

D **3.** The treehouse in my backyard

A **4.** A mysterious event in the school library

A Story
B How-to explanation
C Comparison-contrast
D Description

B The following details are from a paragraph that tells how to set a table. Write sentences in the correct order.

2 **A** Second, put a plate at each place.

4 **B** Then put a fork next to each napkin.

1 **C** Begin by putting placemats or a tablecloth on the table.

5 **D** Finally, put a knife and spoon to the right of the plate.

3 **E** Third, fold a napkin and put it to the left of each plate.

C Tell about a family outing or school field trip that you enjoyed. Use order words such as *first, then,* and *next* to organize the details.

Possible answer on page TR33

Writer's Guide **7**

Improving Organization/Paragraphs

Original

My family went to Grand Beach. We packed some food to take in a cooler. The adults relaxed on lounge chairs and read books. The kids built sandcastles. We used plastic buckets to find sea animals in the shallow water. Before that, though, we found a good place to put our blanket, umbrella, and chairs. Everyone took a long walk on the beach. At lunchtime we had a picnic under the umbrella. Mom joined us swimming. My parents, brother, aunt, uncle, and cousin all squeezed into the van. The sun started to go down, and we packed up everything and left.

Revising Tips

Give important facts at the beginning.   (The second-to-the-last sentence tells who went to the beach and sets the day in motion. It should be put close to the beginning.)

Use an order that makes sense. Tell events in the order they happen.   (Move up information in the sixth sentence.)

Use order words to help your reader understand what happened.   (Add words and phrases such as *then, next,* and *after a short rest.*)

Start a new paragraph when the topic shifts.   (Put the afternoon events in a second paragraph.)

Write a conclusion to tie details together.   (*We were tired but happy after a long day at the beach* sums up the day.)

Improved

Last summer my family went to Grand Beach. My parents, brother, aunt, uncle, and cousin all squeezed into the van. We packed sandwiches, fruit, and juice in a cooler. When we arrived, we found a good place to put our blanket, umbrella, and chairs. Next, everyone took a long walk on the beach. Then the adults relaxed on lounge chairs and read books while the kids built sandcastles. We also used plastic buckets to find sea animals in the shallow water.

At lunchtime we had a picnic under the umbrella. After a short rest, Mom joined us swimming. When the sun started to go down, we packed up everything and left. We were tired but happy after a long day at the beach.

Writer's Corner

Although you won't actually say "the end" after your last written word, readers should know you have finished. A good conclusion (whether it's a question for readers, a summarizing sentence, or an echo of the beginning) makes your writing complete.

TEACHER TALK

Voice

The most important way to get voice into your writing is to write about something you know. All authors draw on their own experiences when writing. I model for students. I tell them that I would like to write a story about a pet. It could be a cat or a dog. I start to write the cat story, but I don't have very much to say because I have never had a cat. Then I write the dog story. Having had a dog as a pet, I have many interesting stories to tell. I can tell how that dog looks and what it does. Now I ask students to think of something they know about and then we do Think, Pair, Share. They tell the person sitting next to them about their topic. Then we share ideas with the whole group. Now students are excited to begin writing their stories with voice.

Your writing shows your special style and personality. Use your writer's **voice** to shape your writing. A writer's voice may be funny or serious. It could be friendly or formal. When your writing voice is strong and clear, readers believe what you have to say.

- I was so tired that I got into bed early. (weak voice)
- I was so worn out that I crawled into bed an hour before dinnertime. I didn't wake up until Dad shouted that breakfast was ready. (strong voice)

Strategies for Developing a Writer's Voice

- Think about your readers and about your reason for writing. Use a light, friendly voice when you write a letter to a cousin or when you tell a funny story. Use a more serious voice for a book report or for directions.
- Your choice of words should match your voice. In informal writing, you might use contractions or slang to make your writing sound like your everyday voice. A letter to the editor of your school newspaper would have a more serious voice.
- Use your writer's voice to speak directly to your audience. If your voice is strong, readers will want to keep on reading.
- Different types of sentences add to voice. Engage readers by asking a question or giving a command.

A Match each opening sentence with the letter of the reader it fits best.

    A Your cousin Jenny in Hawaii
    B The editor of a town newspaper
    C Your teacher and classmates
    D Kids in your neighborhood

B **1.** I believe that everyone in town should support the clean-up project organized by our school.

D **2.** Let's plan the greatest block party ever!

A **3.** You won't believe what happened here last weekend!

C **4.** Marsupials are a fascinating group of animals.

B Match each kind of voice with the writing it would fit best.

  A funny   **B** persuasive   **C** serious   **D** friendly

D **5.** an invitation asking students to attend the class play

B **6.** a letter trying to convince people to come to a school bake sale

C **7.** an article about a recent hurricane

A **8.** a story about a talking cow

C Choose one of the following opening sentences. Add sentences to write a paragraph about the topic. Use a voice that fits your main idea and audience.
Possible answer on page TR33

- If your brothers and sisters drive you nuts, here are some tips for getting along with them.
- You're never too young to help people in your community.

Improving Voice

Original

Dear Editor,

 Our school district said we might not get to take music classes during the school day from now on. This isn't fair! I love singing and learning to play an instrument. Besides, Toby, Alex, and I have a really cool time writing our own songs and singing them together. I guess we would be able to take music on our own after school. But this wouldn't be the same. Everyone wouldn't get to take extra classes, and I would miss my friends. I might also have to stop playing soccer to take music. Don't be so unfair! Don't take our music away from us!

Revising Tips

Keep your audience and purpose in mind. (Readers of letters to the editor do not know you, Toby, or Alex. Use examples that appeal to a wider audience, such as *Many students have other after-school activities*.)

Use appropriate words. (Replace words such as *cool* and contractions such as *wouldn't*. Appropriate modifiers such as *happy* and *well-rounded* strengthen your argument.)

Choose a strong but pleasant voice. (*This isn't fair* makes you sound negative instead of responsible and logical.)

Improved

Dear Editor,

   Our school district said we might not get to take music classes during the school day from now on. This would be a shame. Right now all students can sing and learn to play an instrument in our school's music classes. Music is very different from math and spelling, but it is just as important. In our music classes, students learn new skills and get to be creative. Also, we really enjoy ourselves. It is fun to sing and play music together.

   If music classes are canceled, students would be able to sign up for special music classes after school. Yet everyone would not be able to take extra classes. Many students have other after-school activities such as sports that would conflict with music classes. Learning music makes us happy and well-rounded. Parents and children should try to save music in our schools.

Writer's Corner

Is the voice in your writing the real you? Is it a person people will trust and enjoy listening to? Try reading your work aloud to answer these questions.

Writer's Guide   **13**

Word Choice

The words *things* and *stuff* are outlawed in my class, both orally and during writing time. I want students to have more specificity in their conversation and in their writing. We brainstorm alternative words as a class, or a student and I will conference during writing time to choose a more specific word. For example, instead of *She wants a palace, jewelry, and other things*, the student is encouraged to itemize one or two additional examples. (*servants, elegant clothes, a throne*)

During a lesson about using dialogue, I discourage (but don't outlaw) the use of *said*. We generate many alternatives that would be appropriate for a specific situation and thus create a clearer mood. For example, if a mouse ran across the room, the writer might state, *I shrieked (yelled or screamed) bloody murder, "There's a mouse in our classroom!"*

Word Choice

Words are the writer's handiest tool. Elaborate on your ideas with exact nouns, strong verbs, and vivid adjectives. Your style will be interesting and lively.

- I like the bakery because it smells good. (dull and plain)
- The bakery smells like sweet cinnamon rolls and fresh, crusty bread. (lively and detailed)

Strategies for Choosing the Right Words

- Choose exact nouns. (*spaniel* instead of dog, *broccoli* instead of *vegetable*)
- Use strong verbs. (*shatter* instead of *break*, *shriek* instead of *yell*)
- Replace dull words such as *nice, bad,* and *thing* with clear words. ("The owner was greedy and cruel" instead of "The owner was bad.")
- Include words that use our senses. ("The sun was as warm as a blanket" instead of "The sun was warm.")
- Don't be wordy. (*happily* instead of "with great happiness")
- Elaborate with specific details. ("Dan slurped up soup and ate crackers" instead of "Dan was a noisy eater.")

A Replace the underlined words with more exact words from the box. Write the paragraph.

climbs 2   shrubs and wildflowers 5
observes 4   brisk 1   wanders 3

(1) Each weekend Luis takes a <u>nice</u> hike. (2) He <u>walks</u> up steep hills. (3) The path <u>goes</u> through the forest. (4) He often <u>sees</u> amazing birds and animals. (5) The <u>plants</u> always surprise him.

B Change each underlined word to a more vivid word of your own. Write the sentences.
Possible answers:

6. Luis and Jackie rode horses through a green <u>place</u>. meadow, valley

7. The horses had <u>nice</u> coats. glossy, shiny

8. They came to a fence that was <u>big</u>. enormous, towering

9. Luis's horse <u>went</u> over the fence. leaped, vaulted

10. Jackie's horse stood on the <u>ground</u>. mud, grass

11. Jackie <u>talked</u> to the horse. murmured, whispered

12. The horse seemed <u>upset</u>. nervous, fearful

C Write a description of a certain kind or quality of weather, such as a snowstorm, thunderstorm, wind, or bright sunshine. Use exact nouns, strong verbs, and vivid adjectives.

Possible answer: The winter wind howls around the house. It makes a sound like a freight train as it whips through the trees. Its frosty breath stings my eyes and scrapes my cheeks.

Writer's Guide **15**

Improving Word Choice

Original

Our city has many hills. These hills are of many sizes because some are big and some are not so big. From the top of them you can see the bridge that goes across the river. You can see all the city's big buildings. Cars go slowly up the hills and then go down. Other vehicles have a hard time getting up the hills. People also have a hard time as they walk up the hills. They have to work hard as they go down the hills too, or they would go too fast. Our city's hills are hard to climb.

Revising Tips

Replace vague nouns with precise ones. (Replace *big buildings* with *skyscrapers*. Replace *other vehicles* with *buses and trucks*.)

Replace weak verbs with strong ones. (Use *creep* and *struggle* instead of *go*. Use *trudge* and *shuffle* instead of *walk*.)

Elaborate with words that help readers see, hear, taste, smell, and feel what you are describing. (*glass and concrete skyscrapers, people huff and puff, plunge*)

Replace dull adjectives with vivid ones. (Use *sky-high* instead of *big*, *challenging* instead of *hard*.)

Avoid wordiness. Rewrite sentences that contain unnecessary words. (Shorten and refocus the second sentence.)

Improved

Our city has many hills. Some seem sky-high, while others rise gently above the streets and avenues. From the top of the highest hills you can see the old-fashioned bridge that spans the river. You can see all the city's glass and concrete skyscrapers. Cars creep up the hills and then fly down. Buses and trucks struggle up the hills. People huff and puff as they trudge up the hills. They slant backwards as they shuffle down, using their feet as brakes so they don't plunge headlong down the slope. Our city's hills are challenging, but the city wouldn't be the same without them.

Writer's Corner

Use as few words as possible to express your ideas. For example, you can say a bridge *spans* a river instead of *goes across* it. Choices such as these will make your writing stronger.

TEACHER TALK

Sentences

Students tend to start sentences with either *I* or *The*. I have them write the first four words from each sentence. Then I tell students to revise their work. In the revision, they are not allowed to start more than two sentences in the entire composition with *I* or *The*. They can rewrite sentences by inverting the word order or replacing the beginning. It makes for less repetition and a smoother, more interesting style. I also have students count the words in each sentence. If sentences tend to have many words (twelve or more), they may be wordy or run-ons.

Sentences

Good writing has a natural flow. Different kinds of **sentences** should make it sound smooth and clear. When you hear a story read aloud, listen to the style and the rhythm of the sentences.

Here are some ways to improve your sentences.

- Use different kinds of sentences. Questions, commands, and exclamations add style to your writing.
- Make sure your sentences are not all short and choppy. Sometimes a longer sentence helps the writing flow.
- Use different beginnings. Starting too many sentences with *I, she, the,* or *a* can be boring.
- Use connecting words. Words such as *even though, because, while,* and *but* can join sentences and show how ideas are related.
- Don't write long, stringy sentences. Too many sentences combined with *and* or *so* make your reader lose interest.

Strategy for Improving Your Sentences

Read a piece of your writing.

- Each time you start a sentence with *I, she, the,* or *a*, circle the word.
- Underline all the short, choppy sentences.
- See how many different kinds of sentences you use. Then revise these sentences to make your writing better.

A Use the connecting words in ( ) to join the two sentences. Write the sentences.

Example: Spot barked. He saw his food. (When)

Answer: Spot barked when he saw his food.

1. Chad wanted to bowl. He had never tried it before. (even though) Chad wanted to bowl even though he had never tried it before.

2. Mrs. Jackson read a book. Sophie went to dance class. (while) Mrs. Jackson read a book while Sophie went to dance class.

3. The Taylors went to a fancy restaurant. It was Joey's birthday. (because) The Taylors went to a fancy restaurant because it was Joey's birthday.

4. Tony put on comfortable shoes. His feet still hurt. (but) Tony put on comfortable shoes, but his feet still hurt.

B Rearrange the words in sentences 5–8 so that A is not the first word. Start with the underlined phrase. Possible answers on page TR33

Example: I ate a big lunch today.

Answer: Today I ate a big lunch.

The night was calm and peaceful. **(5)** A big orange moon glowed brightly above the mountains. **(6)** A gentle wind rustled the leaves in the forest. **(7)** A bird began singing just before sunrise. **(8)** A new day was beginning once again.

C Write a story about a person and an animal who are friends. Use different kinds of sentences. Be sure to begin your sentences with different words. Possible answer on page TR33

Writer's Guide **19**

Improving Sentences

Original

My sister Renata is generous. She is just a teenager. She always finds ways to help others. She organized a coat drive. People donated old coats. She gave them to people in need. She heard about an earthquake in Asia, so she collected money from the students in her school, and she sent more than $500 to the earthquake survivors. Renata does other helpful things. She works at a homeless shelter. She visits senior citizens who live in a special home. Renata is always thinking about others. She is my role model.

Revising Tips

Use different beginnings.   Don't start all sentences with the subject. (Reword some sentences that begin with *She*.)

Join choppy sentences with connecting words that show how ideas are related.   (*Although she is just a teenager, she always finds ways to help others* instead of *She is just a teenager. She always finds ways to help others.*)

Rewrite long, stringy sentences.   Use stronger connecting words, and break some sentences into two. (*When Renata heard about an earthquake in Asia, she collected money from the students in her school.*)

Vary kinds and lengths of sentences.   Use questions, exclamations, and commands as well as statements.

Improved

What makes a person truly generous? Listen to some things that my sister Renata does. Although she is just a teenager, she always finds ways to help others. For example, she organized a coat drive. People donated old coats, and Renata gave them to people in need. When Renata heard about an earthquake in Asia, she collected money from the students in her school. She sent more than $500 to the earthquake survivors. Renata does other helpful things as well. She works at a homeless shelter and visits senior citizens who live in a special home. Renata is always thinking about others. Is it any wonder she is my role model?

Writer's Corner

Try using a question, command, or exclamation as an introduction or conclusion. These kinds of sentences will get your readers' attention.

Conventions

I reinforce conventions—spelling, grammar, and usage—when I teach word choice. Trying to get middle-level students to avoid words such as *good*, *bad*, *happy*, and *sad* takes a huge effort. One of the strategies I like involves using upgrades and our "vocabulary wallpaper." I introduce the term *upgrade* to mean a more advanced word that should be a part of their vocabulary. While reading a novel or short story, I plan a lesson around vocabulary. When discussing the words, I have students use index cards to write the upgrade in the middle, its definition under it, its part of speech in the upper right-hand corner, and the student's name at the bottom. These are then taped to the wall (Wallpaper) and arranged by part of speech. When students are looking for an upgrade while writing, they look around the room for the right part of speech category. I also will give an extra credit point for each upgrade that is underlined and spelled and used correctly in their written work. This is added incentive to apply the words, increase their vocabulary, and develop mastery of conventions.

Conventions

> **Conventions** are rules for writing. Capital letters show where a sentence begins. A period, question mark, or exclamation mark signals the end of a sentence. A new paragraph begins with an indentation. Grammar and spelling follow patterns.

- joe asted his techur for a pensul then he could gets to work. (weak conventions)
- Joe asked his teacher for a pencil. Then he could get to work. (strong conventions)

Strategies for Conventions of Writing

- Start sentences with a capital letter and end with the proper punctuation mark.
- Make sure each sentence tells a complete idea. Each subject and verb should agree.
- Use the correct forms of verbs.
- Capitalize all important words in proper nouns.
- Follow rules for punctuation marks.
- Use pronouns and modifiers correctly.
- Use a dictionary or spell checker for difficult words.

Proofreading Marks

¶	New paragraph
≡	Capital letter
/	Lowercase letter
◯	Correct the spelling.
∧	Add something.
ℒ	Remove something.

A Choose the correct word in ( ) to complete each sentence. Write the sentences.

1. My parents and (<u>I</u>, me) rode a train across country.
2. We have (saw, <u>seen</u>) many beautiful sights.
3. Trains (takes, <u>take</u>) much longer than airplanes.
4. You (learning, <u>learn</u>) about the country on a train.
5. The train was fun for me and (they, <u>them</u>).

B Look at each sentence. Correct any mistakes in punctuation, grammar, and spelling. Write the paragraph.
Possible answers on page TR34

(6) Last summer melinda went to hawaii. (7) Did she right you a postcard. (8) The blue ocean and white sand makes the islands beutiful. (9) rainforests beaches and mountains attract many tourists. (10) Dont you want to visit our 50th state.

C Write three sentences about one of the topics below. Follow the rules for capitalization, punctuation, grammar, and spelling. Trade papers with a classmate and look for anything that should be changed.
Possible answers on page TR34

- A hiking or camping trip I took
- My favorite holiday
- Something I collect

Improving Conventions

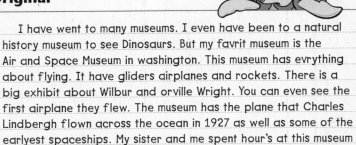

Original

I have went to many museums. I even have been to a natural history museum to see Dinosaurs. But my favrit museum is the Air and Space Museum in washington. This museum has evrything about flying. It have gliders airplanes and rockets. There is a big exhibit about Wilbur and orville Wright. You can even see the first airplane they flew. The museum has the plane that Charles Lindbergh flown across the ocean in 1927 as well as some of the earlyest spaceships. My sister and me spent hour's at this museum and didnt get tired. Does flying interest you. Then go the Air and Space Museum!

Revising Tips

Check for correct capitalization of sentences and of proper nouns.   *(Dinosaurs, washington, orville)*

Look for misspellings.   *(favrit, everythin, earlyest)*

Make sure you have used punctuation, including apostrophes, correctly.   *(hour's, didnt, interest you)*

Check for correct pronoun usage.   *(My sister and me spent)*

Check for correct verb forms.   *(I have went, Charles Lindbergh flown)*

Make sure that subjects and verbs agree.   *(It have)*

Improved

I have gone to many museums. I have even been to a natural history museum to see dinosaurs. But my favorite museum is the Air and Space Museum in Washington. This museum has everything about flying. It has gliders, airplanes, and rockets. There is a big exhibit about Wilbur and Orville Wright. You can even see the first airplane they flew. The museum has the plane that Charles Lindbergh flew across the Atlantic in 1927 as well as some of the earliest spaceships. My sister and I spent hours at this museum and didn't get tired. Does flying interest you? Then go the Air and Space Museum!

Writer's Corner

Sometimes it's hard to catch your own mistakes. Use a ruler to check each line of your paper from start to finish. If you're trying to focus on spelling errors, read your sentences backwards. That way you won't be distracted by their meaning.

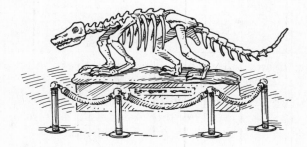

Rubrics and Models

Narrative Writing *Scoring Rubric*

A scoring **rubric** can be used to judge a piece of writing. A rubric is a checklist of traits, or writing skills, to look for. See pages 2–25 for a discussion of these traits. Rubrics give a number score for each trait.

Score	4	3	2	1
Focus/Ideas	Excellent narrative focused on a clear main idea; strong elaboration	Good narrative mostly focused on a main idea; good elaboration	Unfocused narrative with unrelated details; little elaboration	Rambling narrative with unrelated details
Organization/ Paragraphs	Strong beginning, middle, and end, with appropriate order words	Adequate beginning, middle, and end, with some order words	Little direction from beginning to end, with few order words	Lacks beginning, middle, end, with incorrect or no order words
Voice	Writer involved— personality evident	Reveals personality at times	Little writer involvement	Careless writing with no feeling
Word Choice	Vivid, precise words that bring story to life	Adequate words that bring story to life	Few vivid or interesting words	Vague, dull, or misused words
Sentences	Excellent variety of sentences; natural rhythm	Varied lengths, styles, generally smooth	Simple, awkward, or wordy sentences; little variety	Choppy, many incomplete or run-on sentences
Conventions	Excellent control; few or no errors	No serious errors to affect understanding	Weak control; errors affect understanding	Many errors that prevent understanding

Following are four models that respond to a prompt. Each model has been given a score, based on the rubric.

Writing Prompt Write about an experience you enjoyed even though you did not think you would. Be sure your narrative has a beginning, middle, and end.

Narrative Writing Model *Score 4*

Did you ever want to go to the bottom of the ocean? Well, I didn't! Last summer my family visited my grandma in Florida. One day my dad said, "Today we're going snorkeling!" I was excited. Then I found out I would have a mask over my face. I would breathe through a little tube. Snorkelers don't go deep, so the tube sticks up into the air.

I didn't like the idea of breathing underwater. Even though I was nervous, I went to the beach. The water was crystal clear. My dad took his time and helped me use the snorkel. I stayed underwater for longer and longer. The fishes and plants were amazing rainbows of color. Now I can't wait to go snorkeling in Florida again.

Focus/Ideas   Focused on the snorkeling experience; supported with details

Organization/Paragraphs   Events in order and broken into paragraphs; connecting words *(one day, then, now)* that move story along

Voice   Expresses unique personality *(Well, I didn't!)*

Word Choice   Precise word choice and vivid imagery *(mask over my face, little tube, crystal clear, rainbows of color)*

Sentences   Variety of sentence kinds and lengths

Conventions   No errors

Narrative Writing Model *Score 3*

My mom talked me into joining the soccer team. She said that I always liked to run and kick and let off steam. But I just like to play with my friends in the neigborhood. Not on a real team. We have fun kicking the ball around on the playground. I knew that I would have practice twice a week and a game once a week. Who's got time for that? Anyway, I started going to practices and games, and they turned out to be fun. Now I like soccer alot. I've learned teamwork and strategies. My team has won some games, and I feel I've contributed.

Focus/Ideas   Main idea of not wanting to join soccer team clear and most details focused on that experience

Organization/Paragraphs   Beginning and end clear; could use more connecting words

Voice   Writer's feelings and change revealed in the last three sentences and in *Who's got time for that?*

Word Choice   Some precise words (*teamwork, strategies*); some dull words (*fun*)

Sentences   Variety (complex and compound sentences)

Conventions   Sentence fragment (*Not on a real team*); some spelling errors (*neigborhood, alot*)

Narrative Writing Model *Score 2*

The main thing I didn't want to do was go to my swimming lessons because the water was always cold and the teacher made us do excersises and praktis the hole time. I had hard time learning to tread water so the teacher made me keep praktis even thogh I got tired. Well now I can swim and I can also tread water, so I guess its a good thing I took lessons.

Focus/Ideas   Focused on the experience with several supporting details

Organization/Paragraphs   Moves from a beginning to an end; needs introduction that engages reader

Voice   Gives readers a sense of who the writer is

Word Choice   Limited, dull word choice (*do, got*)

Sentences   Wordy and strung together with many *and's* and other connectors

Conventions   Many misspellings; omitted words (*I had hard time*); wording errors (*made me keep praktis*), no paragraph indent

Narrative Writing Model *Score 1*

I didn want go to the party but my mom said I shod so I put on my favrite swettr. Because I just move in the nabor hood and didn no anyone. So I go Everyone was nice and fun and mad the gam the party was fun too. So my frends and me gong to partys if they invite me.

Focus/Ideas   Unclear description of the party

Organization/Paragraphs   Events in sequence but need connecting words

Voice   Errors detract from sense of writer's personality

Word Choice   Limited, dull word choice *(nice, fun)*

Sentences   Long, stringy sentences; overuse of *and, so*

Conventions   Many errors that interfere with meaning

Descriptive Writing *Scoring Rubric*

Score	4	3	2	1
Focus/Ideas	Excellent description with clear main idea and strong, elaborated details	Good description with adequate details focused on main idea	Some descriptive details; some focus on main idea	Little focus on described subject; lacks details
Organization/ Paragraphs	Details arranged in clear order; strong beginning and ending	Details mostly arranged in order; good beginning and ending	Details not well connected; poor beginning and ending	No organization to details; lack of beginning or ending
Voice	Strong personality; clear connection between writer and subject	Writer involved; some connection between writer and subject	Writer lacking involvement; few feelings shown	Writer involvement, point of view missing
Word Choice	Specific, vivid language that appeals to several senses	Accurate, engaging language that appeals to one or two senses	Uninteresting language; little appeal to senses	Limited, vague language; repetitive
Sentences	Superior structure; excellent flow	Some varied beginnings; well constructed	Simple structures; little variety	Many errors; awkward, hard to read
Conventions	Excellent control; few or no errors	No serious errors to affect understanding	Weak control; enough errors to affect understanding	Many errors that prevent understanding

Following are four models that respond to a prompt. Each model has been given a score, based on the rubric.

Writing Prompt   Describe your favorite animal. It may be a pet that you know well or a wild animal that you have read about. Use exact words to help readers see, hear, taste, smell, and feel what you are describing.

Descriptive Writing Model *Score 4*

My cocker spaniel Sadie has blond curly fur and big brown eyes. She has a soft bark and a tongue that feels like sandpaper. Sadie has many ways to let me know how she feels.

Sadie shows some feelings with her face. Sometimes she tilts her head as if she is wondering about something. Sometimes her eyes and mouth look like she is smiling.

The rest of Sadie's body shows feelings too. When she is excited, her tail moves back and forth like a swing at the playground. Her claws make happy little clattering sounds as she runs across the kitchen to greet me.

I guess I am playing favorites, but I think Sadie is the most beautiful and intelligent dog in the world.

Focus/Ideas Strong focus with many supporting details

Organization/Paragraphs Engaging introduction, conclusion, and body paragraphs

Voice Clearly communicates feelings for pet

Word Choice Vivid word choice and images that appeal to touch, sight, and hearing (*a tongue that feels like sandpaper, like a swing at the playground, little clattering sounds*)

Sentences Clear sentences of various kinds and lengths

Conventions No errors

Descriptive Writing Model *Score 3*

 I think tigers are so interesting. First of all, they are beautiful
they have unusul coats, usully with orange and black stripes.
They also have big round heads and long whiskers. They are big
but they are very graceful. They move very smoothly, as if they
are gliding across the ground.

 Tigers are scary when they roar very loud. You can still
tell they are related to cute little kitty cats that run around
the neighborhood. I think tigers are the most beautiful
and interesting animals we have.

Focus/Ideas   Focused on qualities
of tigers and supported with
many details

Organization/Paragraphs   A few transitions
(*First of all, also*); needs better introduction and conclusion

Voice   Writer's appreciation of tigers communicated

Word Choice   Some vivid words (*graceful*); phrases that
appeal to sight (*as if they are gliding across the ground*); some
overused modifiers (*beautiful, big, cute*)

Sentences   Variety in kind and length; many sentences
beginning with *They*

Conventions   A run-on sentence; spelling errors
(*unusul, usully*)

Descriptive Writing Model *Score 2*

Whales are so cool they are huge and live in the water but yet they consider them mammals. A whale has black shinny skin and it dive deep in the water. Then it comes back to the top agin and blows water throgh it's spout. A whale has a funny tail that has two points and sometimes it stiks it's tail out of the water only. Some whales are smaller and don't have black skin.

Focus/Ideas   Focused on the subject, some descriptive details

Organization/Paragraphs   Some organization evident but not consistent; needs clear conclusion

Voice   Shows enthusiasm for topic

Word Choice   Some vivid words appealing to sight and sound; some vague or dull words *(cool, funny)*

Sentences   Run-on at beginning; other sentences are grammatical but have little variety

Conventions   Many misspellings; vague pronoun references *(they consider them mammals)*; errors in subject-verb agreement *(it dive)*

Descriptive Writing Model *Score 1*

> My cats cute. With long fur. He is fluffy and he has a long tail and he has wite spots on his stomik. He has wite paws too and you cant hear him. He comes into the room. He meow sometimes but he dont like most peeple only the ones that take care of.

Focus/Ideas   Attempts specific descriptions but loses focus with details on cat's relationship with people

Organization/Paragraphs   Descriptions in no logical order; no ending

Voice   Little voice evident

Word Choice   Limited word choice; some appeal to sight and sound

Sentences   Overuse of the connecting word *and*; many sentences beginning with *He*

Conventions   A fragment; omission of apostrophes for contractions; many misspellings; errors in subject-verb agreement *(he meow, he dont)*

Persuasive Writing *Scoring Rubric*

Score	4	3	2	1
Focus/Ideas	Excellent persuasive essay with clearly stated opinion and strong elaboration	Clear opinion supported by mostly persuasive reasons	Opinion not clearly stated, weak reasons or not enough support	No stated opinion, details not focused on topic
Organization/ Paragraphs	Strong, convincing introduction; reasons presented in order of importance	Interesting introduction; reasons in order of importance	Weak or unclear introduction; reasons not clear or not in order of importance	No introduction; few reasons; order not logical
Voice	Concerned, committed writer behind words	Some sense of caring; concerned writer behind words	Little sense of writer involvement	No sense of writer's personality or feelings evident
Word Choice	Effective use of persuasive words	Use of persuasive words adequate to good	Few persuasive words used in essay	No persuasive words used in essay
Sentences	Varied sentence structures; excellent flow and rhythm	Some varied sentence structures; few sentence errors	Limited to simple sentences; some errors	Simple, choppy sentences; fragments and run-ons
Conventions	Excellent control of all mechanical aspects of writing	Few errors in grammar, spelling, punctuation, paragraphing	Some distracting mechanical errors	Many errors that prevent understanding

Following are four models that respond to a prompt. Each model has been given a score, based on the rubric.

Writing Prompt   Think about a new activity or some other change that would improve your school. Write a letter to your principal. Try to persuade him or her to make the change by giving several good reasons for it.

Persuasive Writing Model *Score 4*

Dear Mr. Henry,

    I think we should start a school orchestra. First of all, many students take music lessons and could join. I play the piano. I have friends who play horns, flutes, violins, and guitars. Sometimes we play together, but it is usually too hard to get everyone in one place. Second, an orchestra would be a great after-school activity for some students. Not everyone likes to do sports after school. Students should have the choice of playing music. Finally, music is an excellent way to bring people together. We could hold one or two concerts each year. The other students, parents, and family members would enjoy hearing us play. I hope you will let us organize an orchestra for our school.

    Yours truly,

Shannon Jordan

Focus/Ideas Focused on the request, supported with logical reasons

Organization/Paragraphs Clear introduction, transitions indicate reasons in order from least to most important

Voice Strong voice indicates reasonable, committed personality

Word Choice Uses persuasive words *(should, excellent)*

Sentences Varied, clear sentences with good rhythms

Conventions No errors

Persuasive Writing Model *Score 3*

Dear Mr. Gregory,

  Our school has a lot of good spellers. That is why a school spelling bee is a great idea. Students from each grade could compeat and pick two or three winners. Then the winners from all the grades could compeat in one big spelling bee or maybe grades 1 and 2, 3 and 4, and 5 and 6 could go together. The whole school and parents could come to the autorium and watch the spellers. This would be fun and educational and it would encourage kids to be good spellers.

  Yours truly,

  Matt Sanchez

Focus/Ideas   Focused on the request, some distracting information on procedures

Organization/Paragraphs   Good introduction and conclusion, reasons need better transitions and organization

Voice Believable, enthusiastic voice

Word Choice   Good use of verbs *(compete, encourage)*; some use of persuasive words *(great idea)*

Sentences   Several stringy sentences with unclear connecting words *(. . . or maybe grades 1 and 2, 3 and 4, . . .)*

Conventions   Some missing commas in compound sentences; some spelling errors *(compeat, autorium)*

Persuasive Writing Model *Score 2*

Dear Ms. Lee,

    Can our school have a school Fair this year? I know we havnt had one for the last two years becuase it costs a lot. But it is really fun. The students will do the work it will not cost much. We will plan the games and set up the classrooms for them. We will get our parents to help us. They will make bake goods and help set up the games. Theyll also help run the games. Could we have the Fair on a saturday in February? Becuase that is a quiet month. Please let us do this becuase it is really fun.

               Yours truly,
               Rodney Jackson

Focus/Ideas   Focused on the request

Organization/Paragraphs   Needs clear arrangement of reasons from least important to most important

Voice   Feelings about topic communicated

Word Choice   Limited, dull word choice *(please, fun)*; no persuasive words; repetition *(it is really fun)*

Sentences   Little sentence variety

Conventions   Run-on sentence and a fragment; lack of apostrophes for contractions *(havnt, theyll)*; spelling and capitalization errors *(becuase, Fair, saturday)*

Persuasive Writing Model *Score 1*

Dear Mrs. Brady

    I thik we should be abel to have recess after lunch. Instad of just go back to class after lunch. We allredy have two recesses. But the problm is it is too hard to go rite back to work after eating. A little time to relax after eating. Evryone thiks this a good idea.

Tara Schmidt

Focus/Ideas   Clear request, but not enough focused reasons

Organization/Paragraphs   Reasons not organized; no transitions

Voice Identifiable voice

Word Choice   Limited word choice; use of persuasive word *should*

Sentences   Little natural flow; fragments

Conventions   Many misspellings; does not observe letter format; awkward constructions *(Instad of just go back to class)*; omitted words *(this a good idea)*

Expository Writing *Scoring Rubric*

Score	4	3	2	1
Focus/Ideas	Excellent explanation; main idea developed with strong details	Good explanation of main idea; details that mostly support it	Some focus on main idea, few supporting details	Main idea unfocused or lacking; few supporting details
Organization/ Paragraphs	Main idea in clear topic sentence; details in time order; appropriate connecting words	Adequate topic sentence; most details in correct order; some connecting words	Topic sentence, important details missing or in wrong order; few connecting words	No clear order to details or connecting words to show relationships; no clear topic sentence
Voice	Engaging, but serious and rather formal	Mostly serious, but with some inappropriate shifts	Voice not always appropriate to subject matter	Voice lacking or inappropriate
Word Choice	Carefully chosen, precise words	Topic portrayed with clear language	Some vague, repetitive, or incorrect words	Dull language; very limited word choices
Sentences	Well-crafted, varied sentences	Accurate sentence construction; some variety	Little variety; overly simple constructions, some errors	Many fragments, run-ons; sense hard to follow
Conventions	Excellent control of all mechanical aspects of writing	Few mechanical errors	Some distracting mechanical errors	Many errors in mechanics that prevent understanding

Following are four models that respond to a prompt. Each model has been given a score, based on the rubric.

Writing Prompt Think of a natural feature such as a mountain, body of water, or canyon. Write a paragraph explaining some important facts about it. For example, you might include information about how it was formed or what it is used for.

Expository Writing Model *Score 4*

The Grand Canyon is one of the great natural wonders of the world. Located in Arizona, it is 277 miles long and one mile deep in some places. The widest parts of the canyon are 18 miles wide. The Colorado River flows at the bottom of the canyon. How was the canyon formed? Erosion by the river created it millions of years ago. The rocks of the canyon walls are many shades of red, yellow, and brown. The canyon is so beautiful and so enormous that millions of people visit it every year. They can drive on roads around the canyon or hike on trails. Adventurous visitors can ride mules all the way down the canyon to the bottom. We are lucky to have such an amazing place in our country.

Focus/Ideas   Focused on the topic, supported with many facts and details

Organization/Paragraphs   Good introduction and conclusion; logical arrangement of details

Voice   Knowledgeable voice

Word Choice   Precise word choice and images (*many shades of red, yellow, and brown*)

Sentences   Clear sentences of varied lengths and kinds

Conventions   Excellent control

Expository Writing Model *Score 3*

The Mississippi River is one of the chief Rivers in the United States. The name <u>Mississippi</u> comes from an Indian word that means "big river." The Mississippi starts in Minnesota and flows south all the way to the Gulf of Mexico. It goes 2,348 miles. Ships carry goods down the River. It's widest part is 4,500 feet at Cairo, Illinois. One interesting thing about the Mississippi River is that it forms the boundarys of many states such as Illinois, Kentucky, Missouri, and Arkansas. That's what I know about the Mississippi.

Focus/Ideas   Focused on the topic and supported with many details

Organization/Paragraphs   Needs transitions to make organization of details logical; weak conclusion

Voice   Trustworthy voice, needs more individuality

Word Choice   Precise verbs *(flows, forms)*

Sentences   Varied sentence lengths; many begin with *the*

Conventions   Mistakes with apostrophes *(It's widest part)* and capitalization *(Rivers, River)*, spelling error *(boundarys)*

Expository Writing Model *Score 2*

> Mount Shasta is a moutain. It is in northern California. About 14,000 feet high. The resons it is famous is it has twin peeks. They are both volcanos. But they dont erupt. The second peek is 2,500 feet lower than the main one. The moutain is located in north central California. Mount Shasta is high and it is very beautiful.

Focus/Ideas   Focused on the topic but needs more supporting details

Organization/Paragraphs   Topic sentence included; details need more logical organization

Voice   No strong voice; reads like a list of facts

Word Choice   Limited word choice (*high, beautiful*), some wordiness

Sentences   Fragment (*About 14,000 feet high*); short, choppy sentences that could be combined

Conventions   Many misspellings, subject-verb agreement error (*reasons . . . is*)

Expository Writing Model *Score 1*

> Lake Michigan is near us it is big it is a Great lake it is the thrid bigest. It is totaly in the United states it is not in canada at all. Did you know a ship cold go all the way from Lake michigan to the gulf of Mexico.

Focus/Ideas   Generally focused on the topic

Organization/Paragraphs   No logical organization, no introduction or conclusion

Voice   Writer not involved except in final sentence

Word Choice   Limited, dull word choice

Sentences   Run-ons

Conventions   Incorrect end punctuation; many misspellings; errors in capitalization; no paragraph indent

Evaluate Your Writing

You can evaluate your own writing by reading it over carefully. Think about what is good as well as what you can improve. As you read, ask yourself the following questions.

How does my writing sound?   Read it aloud to find out.

- If it sounds choppy, you might combine short sentences.
- Are there many sentences strung together with *and, because,* or *then?* "Unhook" a long stringy sentence by separating it into several sentences.
- Do most sentences begin with *I, the, it, she,* or *he?* Think of other ways to begin these sentences. Simply rearranging words might do the trick.
- Do ideas seem connected? If not, add transition words or phrases such as *finally* or *on the other hand*. These words connect ideas and help your sentences flow.

Is the style appropriate?   Who is your audience? (friends, your principal, a newspaper editor) What is your purpose? (to inform, to persuade, to entertain) Sentence fragments, informal language, and slang may be appropriate for e-mails or quick notes among friends. A more formal style suits written assignments.

Does your writing address the assignment?

- Look for key words in the writing prompt. For example:

    Compare and contrast a bike and a car.
    Tell two similarities and two differences.

    Topic: bike and car

    What you need to do: Compare and contrast

    What to include: Two similarities and two differences

- Other kinds of key words in writing prompts include *describe, explain, summarize, examples, why,* and *how.*

Is your writing focused? Are all the sentences about the main idea? Take out or refocus sentences that wander off into unimportant details.

Is there enough elaboration and support? Your writing may be unclear if you don't elaborate on your ideas. Supply information that readers need to know.

- Use sensory details to make your writing seem fresh and to give readers pictures, but avoid sounding flowery.
- If you give an opinion, supply strong supporting reasons.
- Expand on a main idea with several telling details.
- When necessary, define a term or give examples.

Is your beginning strong? Does a question, a surprising fact, or an amusing detail capture a reader's interest?

Is your ending satisfying? A conclusion may restate the main idea in a new way, tell what you feel or what you have learned, or pose a question to readers to think about. Whatever it does, it should signal that you have finished.

Have you used effective words—and not too many of them? Have you chosen your words carefully?

- Strong verbs, precise nouns, and vivid adjectives make your writing clear and lively.
- Are there awkward phrases you can replace with a word or two? For example, replace *due to the fact that* with *because* and *at this point in time* with *now.*

Checklist

- ☐ My writing sounds smooth and easy to read.
- ☐ I have used an appropriate style for my audience and purpose.
- ☐ My writing addresses the prompt or assignment.
- ☐ My writing is focused.
- ☐ I have used enough elaboration and support.
- ☐ I have a strong beginning.
- ☐ I have a satisfying conclusion.
- ☐ I have used effective words and avoided wordiness.

Grammar and Writing Lessons

Sentences

TEACH

Read aloud the definitions and examples in the box on p. 50. Point out that although the fragment begins with a capital letter and ends with a period, it is not a complete sentence because it does not tell what the person in the sentence is or does.

Think Aloud **Model** The sentence tells about someone: girls. It tells what the girls did: ate strawberries. The fragment also tells about someone: a farmer. It even describes where he was: in the big field. But it doesn't tell about the farmer being something or doing something. So that's how I know it is a fragment, not a sentence.

LESSON 1

Sentences

A **sentence** tells a complete thought. It names someone or something and tells what that person or thing is or does. An incomplete sentence is called a **fragment**.

Sentence   The girls ate strawberries.
Fragment   A farmer in the big field.

Words in a sentence are in an order that makes sense. A sentence always begins with a capital letter and ends with an end mark.

A Write *S* if the group of words is a sentence. Write *F* if the group of words is a fragment.

1. The bakery sells fresh bread. S
2. Serving lunch at the café. F
3. The banker eats there each day. S
4. At a quiet table in the corner. F
5. Sometimes the miners come to town. S
6. The shops are busy. S
7. Selling tools and groceries. F
8. Everyone works hard all week. S
9. Each person has a job. S
10. In town or on a farm. F
11. The farmer rests. S
12. Out in the field under a tree. F

50   Grammar

RESOURCES

Daily Fix-It Lesson 1
   See p. TR1.
   See also Daily Fix-It Transparency 1.
Grammar Transparency 1

B Write the group of words in each pair that is a sentence.

1. <u>Who will build a store?</u>
   Selling food and other goods?

2. Need cloth for shirts and pants.
   <u>One shop sells bolts of cloth.</u>

3. Builders, cooks, and bankers.
   <u>A new town needs many workers.</u>

4. <u>Soon the town will be full of people.</u>
   Going to town on errands.

5. Milk, eggs, bread, and a toothbrush.
   <u>People rush from store to store.</u>

6. <u>Did I forget something?</u>
   Ten things on my shopping list.

C Add your own words to make complete sentences. Write the new sentences. Remember to use capital letters and punctuation marks.
Possible answers:

7. Apple pie ____. Apple pie is my favorite dessert.

8. The kitchen in my house ____. The kitchen in my house is warm and cozy.

9. ____ tastes good after lunch. Dessert tastes good after lunch.

10. ____ are easy to bake. Muffins are easy to bake.

11. All kinds of fruit ____. All kinds of fruit can be used for dessert.

12. ____ is my favorite thing to cook. Baked chicken is my favorite thing to cook.

13. I like ____. I like the smell of baked apples.

14. For lunch, we ____. For lunch, we had grilled cheese sandwiches.

Grammar **51**

PRACTICE

Guided Practice Ⓐ

Work through the exercise with students. Then have them tell what sentence part or parts are missing in each fragment.

TEACHING TIP

- Tell students that when we speak in a casual conversation, we don't always use complete sentences. Our meaning depends on context. For example, if someone asks what you had for lunch, you might answer, "A turkey sandwich and an apple." Have students imagine that you simply said this phrase out of the blue, without being asked a question. Because it is a fragment, it would not make sense.

Independent Practice Ⓑ and Ⓒ

Have students complete the exercises. For Differentiated Instruction and Extra Practice, see p. TR11.

Differentiated Instruction

Strategic Intervention

Find a paragraph of simple sentences in a reading text. Ask pairs of students to take turns reading the sentences aloud. After one partner reads aloud a sentence, the other partner tells who or what the sentence is about. Then that partner reads the sentence aloud again. This time the other partner tells what the person or thing in each sentence is or does.

Advanced

Have students write five sentences about their community. Ask them to include one fragment among their sentences. Have students exchange papers with a partner. Partners circle the fragment and rewrite it so that it is a complete sentence. Then students exchange papers again and discuss the part or parts that are missing in the sentence fragments.

ELL

Have students look at the illustration on p. 50 and identify the setting. Pair children of different abilities and have them make up sentences about farms. Write their sentences on the board. Have students tell what each sentence names and what it tells about what the subject is or does.

Point out that to distinguish a sentence from a fragment, students should ask two questions: *Does this name someone or something? Does this tell what that person or thing is or does?* If the answer to both questions is yes, they are looking at a sentence.

Monitor Progress

Check Grammar

If... students have difficulty identifying complete sentences,	**then...** work through the test items with them and talk about what makes each of the three incorrect answers wrong.

Test Preparation

Write the letter of the sentence that has correct capitalization and punctuation.

1. A What is a ghost town.
   B what is a ghost town?
   C what is a ghost town.
   D What is a ghost town?

2. A Miners didn't find gold
   B Miners didn't find gold.
   C miners didn't find gold.
   D miners didn't find gold

3. A They had to move away
   B they had to move away
   C they had to move away.
   D They had to move away.

4. A They left their houses
   B they left their houses.
   C They left their houses.
   D they left their houses

Write the letter of the complete sentence.

5. A Houses and stores.
   B Standing in many towns.
   C Buildings stayed empty.
   D Weren't needed anymore.

6. **A** People went to cities.
   B Working in other jobs.
   C Gave up dreams.
   D Getting rich quickly.

7. A Towns with houses and shops.
   B Some towns didn't last long.
   C Families of the miners.
   D People suddenly gone.

8. A In many areas of the West.
   B Empty towns still stand.
   C Streets and buildings.
   D Looking broken down.

Review

Write *S* if the group of words is a sentence. Write *F* if the group of words is a fragment.

1. Drake explored California. s
2. Sailed on the coast in 1579. F
3. Many people from Spain. F
4. They settled in villages. s
5. Big ranches with cattle. F
6. American trappers in the 1800s. F
7. They came to California too. s
8. Many pioneers soon settled there. s
9. Farming and ranching. F
10. Became a state in 1850. F

Decide whether each group of words is a sentence or a fragment. If it is a sentence, write the sentence with correct capitalization and punctuation. If it is a fragment, write *F*.

11. a man owned land in California in 1848
    A man owned land in California in 1848.
12. wanted to build a sawmill F
13. a worker found gold in Sutter's river
    A worker found gold in Sutter's river.
14. told everyone about the discovery F
15. thousands of people rushed to Sutter's mill
    Thousands of people rushed to Sutter's mill.
16. a few people made their fortunes
    A few people made their fortunes.
17. returned home with no gold F
18. others opened businesses
    Others opened businesses.

Summarize

Ask students to describe complete sentences and fragments and ways to identify them.

- A sentence tells a complete thought. It begins with a capital letter and ends with an end mark.
- A fragment is an incomplete sentence. It is missing an important sentence part. It may not name someone or something that the sentence is about, or it may not tell what the person or thing is or does.

Grammar-Writing Connection

Remind students that a sentence begins with a capital letter, ends with an end punctuation mark, and tells a complete thought. Punctuating sentences correctly and including the necessary parts help readers understand a writer's message.

Unclear: I play soccer every Saturday morning My friends on the field with me.

Clear: I play soccer every Saturday morning. My friends are on the field with me.

Voice

- Identify characteristics of a character description.
- Write a character description with a strong voice.
- Develop criteria for judging a piece of writing.

TEACH

- Read aloud the information about voice in the box.
- Ask students to tell in their own words what voice is. *(the sense of the writer's personality that makes one person's writing different from everyone else's)*

Guided Writing

Read each item in Exercise 1 with students. Help them identify specific words, details, and author's purpose that create an identifiable voice in each paragraph.

Independent Writing

Ask volunteers to read aloud their responses to Exercise 2. Have students describe the voice of each piece of writing and identify specific items that created the voice.

Monitor Progress

Check Voice

If... students need more help with voice,	**then...** find passages in which the voice can be identified as funny, suspenseful, or serious. Have students identify the voices and the characteristics that create them.

 WRITER'S CRAFT

Voice

> **Voice** shows a writer's personality. It shows feelings and makes one person's writing sound different from everyone else's.

 Write a word from the box to describe the voice of each writer.

> persuasive   serious   imaginative

1. Are you tired of working hard every day? Would you like to make a lot of money? Then come to the gold mines of California. After you pan for gold for a few days, you may never have to work again. The gold you find will buy you a beautiful new home and time to enjoy it. persuasive

2. Can you picture a gold miner in California in 1848? "Yahoo! I just found gold at Sutter's mill. It was a nugget as big as a loaf of bread! I will take it to town. By this time tomorrow I will be rich! I will probably never have to work again!" imaginative

3. The Gold Rush brought many people to California. They all hoped to find gold and get rich. But many of them did not find gold. Still, they decided to stay in California. The land was rich even if the gold mines were not. They stayed and built homes, farms, and towns. serious

 Would you have gone to California to find gold? Write two or three sentences telling why or why not. Use a voice that helps express your feelings about mining for gold.
Possible answer is on page TR34.

54   Writing

RESOURCES

Writing Transparencies 1A, 1B
Writing Rubrics and Anchor Papers p. 9

Character Description

A **character description** makes a person or story character come alive for the reader. It vividly describes the person's actions and character traits.

Topic sentence "sets up" three character traits.

Detail sentences tell actions for each trait.

Conclusion tells writer's feelings about the character.

My Favorite Artist

My Aunt Jen is the most creative, patient, and fun person I know. She is an artist. She usually paints pictures of places. Aunt Jen makes a place seem real and inviting. I always wish I could somehow get inside the painting and experience that place.

Aunt Jen is a busy artist, but she finds time to teach others. She gives me an art lesson each Saturday. She is patient even when I am all thumbs with my paintbrush.

Finally, Aunt Jen is fun. She loves art, but she also likes to sing and play catch in the backyard. Aunt Jen is one of my favorite people to spend time with. I want to be like her when I grow up.

Writing **55**

Character Description

ANALYZE THE MODEL

Read aloud the model and the callouts to the left of it. Prepare students to write their own character descriptions.

PROMPT

Write about a person you admire. Use details that bring several traits of the person to life.

Getting Started Students can do any of the following.

- Use an organizer (pp. TR28–TR32).
- Write a list of things that the person does.
- Use vivid adjectives and strong verbs to describe each thing.

Editing/Revising Checklist

☑ Do my details make the person come alive?

☑ Do my feelings and personality show in my writing?

☑ Are my sentences complete?

Self-Evaluation Distribute copies of p. TR26 for students to fill out.

Scoring Rubric — Character Description

Rubric 4 3 2 1	4	3	2	1
Focus/Ideas	Vivid description of person; many actions and traits described	Good description of person; some actions and traits described	Few details in description about person's actions and traits	Not a description: lacks clarity and development
Organization/ Paragraphs	Key traits arranged and developed with details and examples	Development of key traits orderly and logical	Traits and details not arranged logically	Lacks organization
Voice	Writer very involved with subject	Writer involved with subject	Tries to deal with subject but does not get very involved	Writer not involved with subject
Word Choice	Character traits conveyed through specific words for traits and actions	Character traits portrayed through clear language	Some vague, repetitive, or incorrect words	Incorrect or limited word choice
Sentences	Structure varied and adds interest	Control over simple sentence structure but not over complex ones	Choppy sentences; lack variation	Fragments or run-on sentences
Conventions	Excellent control and accuracy	Reasonable control with few distracting errors	Errors that may prevent understanding	Frequent errors that interfere with meaning

For 5- and 6-point rubrics, see Writing Rubrics and Anchor Papers p. 9.

Subjects and Predicates

- Define and identify the subject and predicate of a sentence.
- Use subjects and predicates correctly in writing.
- Become familiar with subject and predicate assessment on high-stakes tests.

TEACH

Read aloud the definitions and examples in the box on p. 56. Explain that when deciding whether words in a sentence are part of the complete subject or the complete predicate, students can ask the following questions: *Does this word or group of words tell whom or what the sentence is about? Does this word or group of words tell what the subject is or does?*

Model In the first example, I know that *people* is the subject. It is the word that tells whom the sentence is about. The word *most* tells more about *people*, so I know it is part of the complete subject. I know that *learn* is the predicate of the sentence because it tells what the subject, *people*, do. The word *something* tells what people learn, so it is part of the complete predicate. The phrase *each day* tells when people learn, so it is also part of the complete predicate.

LESSON 2

Subjects and Predicates

A sentence has a **subject** and a **predicate.** The subject is the sentence part that tells whom or what the sentence is about. All the words in the subject are called the **complete subject.** The predicate is the sentence part that tells what the subject is or does. All the words in the predicate are called the **complete predicate.**

In the following sentences, the complete subject is underlined once. The complete predicate is underlined twice.

<u>Most people</u> <u>learn something each day</u>.
<u>The boy on that bike</u> <u>is my brother</u>.

A Write the complete subject of each sentence.

1. <u>We</u> find knowledge in many places.
2. <u>The students in our class</u> ask questions.
3. <u>The library</u> has books about many subjects.
4. <u>Teachers</u> help students with their lessons.
5. <u>Books about animals</u> are my favorites.
6. <u>My two friends</u> like mysteries.

Write the complete predicate of each sentence.

7. The class <u>studied whales</u>.
8. The school librarian <u>knows all about caves</u>.
9. James <u>read about pirates</u>.
10. People <u>learn about animals at the zoo</u>.

56 Grammar

RESOURCES

Daily Fix-It Lesson 2
   See p. TR1.
   See also Daily Fix-It Transparency 2.
Grammar Transparency 2

B Write each sentence. Underline the complete subject. Circle the complete predicate.

1. The farmers (raise goats.)
2. They (sell the goats' wool.)
3. Wool from goats (feels soft and fluffy.)
4. Mom (made a wool sweater.)
5. Some people (drink goat's milk.)
6. Goats and sheep (are important farm animals.)
7. Sheep (have thick, curly fur.)
8. My new winter coat (is made from sheep's wool.)

C Add a predicate to each subject to make a complete sentence. Write the sentence with correct punctuation.
Possible answers:
9. My favorite farm animal ___. My favorite farm animal is a big black sheep.
10. Farms in my state ___. Farms in my state grow corn.
11. Wool ___. Wool comes from sheep.
12. Cows ___. Cows give milk.

Add a subject to each predicate to make a complete sentence. Write the sentence with correct punctuation.
Possible answers:
13. ___ wears sweaters.
Everyone wears sweaters.
14. ___ keeps me warm.
My parka keeps me warm.
15. ___ is cold in winter.
The temperature is cold in winter.
16. ___ feels good in winter.
A warm sweater feels good in winter.

Grammar **57**

Guided Practice Ⓐ

Work through the exercise with students. Afterwards, you might choose words and phrases from the complete subjects and complete predicates and have students explain why each is part of the complete subject or the complete predicate.

TEACHING TIP

Make sure students don't assume that the first part of a sentence is always the subject and the second part is always the predicate. Write the following sentence on the board and help students identify the complete subject and complete predicate:

In the yard sat a big brown dog.
(Subject: *a big brown dog*; Predicate: *In the yard sat*)

Independent Practice
Ⓑ and Ⓒ

Have students complete the exercises. For Differentiated Instruction and Extra Practice, see p. TR11.

Differentiated Instruction

Strategic Intervention

On paper, write several complete subjects and complete predicates. *(Thick green forests; Squirrels with fluffy tails; Are good homes for animals; Live in dead trees)* Cut out each so that it appears on a separate strip of paper. Mix up the strips and lay them face up on a table. Have students take turns choosing one subject and one predicate and putting them together to form a sentence.

Advanced

Have students write a sentence about pets or other animals using only a simple subject and a simple predicate. *(Bingo barks.)* Have students exchange papers with a partner and write details that elaborate on both the subject and the verb. *(My silly dog Bingo barks every morning.)* Encourage students to add as many details as possible to both the subject and the predicate without adding additional subjects or verbs.

ELL

Extend the grammar concept of the lesson. Have students tell you about events that happened outside during a recent recess. Write their ideas as sentences on the board. *(Some fourth-grade girls played kickball on the soccer field.)* Have volunteers underline the complete subject and circle the complete predicate in each sentence.

A test may ask you to identify the subject of a sentence. The subject may include more than one person, place, or thing. Be sure to include the complete subject.

Example: Jay and I can hike.

Subject?:   Jay and I

Monitor Progress

Check Grammar

If... students have difficulty identifying subjects and predicates,	**then...** discuss each incorrect answer in the test items and have volunteers explain why it is incorrect.

Test Preparation

✔ Write the letter of the complete subject of each sentence.

1. All of my friends like gifts.

  A All

  B my friends

  C All of my friends

  D friends like gifts

2. Birthday presents are nice surprises.

  A Birthday

  B Birthday presents

  C presents are

  D nice surprises

3. We get gifts every day.

  A We

  B We get

  C get

  D get gifts

4. Some gifts are not wrapped up.

  A Some gifts

  B gifts

  C gifts are

  D not wrapped up

✔ Write the letter of the complete predicate of each sentence.

5. My favorite gift was a bicycle.

  A My favorite

  B favorite gift

  C gift was

  D was a bicycle

6. The bicycle goes fast.

  A The bicycle

  B bicycle goes

  C goes fast

  D goes

58   Grammar

Review

◉ Write the complete subject of each sentence.

1. Carpets make floors soft and colorful. Carpets
2. Animal skin rugs covered cave floors. Animal skin rugs
3. People in the Middle East wove rugs long ago.
   People in the Middle East
4. Rugs from different countries have different patterns.
   Rugs from different countries
5. That Persian rug has birds and leaves. That Persian rug
6. The rug in my room is blue with white dots. The rug in my room

◉ Write the complete predicate of each sentence.

7. Bright colors make that rug unusual. make that rug unusual
8. The Chinese rug is red and blue. is red and blue
9. American colonists made braided rugs. made braided rugs
10. Machines make many rugs today. make many rugs today
11. People weave rugs by hand also. weave rugs by hand also
12. Those rugs last for many years. last for many years

◉ Write each sentence. Underline the complete subject.
Circle the complete predicate.

13. <u>Weavers</u> (made this rug from wool.)
14. <u>The rug</u> (looks soft and colorful.)
15. <u>The pattern</u> (has squares and circles.)
16. <u>People in France</u> (wove the rug.)
17. <u>Our family room</u> (needs a rug like this.)
18. <u>The old rug</u> (is thin and worn.)

Grammar **59**

Summarize

Ask students to define *subject* and *predicate*. Then have them define *complete subject* and *complete predicate* and explain how to identify them in a sentence.

- The subject names something or someone that the sentence is about.
- The predicate states what the subject is or does.
- All the words that tell more about the subject are part of the sentence's complete subject. All the words that tell more about the predicate are part of the sentence's complete predicate.

Grammar-Writing Connection

Sometimes you can give readers better pictures by adding details to both subjects and predicates.

Vague: The cat ran.

More vivid: The <u>scared</u> cat ran <u>under the porch</u>.

Repetition and Rhyme

TEACH

- Read aloud the information about repetition and rhyme in the box.
- Ask students to tell in their own words what repetition and rhyme are. *(Repetition is using a word or group of words more than once; rhyme is using two words that have the same ending sounds.)*

Guided Writing

Read aloud each item in Exercise 1. Have students listen for and identify repeated words and phrases. Do the same with Exercise 2 for rhyming words.

Independent Writing

Ask volunteers to read aloud their responses to Exercise 3. Ask listeners to identify the rhyming words.

Monitor Progress

Check Repetition and Rhyme

If... students need more help with repetition and rhyme,	**then...** locate poems with repetition and rhyme. Read them aloud and have students identify repeated and rhyming words.

WRITER'S CRAFT

Repetition and Rhyme

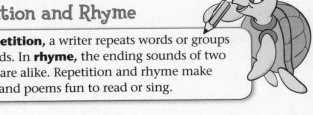

> In **repetition,** a writer repeats words or groups of words. In **rhyme,** the ending sounds of two words are alike. Repetition and rhyme make songs and poems fun to read or sing.

Write the repeated words or groups of words in each story.

1. The goat grew the wool. A farmer cut the wool. That spinner spun the wool. The woman knit the wool. And on a cold winter day, I wore the wool! the wool

2. The kids were messy. The kids were playful. The kids were covered with soft fur. The kids were baby goats! the kids were

Write the words that rhyme in each poem.

3. My sweater's made of bright red wool.
   It will unravel if you pull! wool, pull

4. The sheep and goats are free to roam,
   But when the sun sets, they come home. roam, home

5. The farmer went up to the goat
   And said, "It's time to trim your coat."
   The goat went on his happy way
   And thought, "He won't catch me today!"
   goat, coat; way, today

Write two lines about animals on a farm. Make the lines rhyme. Repeat at least one word or group of words.
Possible answer:
I see a horse and a pig, a pig.
The pig is small, and the horse is big.

60 Writing

RESOURCES

Writing Transparencies 2A, 2B
Writing Rubrics and Anchor Papers p. 10

Song

> A **song** can describe a feeling or event that is important to the writer. It uses repetition and rhyme to vividly express the writer's personality.

Repetition such as *funny dog* makes the song fun.

Rhymes (*dog/log, pup/up, ball/fall, pet/yet*) make the song lively.

Repetition such as *crazy pet* shows the writer's personality.

I Got a Funny Dog

I got a funny dog, funny dog, funny dog.
I taught him how to jump, but he lay like a log.

I got a silly pup, silly pup, silly pup.
I told him to lie down, but he kept standing up.

I got a bouncy ball, bouncy ball, bouncy ball.
I threw it to my dog, but he just let it fall.

I got a crazy pet, crazy pet, crazy pet.
He's sure to learn some tricks, but he hasn't done it yet.

Writing **61**

Song

ANALYZE THE MODEL

Read aloud the model and the callouts to the left of it. Prepare students to write their own songs.

> **PROMPT**
>
> Write a song about something that happened to you. Use repetition and rhyme to make the song fun.

Getting Started Students can do any of the following.

- Use an organizer (pp. TR28–TR32).
- Write details that tell why the event was interesting, funny, or unusual.
- Make some lines rhyme and repeat some words to make the song lively.

Editing/Revising Checklist

✓ Does my song tell about something that happened to me?

✓ Do I repeat words or use rhyming words in my song?

✓ Do my sentences have subjects and predicates?

Self-Evaluation Distribute copies of p. TR26 for students to fill out.

Scoring Rubric Song

Rubric 4 3 2 1	4	3	2	1
Focus/Ideas	Song with vivid description of experience; well-chosen supporting details	Song with fairly vivid description of experience; some good details	Song with few details about experience; lack of focus on the experience	Song with no focus on experience; lacks development
Organization/ Paragraphs	Strong understanding of song format	Uses song format with some assurance	Uses song format somewhat, but not in organized or coherent way	Does not use song format; does not organize lines coherently
Voice	Writer's personality clearly conveyed	Shows some involvement of writer with subject	Only one or two details that reveal writer	Writer not involved with subject at all
Word Choice	Uses repetition and original rhymes effectively	Some repetition and original rhymes	Few uses of rhyme and repetition	No understanding of rhyme or repetition
Sentences	Includes clear, complete sentences	Includes sentences that are easy to read	Some sentences, some fragments; lack of variety	Fragments or incoherent sentences
Conventions	Excellent control and accuracy	Few errors	Many errors that may prevent understanding	Serious errors that interfere with meaning

For 5- and 6-point rubrics, see Writing Rubrics and Anchor Papers p. 10.

Statements and Questions

- Define and identify statements and questions.
- Use statements and questions correctly in writing.
- Become familiar with statement and question assessment on high-stakes tests.

TEACH

Read aloud the definitions and examples in the box on p. 62. Explain that students can distinguish between a statement and a question by considering the purpose of the sentence and by looking at the end punctuation.

Think Aloud **Model** I know the first example is a statement because its purpose is to tell something. It tells something about people. I know that the second example is a question because its purpose is to ask something. It asks to find out something. When I check the end punctuation of both sentences, I see I am right because the first sentence ends with a period. Statements end with periods. The second sentence ends with a question mark. Questions end with question marks.

LESSON 3

Statements and Questions

A sentence that tells something is a **statement**. A sentence that asks something is a **question**.

Statement Most people save money.
Question Do you save money?

A statement begins with a capital letter and ends with a period. A question begins with a capital letter and ends with a question mark.

A Write *statement* if the sentence tells something. Write *question* if the sentence asks something.

1. There are a few different ways to save money. statement
2. You can put money away each week. statement
3. Do you always save your allowance? question
4. You can buy the things you need on sale. statement
5. What is the best way to save money? question

Write each sentence. Use correct capitalization and the correct punctuation mark.

6. my sister Annie saves one dollar each week.
7. frank does not spend money on candy.
8. did you save your birthday money?
9. could we put the money in the bank?
10. saving money can be fun.

RESOURCES

Daily Fix-It Lesson 3
   See p. TR1.
   See also Daily Fix-It Transparency 3.
Grammar Transparency 3

B Use one word from the box to make each statement into a question. Write the new sentences. Use correct capitalization and punctuation. You can use a word more than once.

can	will	should	do

Example: You need money in the future.
Answer: Will you need money in the future?
Possible answers:
1. You put money in the bank. Do you put money in the bank?
2. The dollars add up over the years. Will the dollars add up over the years?
3. You save money for college. Can you save money for college?
4. Your friends save money in the bank too. Should your friends save money in the bank too?
5. The banks help you save money. Will the banks help you save money?
6. You save as much as you can. Do you save as much as you can?

C Add words to expand each item below into an interesting sentence. Each item will tell you whether to write a statement or a question.

7. Statement: tellers work
8. Question: banks pay
9. Statement: banks lend
10. Statement: families save
11. Question: boys and girls learn
12. Question: money help

Possible answers:
7. Tellers work in a bank.
8. Do banks pay money to savers?
9. Banks lend money to people.
10. Families save money for houses and cars.
11. Should boys and girls learn about banks?
12. Can money help you in the future?

Grammar **63**

Guided Practice **A**

Work through the exercise with students. Then call on them to read each sentence aloud, using vocal inflections to differentiate between statements and questions.

TEACHING TIP

- Point out that certain words, such as *what, who, when, did, would,* and *could,* often introduce questions. However, other kinds of sentences may also begin with these words. (<u>When</u> the snow falls, we'll go skiing.)

- Have pairs of students take turns asking and answering the questions in Exercise B.

Independent Practice
B and **C**

Have students complete the exercises. For Differentiated Instruction and Extra Practice, see p. TR11.

Differentiated Instruction

Strategic Intervention

Make copies of an article in a book or magazine that includes both statements and questions. Give each student a copy. Have students underline each statement and circle each question. Check their sentence identification together.

Advanced

Have each student locate an article about a current event in a news magazine for kids or another magazine or newspaper. Have students write five questions about the facts that are answered in the article. Have students exchange articles and questions with a partner and answer the questions.

ELL

Make pairs of cards with a period and a question mark on them. Give a pair of cards to each student. Say a statement or a question. Ask students to hold up the punctuation mark that goes at the end of the sentence. After students have done so, write the sentence on the board and have a volunteer add the end mark.

You might be asked to identify statements and questions. Don't assume that any sentence that begins with a word such as *what* or *why* is a question. It may be a statement or another kind of sentence.

Statements: <u>What</u> I saw in the
(tell something) sky was an airplane.

<u>Why</u> he did that is a mystery to me.

Questions: <u>What</u> is in the sky?
(ask something) <u>Why</u> did he do that?

Monitor Progress

Check Grammar

If… students have difficulty identifying statements and questions,	**then…** have them find an example of each in their own writing and read the two sentences aloud. Other students can identify each as a statement or question.

Test Preparation

✓ Write the letter of the sentence that is written correctly.

1. A the colonists didn't make coins.
   B The colonists didn't make coins
   Ⓒ The colonists didn't make coins.
   D the colonists didn't make coins

2. A How did they buy things.
   Ⓑ How did they buy things?
   C how did they buy things?
   D How did they buy things

3. A They traded goods
   B they traded goods?
   C they traded goods.
   Ⓓ They traded goods.

4. A What did they trade
   B What did they trade.
   C what did they trade?
   Ⓓ What did they trade?

5. A Did they trade crops.
   Ⓑ Did they trade crops?
   C did they trade crops.
   D did they trade crops?

6. Ⓐ They also traded furs.
   B they also traded furs.
   C they also traded furs
   D They also traded furs

7. A Some people had Spanish money
   B some people had Spanish money.
   Ⓒ Some people had Spanish money.
   D some people had Spanish money

8. A Was it made of gold.
   B was it made of gold
   C was it made of gold?
   Ⓓ Was it made of gold?

Review

✓ Write *statement* if the sentence tells something. Write *question* if the sentence asks something.

1. Who made the first money? question
2. The Chinese used paper money long ago. statement
3. Did American colonists use paper money? question
4. They had no bills until the 1700s. statement
5. They traded goods instead of money. statement

✓ Write each sentence with the correct punctuation mark.

6. Did the first Americans have banks?
7. Most colonists lived on farms.
8. Alexander Hamilton wanted large banks.
9. What did Thomas Jefferson think about banks?
10. Jefferson thought farmers didn't need banks.

✓ Use a word from the box to make each statement into a question. Write the new sentence. Use correct capitalization and punctuation. You can use a word more than once.

can	will	should	do

11. You know what kinds of money other countries have.
    Do you know what kinds of money other countries have?
12. You remember that Mexico uses *pesos*.
    Do you remember that Mexico uses *pesos*?
13. You spend dollars in Mexico.
    Can you spend dollars in Mexico?
14. You change your dollars to *pesos*.
    Should you change your dollars to *pesos*?
15. You buy things in Mexico.
    Will you buy things in Mexico?

Grammar **65**

Summarize

Ask students to describe statements and questions and explain how to identify them.

- A statement tells something. It begins with a capital letter and ends with a period.
- A question asks something. It begins with a capital letter and ends with a question mark.
- The best way to tell whether a sentence is a statement or a question is to think about its purpose and look at its end mark.

Grammar-Writing Connection

Explain that variety makes writing more interesting. Using questions occasionally instead of only statements adds variety.

Statements only:	I helped rake leaves. Mom gave me $5. I will put it in the bank.
Statements and a question:	I helped rake leaves. Mom gave me $5. What will I do with it? I will put it in the bank.

Time-order Words

OBJECTIVES

- Identify characteristics of a math story.
- Write a math story using time-order words.
- Develop criteria for judging a piece of writing.

- Read aloud the information about time-order words in the box.
- Ask students to tell in their own words what time-order words are. *(words such as* then *and* today *that tell when something happens)*

Guided Writing

Read each sentence in Exercise 1. Tell students to find the word that answers the question *when?* about each sentence. For Exercise 2, suggest students review the time-order words in Exercise 1 before they write the sentences.

Independent Writing

Ask volunteers to read aloud their responses to Exercise 3. Have students identify the time-order words that each writer used.

Monitor Progress

Check Time-order Words

If... students need more help with time-order words,	**then...** find a passage with several time-order words. Read it aloud without and then with the time-order words. Call students' attention to each time-order word as you read it.

 WRITER'S CRAFT

Time-order Words

> **Time-order words,** such as *then* and *today,* tell you when something happens.
>
> <u>After</u> I got my allowance, I went to the store.

Write the time-order word in each sentence.

1. <u>Yesterday</u> Jon had a money-making idea.
2. <u>First</u> he bought some sturdy paper.
3. <u>Then</u> he bought some wooden sticks.
4. <u>Next</u> he picked up a ball of string.
5. He looked for some colorful rags <u>later</u>.
6. Jon worked in the garage <u>afterwards</u>.
7. <u>Finally</u>, he had made six kites.
8. <u>Tomorrow</u> he will sell the kites to his friends.

Add a time-order word to each sentence. Write the sentences.
Possible answers:
9. ____ Jon sold the six kites. First . . .
10. ____ he made some more kites. Then . . .
11. ____ he sold all those kites too. Later . . .
12. ____ he will make something else. Now . . .

 Write two or three sentences about a time when you sold or bought something. Use two or more time-order words to tell when something happened.
Possible answer: Yesterday I made lemonade. Then I sold the lemonade at a stand in front of my house.

66 Writing

RESOURCES

Writing Transparencies 3A, 3B
Writing Rubrics and Anchor Papers p. 11

Math Story

A **story** tells about some related events that happened to someone. A math story tells about something that happened that had to do with numbers and math.

Last fall tells when the story takes place.

First and *next* show the sequence of events.

Questions give the paragraph variety.

A Wrapping-Paper Problem

(Last fall) my soccer team needed money for uniforms. Each player would sell ten rolls of wrapping paper for $4 each. (First,) I sold three rolls to the Hongs next door. (Next,) the Lanes bought two rolls. Mrs. Sanchez also bought two rolls. On the way home I saw Mr. Collins. He bought three rolls. (How many rolls of wrapping paper had I sold? How much money did I earn for uniforms?)

Writing **67**

Math Story
ANALYZE THE MODEL

Read aloud the model and the callouts to the left of it. Prepare students to write their own math stories.

PROMPT

Write a story about something that happened with numbers and math. Use time-order words.

Getting Started Students can do any of the following.

• Use an organizer (pp. TR28–TR32).

• List story topics that involve numbers.

• Write a math problem to build on.

Editing/Revising Checklist

☑ Does my story involve numbers and math?

☑ Do time-order words make the order of events clear?

☑ Have I used statements and questions in my math story?

Self-Evaluation Distribute copies of p. TR26 for students to fill out.

Scoring Rubric Math Story

Rubric 4 3 2 1	4	3	2	1
Focus/Ideas	Interesting story built around numbers and math	Reasonably interesting story with some math	Uses some math, but focus not entirely clear	Does not focus on narrating an event involving math
Organization/ Paragraphs	Sequence of events clear	Sequence of events fairly clear	Some lapses in clarity of sequence of events	Sequence of events unclear
Voice	Reveals a lively, engaging personality	Writer involved with subject	Weak voice	Writer not involved with subject
Word Choice	Variety of appropriate time-order words used	Some time-order words used	A few time-order words used	No appropriate time-order words used
Sentences	Well-crafted sentences; includes questions	Easy-to-read sentences; includes some questions	Choppy sentences; includes only one kind of sentence	Fragments or incoherent sentences
Conventions	Excellent control and accuracy	Few errors	Many errors that may hinder understanding	Serious errors that interfere with meaning

For 5- and 6-point rubrics, see Writing Rubrics and Anchor Papers p. 11.

Commands and Exclamations

- Define and identify commands and exclamations.
- Use commands and exclamations correctly in writing.
- Become familiar with command and exclamation assessment on high-stakes tests.

TEACH

Read aloud the definitions and examples in the box on p. 68. Point out that, like statements and questions, commands and exclamations can be identified by their purposes and by their end punctuation.

Think Aloud

Model I can tell that the first two sentences are commands because they both tell someone to do something. The first sentence tells someone to put; the second sentence tells someone to give. Also, both sentences end with periods. I can tell that the next two sentences are exclamations. They both express strong feelings, and they both end with exclamation marks.

Commands and Exclamations

A sentence that tells someone to do something is a **command.** A sentence that shows strong feelings is an **exclamation.**

Command	Put a dollar on the counter. Please give me a quarter.
Exclamation	What a bright penny that is! I can't wait to show it to you!

Some commands begin with *please*. Commands usually end with periods. The subject of a command is *you*. The word *you* is not written or said, but it is understood. Exclamations can express feelings such as surprise, anger, or excitement. Exclamations begin with a capital letter and end with an exclamation mark.

A Write *command* if the sentence is a command or *exclamation* if the sentence is an exclamation.

1. Please give me change for a dollar. command
2. Put the money in your pocket. command
3. What a big bag of pennies that is! exclamation
4. Count the pennies carefully. command
5. I am so tired of counting! exclamation
6. That castle is so beautiful! exclamation
7. Please take a picture of the gardens. command
8. How expensive it must be! exclamation

68 Grammar

RESOURCES

Daily Fix-It Lesson 4
    See p. TR2.
    See also Daily Fix-It Transparency 4.
Grammar Transparency 4

B Write the sentences. Add the correct end punctuation. Write *C* if the sentence is a command and *E* if the sentence is an exclamation.

1. What a great coin collection you have
   What a great coin collection you have! E
2. I can't believe that penny is 100 years old
   I can't believe that penny is 100 years old! E
3. Look at this old nickel
   Look at this old nickel. C
4. Start a coin collection of your own
   Start a coin collection of your own. C
5. Look for interesting coins everywhere
   Look for interesting coins everywhere. C
6. You will have a wonderful time
   You will have a wonderful time! E
7. Begin the search today
   Begin the search today. C

C Write a sentence for each item. Follow the directions.
   Possible answers:

8. Write an exclamation about an interesting collection.
   Your doll collection is wonderful!
9. Write a command about how to collect something.
   Look for dolls at garage sales.
10. Write a command to someone in a store.
   Please show me your dolls.
11. Write an exclamation about finding something special at a garage sale.
   What a cute stuffed dog I found!
12. Write a command to someone who wants to see your collection.
   Please be careful with that old teddy bear.
13. Write an exclamation about your favorite toy.
   I love the doll Grandpa gave me!
14. Write a command about how to care for a collection.
   Always keep the cards out of the light.

Grammar **69**

Guided Practice Ⓐ

Work through the exercise with students. Afterwards, ask them to explain how they decided whether each sentence was a command or an exclamation.

TEACHING TIP

- Demonstrate that the subject of a command is always *you* by having students give you a simple command, such as *Pick up a book.* Ask: *Who do you want to pick up a book?* The answer should be *you.*

- Explain that exclamations should not be overused in students' writing. An occasional exclamation livens up a piece of writing. However, too many exclamations may tire readers or make them feel that the writer is exaggerating.

Independent Practice Ⓑ and Ⓒ

Have students complete the exercises. For Differentiated Instruction and Extra Practice, see p. TR11.

Differentiated Instruction

Strategic Intervention

Write several commands and exclamations on the board omitting their end punctuation. Read aloud each sentence. Use your voice to give students clues about the sentence. Have them identify the kind of sentence. Then ask a volunteer to add a period or an exclamation mark at the end of the sentence.

Advanced

Tell students to imagine they are in a boat on a river. Have them write an exclamation that shows each of these emotions: excitement, fear, and surprise. For example, *Those waves are high!* (fear) Remind students to write complete sentences. Have them share their exclamations in small groups while group members identify the feeling that each exclamation shows.

ELL

Provide a word bank of verbs such as *describe, open, smile, shake,* and *stretch.* Have students take turns choosing a verb and saying a command that begins with the verb. For example, *Open your book to page 100.* Write the command on the board and read it with students. Then have them perform the action named in the command.

Test Preparation

✓ Write the letter of the answer that best completes the kind of sentence in ( ).

1. Tell me about your __A__ (command)

   A job.   **C** job?
   B job   **D** Job!

2. __D__ an interesting job you have! (exclamation)

   A what!   **C** What!
   B what   **D** What

3. Explain how you became an animal __B__ (command)

   A trainer   **C** trainer?
   B trainer.   **D** trainer!

4. What beautiful animals you __A__ (exclamation)

   A have!   **C** have
   B have.   **D** have?

5. Let me pet an __B__ (command)

   A elephant!   **C** elephant
   B elephant.   **D** elephant?

6. That elephant is __C__ (exclamation)

   A huge   **C** huge!
   B huge?   **D** huge.

7. __C__ help me reach the elephant's ear. (command)

   A Please.   **C** Please
   B please   **D** Please!

8. __C__ rough the elephant's skin is! (exclamation)

   A How!   **C** How
   B how!   **D** how

9. Show me the elephant's __B__ (command)

   A food!   **C** food
   B food.   **D** food?

10. What fun this has __A__ (exclamation)

    A been!   **C** been.
    B been?   **D** been

Review

✓ Write *command* if the sentence is a command or *exclamation* if the sentence is an exclamation.

1. Show me your silver dollars. command
2. How shiny they are! exclamation
3. That coin is very strange! exclamation
4. Turn the coin over. command
5. What an unusual picture that is!
   exclamation
6. Please put the coin back. command

✓ Write the sentences. Add the correct end punctuation. Write *C* if the sentence is a command and *E* if the sentence is an exclamation.

7. Learn about coins at the library
   Learn about coins at the library. C
8. I can't believe there are so many books about coins
   I can't believe there are so many books about coins! E
9. Look in the index for facts about dimes
   Look in the index for facts about dimes. C
10. That's the strangest dime I've ever seen
    That's the strangest dime I've ever seen! E
11. Don't clean your coins
    Don't clean your coins. C
12. Don't handle them too much
    Don't handle them too much. C
13. Collecting coins is a great hobby
    Collecting coins is a great hobby! E
14. Arrange the coins in the school display case
    Arrange the coins in the school display case. C
15. What an artistic arrangement you made
    What an artistic arrangement you made! E
16. You have the best collection in the whole school
    You have the best collection in the whole school! E
17. Please let me hold that coin
    Please let me hold that coin. C
18. That coin is very heavy
    That coin is very heavy! E

Grammar **71**

Summarize

Ask students to describe commands and exclamations and ways to identify them.

- A command tells someone to do something. The subject is *you,* but it does not appear in the sentence. A command begins with a capital letter and usually ends with a period.
- An exclamation shows strong feelings, such as surprise, anger, or excitement. It begins with a capital letter and ends with an exclamation mark.

Grammar-Writing Connection

The subject of a command is *you.* Because a command addresses, or talks to, readers, it gets their attention. An exclamation can make writing more vivid by expressing surprise, anger, or excitement.

Command and exclamation: Look at this coin. It is 150 years old!

Commands and Exclamations

OBJECTIVES

- Identify characteristics of an e-mail.
- Write an e-mail that includes commands and exclamations.
- Develop criteria for judging a piece of writing.

TEACH

- Read aloud the information about commands and exclamations in the box.

- Ask students to tell in their own words why they should use commands and exclamations in their writing. *(They add variety.)*

Guided Writing

Read each item in Exercise 1. Ask students how they matched each sentence and kind of writing. Read each sentence in Exercise 2 with appropriate expression. Have students decide what feeling each sentence shows.

Independent Writing

Ask volunteers to read aloud their responses to Exercise 3. Have students identify which sentence is the command and which is the exclamation.

Monitor Progress

Check Commands and Exclamations

If... students need more help with exclamations,	then... find and read aloud exclamations from several sources. Have students identify the feelings expressed in each.

 WRITER'S CRAFT

Commands and Exclamations

Sometimes you will use **commands** and **exclamations** in writing. If you want to tell someone to do something, you can use a command. If you want to express a strong feeling such as surprise, anger, or excitement, you can use an exclamation. Commands and exclamations add variety to your writing.

Write the name of a kind of writing in which each command might appear. Choose a name from the box.

> story   persuasive letter   ad

1. Think how much you would enjoy riding a Model K bike.
   ad
2. Please consider me for the job because I am a very hard worker.
   persuasive letter
3. Read this strange tale of a talking fish.
   story

Write the name of a feeling that each exclamation shows.
Possible answers:

4. I found a rare silver dollar at the coin fair!
   excitement
5. Someone bought it before I had a chance!
   disappointment
6. My dad promised to take me to next month's fair!
   happiness

Imagine you have found a wonderful addition for your collection. Write a command and an exclamation about the item.

Possible answer: This is the oldest penny I have ever seen! Look how worn out it is.

72 Writing

RESOURCES

Writing Transparencies 4A, 4B
Writing Rubrics and Anchor Papers p. 12

E-mail

An **e-mail** is a note or letter sent to someone on a computer. Often brief and informal, e-mails are an easy way to keep in touch.

An e-mail to a friend uses informal words. A business e-mail is more formal.

These are commands.

Exclamations express the writer's excitement.

Subject: New Pet
Date: Thursday, May 16, 2007 6:22:17 PM
From: Jane.Sherman@netbiz.com
To: Christina.Sanchez@abc.net

Hey! Guess what happened. I saw a cute kitten on my way home from school. It had soft fur with gray and white stripes. It was sitting all by itself on the sidewalk near my house. I took it home. It followed me all over the house, meowing in a tiny voice. My mom said we should look for its owner. We took the kitten down the street. Soon we saw our neighbor. She was so happy to see the kitten! Guess what she said. She said I could buy the kitten for $10. I had just earned $10 for cleaning the garage. This was such a lucky day for me! If you come over tomorrow, you can see Zippy.

Writing **73**

E-mail
ANALYZE THE MODEL

Read aloud the model and the callouts to the left of it. Prepare students to write their own e-mails.

PROMPT
Imagine something exciting has just happened to you. Write an e-mail to a friend and tell what happened.

Getting Started Students can do any of the following.

- Use an organizer (pp. TR28–TR32).
- Recall times when they felt excited and why.
- Brainstorm vivid details.

Editing/Revising Checklist
☑ Does my e-mail tell about an exciting experience?
☑ Do I use vivid details?
☑ Have I used commands and exclamations?

Self-Evaluation Distribute copies of p. TR26 for students to fill out.

Scoring Rubric E-mail

Rubric 4 3 2 1	4	3	2	1
Focus/Ideas	Vivid e-mail message with well-chosen details	Fairly vivid e-mail message with some details	E-mail message with few details and/or lack of focus on event	No e-mail message; lacks clarity and development
Organization/ Paragraphs	Many details clearly describing writer's feelings	Several details describing feelings	Main idea undeveloped with few descriptive details	Lack of order creates incoherence
Voice	Lively, engaging personality	Some imagination shown	Little or no imagination shown; weak voice	Writer not involved with subject
Word Choice	Vivid verbs and adjectives that describe writer's feelings	Some vivid verbs and adjectives used	Verbs and adjectives vague or unoriginal	Verbs and adjectives not used effectively
Sentences	Both commands and exclamations included	Includes at least one command and one exclamation	Choppy sentences; no commands or exclamations	Fragments or incoherent sentences
Conventions	Excellent control and accuracy	Few errors	Many errors that may prevent understanding	Serious errors that interfere with meaning

For 5- and 6-point rubrics, see Writing Rubrics and Anchor Papers p. 12.

Compound Sentences

- Define and identify simple and compound sentences.
- Use simple and compound sentences correctly in writing.
- Become familiar with simple and compound sentence assessment on high-stakes tests.

TEACH

Read aloud the definitions and examples in the box on p. 74. Point out that all the sentences that students have learned about so far have been simple sentences. Now they will learn about a different kind of sentence: compound sentences.

Think Aloud

Model I know that a simple sentence has a subject and predicate and that it tells a complete thought. The first two examples are both simple sentences. Since each sentence mentions the boy's mother, these two simple sentences can be joined together to make a compound sentence. The example compound sentence shows how. A comma and the word *and* was used to join the two simple sentences into a compound sentence.

LESSON 5

Compound Sentences

A **simple sentence** has one subject and one predicate. **A compound** sentence contains two simple sentences joined by a comma and a word such as *and, but,* or *or.*

Simple Sentence	The boy helped his mother.
Simple Sentence	His mother got him a bicycle.
Compound Sentence	The boy helped his mother, and his mother got him a bicycle.

The two parts of a compound sentence have ideas that make sense together. A comma goes after the first sentence, before the word *and, but,* or *or.*

A Write *S* if the sentence is a simple sentence. Write *C* if the sentence is a compound sentence.

1. The family had a farm. S
2. The boy planted beans, and his mom planted pumpkins. C
3. The family ate bananas and spinach. S
4. The spinach tasted good, but the bananas tasted better. C
5. The boy picked the crops, and his father sold them. C
6. A wheelbarrow carries crops. S
7. You can pick peas, or you can dig sweet potatoes. C
8. It rains in spring, and the crops grow quickly. C
9. Coffee grows on trees, and pumpkins grow on vines. C
10. Work on a farm is often hard. S

74 Grammar

RESOURCES

Daily Fix-It Lesson 5
  See p. TR2.
  See also Daily Fix-It Transparency 5.
Grammar Transparency 5

B Write each compound sentence. Add a comma to punctuate the sentence correctly.

1. Rob walks to school and Will rides his bike.
Rob walks to school, and Will rides his bike.

2. Bicycle accidents are common but Will rides carefully.
Bicycle accidents are common, but Will rides carefully.

3. Will signals his turns and he always walks his bike across the street.
Will signals his turns, and he always walks his bike across the street.

4. Will rides his bike on weekends or he may hike with his family.
Will rides his bike on weekends, or he may hike with his family.

5. Will's brother doesn't like bike trips but Will enjoys them.
Will's brother doesn't like bike trips, but Will enjoys them.

6. Rob will buy a bike or he may get one for his birthday next month.
Rob will buy a bike, or he may get one for his birthday next month.

C Use the word in ( ) to combine each pair of simple sentences. Write the compound sentence.

7. The first bicycle was wooden. It looked like a scooter. (and)
The first bicycle was wooden, and it looked like a scooter.

8. Another bike had handlebars. It had no pedals. (but)
Another bike had handlebars, but it had no pedals.

9. The high-wheeler had a big front wheel. The back wheel was small. (but)
The high-wheeler had a big front wheel, but the back wheel was small.

10. People rode bikes for fun. Soon the roads were full of them. (and)
People rode bikes for fun, and soon the roads were full of them.

11. People might walk to work. They might bike. (or)
People might walk to work, or they might ride a bike.

12. You can see early bikes at a museum. You might find them in an antique shop. (or)
You can see early bikes at a museum, or you might find them in an antique shop.

Guided Practice Ⓐ

Work through the exercise with students. Then have them identify the two simple sentences that make up each compound sentence and the word that joins the two simple sentences.

TEACHING TIP

- Discuss how the words *and, but,* and *or* have different meanings. Help students make up examples of compound sentences using each word.

- Explain that when writing compound sentences, students should join together only two simple sentences. They should avoid stringing several simple sentences together with *and* or *but.*

Independent Practice Ⓑ and Ⓒ

Have students complete the exercises. For Differentiated Instruction and Extra Practice, see p. TR11.

Differentiated Instruction

Strategic Intervention

Write simple sentences on the board. *(Leaves are falling. The air is chilly.)* Number the sentences. Give directions for joining the sentences to make compounds. *(Combine sentences 1 and 4 using* and. *Leaves are falling, and the air is chilly.)* Call on volunteers to write the compound sentences on the board. Make sure they use correct punctuation.

Advanced

Have students write on paper six simple sentences about a sport they like. *(I play baseball in summer.)* Have them exchange papers with a partner. Partners choose sentences that could be combined to make compound sentences. Have them write at least one and more if possible. Remind them that simple sentences must have ideas that make sense together to be combined into a compound sentence.

ELL

Ask students this question: *What is your favorite food?* Write their answers on the board as complete sentences. Help students make up compound sentences using their responses. *(Carlos likes pizza, but Lee likes hamburgers. Sue likes tacos, and Jamie likes spaghetti.)* Write the compound sentences on the board and let volunteers punctuate them.

You may be asked to identify a compound sentence. A compound sentence combines two simple sentences. Each part of a compound combined sentence has its own subject and predicate.

Not a compound sentence:	Tim and Mary rode their bikes.
Not a compound sentence:	Sam talked and laughed.
Compound sentence:	<u>Tim</u> <u>rode</u> his bike, and <u>Sam</u> <u>talked</u>.

Monitor Progress

Check Grammar

If... students have difficulty identifying compound sentences,	**then...** point out simple and compound sentences in their reading materials. Discuss why each example is or is not a compound sentence.

Test Preparation

✔ Write the letter of the words that complete each sentence correctly.

1. Bike races are __B__ are also challenging.
   - **A** popular, And they
   - **B** popular, and they
   - **C** popular and they
   - **D** popular or they

2. Some races are __C__ are very long.
   - **A** short and some
   - **B** short, And some
   - **C** short, but some
   - **D** short or some

3. Some races include __A__ do not.
   - **A** teams, but others
   - **B** teams or others
   - **C** teams and others
   - **D** teams, But others

4. Some races are __C__ are run on special tracks.
   - **A** indoors and they
   - **B** indoors but they
   - **C** indoors, and they
   - **D** indoors, And they

5. Others are __D__ go many miles.
   - **A** outdoors. and they
   - **B** outdoors but they
   - **C** outdoors and they
   - **D** outdoors, and they

6. Racers may train __D__ use indoor tracks.
   - **A** outdoors and they may
   - **B** outdoors or they may
   - **C** outdoors but they may
   - **D** outdoors, or they may

Review

☑ Write *S* if the sentence is a simple sentence. Write *C* if the sentence is a compound sentence.

1. We had a bicycle race through our town. S
2. I did not ride in the race, but Carla did. C
3. The race began on Main Street, and it went for five miles. C
4. Carla got a good start. S
5. Carla's friends stood on the street, and they cheered her on. C
6. There were many racers, and they were all fast. C
7. Carla looked strong, but she was stuck in fourth place. C
8. The race was nearly over, and Carla finally pulled ahead. C
9. Carla crossed the finish line first. S
10. We all had lemonade and ice cream after the race. S

☑ Choose one of the words in ( ) to combine each pair of simple sentences. Write the compound sentence.

11. Julio wants a new racing bike. It is costly. (but, or)
    Julio wants a new racing bike, but it is costly.
12. He has a job. It is hard to save money. (but, and)
    He has a job, but it is hard to save money.
13. He goes to the shop often. He looks at all the bikes.
    (or, and) He goes to the shop often, and he looks at all the bikes.
14. He will get a red bike. He will choose a blue one. (or, but) He will get a red bike, or he will choose a blue one.
15. He will soon have enough money. He will finally get his bike. (and, but)
    He will soon have enough money, and he will finally get his bike.

Summarize

Ask students to define *simple sentences* and *compound sentences*.

- A simple sentence has one subject and one predicate.
- A compound sentence is made by joining together two simple sentences. The ideas in the two sentences must make sense together.
- The two parts of a compound sentence are joined by a comma and the word *and, but,* or *or.*

Grammar-Writing Connection

Explain that one way to make writing sound smoother is to use compound sentences to replace short, choppy sentences.

Choppy: The dog barked. The cat ran away. I chased the cat. I did not catch her.

Smoother: The dog barked, and the cat ran away. I chased the cat, but I did not catch her.

Show, Don't Tell

- Identify characteristics of a narrative paragraph.
- Write a narrative paragraph using details that show instead of tell.
- Develop criteria for judging a piece of writing.

TEACH

- Read aloud the information about show, don't tell in the box.
- Ask students to tell in their own words what show, don't tell means. *(use words that make better, more vivid pictures in readers' minds)*

Guided Writing

Read the items in Exercises 1 and 2. Discuss with students how the phrases in the box and the second sentence in each pair show rather than tell.

Independent Writing

Have volunteers read aloud their responses to Exercise 3. Ask students to identify details and tell which sense each appeals to.

Monitor Progress

Check Show, Don't Tell

If... students need more help with show, don't tell,	**then...** read aloud passages with sensory details from students' reading materials. Have students identify the senses that are appealed to.

WRITER'S CRAFT

Show, Don't Tell

When you write about yourself, *show*—don't *tell*—how you feel.

No I was nervous.

Yes My voice croaked, and my knees trembled.

Use words from the box or your own words to improve sentences 1–4.

packed with tents and food	chattered and cheered
shimmered like glass	jumped out of bed

(1) I (woke up excited) ____. It was the first day at Camp Kanaho. **(2)** The lake (looked pretty) ____. **(3)** The kids (were noisy) ____. **(4)** Canoes were (ready) ____.
Answers are on page TR34.

Read the pair of sentences. Write the letter of the sentence that *shows* instead of *tells*.

5. A Marisa was excited and happy about the surprise party.

   B Marisa squealed and jumped up and down when her friends threw a surprise party for her.

6. A Fog was in the valley and made it difficult to see.

   B Fog covered the valley like a thick white blanket.

Imagine that you are in a strange place, such as a jungle, attic, or cave. Describe what you see, feel, hear, touch, and smell.
Possible answer is on page TR34.

78 Writing

RESOURCES

Writing Transparencies 5A, 5B
Writing Rubrics and Anchor Papers p. 13

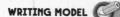

Writing for Tests

Prompt Think about the <u>first time</u> you did something. It might have been going to a new school, moving to a new place, or joining a team. Write a <u>narrative paragraph</u> to a <u>friend</u> showing how you felt.

Details create a vivid mood. Specific verbs paint word pictures.

Writer *shows* that she was early and nervous.

Writer *shows* that she felt proud and excited.

The First Game

The air chilled my nose and hands on Saturday morning. The wet grass squeaked under my new shoes. But I didn't even notice the weather. It was my first soccer game! I paced around the empty field as I waited for the rest of the team to arrive. Soon the game had started. I lost all track of time as I joined the herd of players racing up and down the field. Suddenly I got the chance I was waiting for. The ball was at my feet, and the goal was straight ahead. I took a deep breath and aimed for the goal. The goalkeeper dove for the ball, but she was too late. I scored a goal! The crowd on the sidelines roared, but I didn't even notice it. The roar in my ears came from my own heart.

Writing **79**

Writing for Tests

ANALYZE THE MODEL

Read aloud the model and the callouts to the left of it. Prepare students to write their own narrative paragraphs.

PROMPT

Think about when you did something for the first time. Write a narrative paragraph showing how you felt.

Getting Started Students should do the following.

• Read the prompt and develop a plan for what they want to say.

• Support their ideas with facts, examples, and details.

• Check their writing for errors.

Editing/Revising Checklist

☑ Do I show rather than tell readers how I felt?

☑ Do I stick to the topic?

☑ Have I used compound as well as simple sentences?

Self-Evaluation Distribute copies of p. TR26 for students to fill out.

Scoring Rubric   E-mail

Rubric 4 3 2 1	4	3	2	1
Focus/Ideas	Vivid narrative with well-chosen supporting details	Fairly vivid narrative with some details	Few details and/or lack of focus in narrative	Not a narrative; lacks clarity and development
Organization/ Paragraphs	Uses paragraphs with clear sequence of events	Uses paragraphs; sequence understandable	No paragraphs; sequence of events not clear	No paragraphs or sequence of events
Voice	Sense of writer's personality clearly conveyed	Writer engaged with subject	Weak voice	Writer not engaged with subject
Word Choice	Many vivid verbs and adjectives that describe the experience	Some vivid verbs and adjectives used to show the experience	Experience told in general terms, not shown with specific details	No evidence of trying to show instead of tell
Sentences	Well-crafted sentences; some compound	Fairly well-crafted sentences; some variety	Simple sentences only; no variety	Fragments or incoherent sentences
Conventions	Excellent control and accuracy	Few errors	Many errors that may prevent understanding	Serious errors that interfere with meaning

For 5- and 6-point rubrics, see Writing Rubrics and Anchor Papers p. 13.

Common and Proper Nouns

TEACH

Read aloud the definitions and examples in the box on p. 80. Point out to students that we use common nouns to write or talk about *any* person, place or thing. We use proper nouns to write or talk about a *particular* person, place, or thing.

Model When I read the first example, I know that *birds* and *places* are both nouns. The word *bird* names a thing, and the word *place* names a place. Many nouns, such as *bird* and *place,* are things you can see or touch. In the second example, I see that *Antarctica* is a proper noun because it names a particular place. *July* is a proper noun because it names a particular month.

Common and Proper Nouns

A **common noun** names any person, place, or thing. A **proper noun** names a particular person, place, or thing. Proper nouns begin with capital letters.

Common Nouns	These <u>birds</u> live in cold <u>places</u>.
Proper Nouns	It is cold in <u>Antarctica</u> in <u>July</u>.

The names of days, months, and holidays are proper nouns. They begin with capital letters. Capitalize each important word in a proper noun: *Fourth of July.*

A Write *C* if the underlined noun is a common noun. Write *P* if the underlined noun is a proper noun.

1. Penguins have black and white <u>feathers</u>.C
2. Some penguins live in zoos in the <u>United States</u>.P
3. Penguins have webbed <u>feet</u>.C
4. <u>New Zealand</u> has many penguins.P
5. This penguin hatched in <u>August</u>.P
6. Penguins eat fish from the <u>water</u>.C
7. There is much food in the <u>ocean</u>.C
8. Some penguins live in <u>Australia</u>.P
9. <u>Seals</u> and whales live in Antarctica.C
10. Did you see penguins at the zoo on <u>Labor Day</u>?P

80 Grammar

RESOURCES

Daily Fix-It Lesson 6
　See p. TR2.
　See also Daily Fix-It Transparency 6.
Grammar Transparency 6

B Write the headings *Common Nouns* and *Proper Nouns* on your paper. Write each noun in the sentences under the correct heading. There are nine common nouns and three proper nouns.

Answers are on page TR35.

1. Many birds can be found in Antarctica.
2. Most birds do not live near the South Pole in winter.
3. Their home then is far across the ocean.
4. South America is one destination.
5. The sea can also be a source of food.

C Write the sentences. Capitalize the proper nouns correctly. The number in ( ) tells how many proper nouns are in each sentence.

6. We left on our trip to alaska on new year's day. (2)
7. Some whales and seals live in the pacific ocean. (1)
8. One day david and I took pictures of a whale. (1)
9. We saw a polar bear in january. (1)
10. It was near the coast of the arctic ocean. (1)
11. We saw many birds near the city of anchorage. (1)
12. They live in the pine forests in denali national park. (1)
13. Brown bears live on kodiak island. (1)
14. The largest glacier in north america is in alaska. (2)
15. Mr. murphy and I saw many glaciers. (1)
16. We stopped at sitka and ketchikan on our way home. (2)

Grammar **81**

Guided Practice Ⓐ

Work through the exercise with students. Afterwards, write *Common Nouns* and *Proper Nouns* as headings on the board and call on volunteers to write the underlined words in the correct column.

TEACHING TiP

- Point out that the thing or person that a sentence tells about is a noun.

- To decide whether a noun such as *ocean* is common or proper, students can ask themselves whether it names something that is one-of-a-kind or if there are many different ones.

Independent Practice Ⓑ and Ⓒ

Have students complete the exercises. For Differentiated Instruction and Extra Practice, see p. TR12.

Differentiated Instruction

Strategic Intervention

Have groups of three or four students play Twenty Questions. One student thinks of a person, place, or thing in the school. He or she says, "I am thinking of a common noun" or "I am thinking of a proper noun." The other students ask questions until they are able to guess the noun. The person who guesses correctly takes the next turn.

Advanced

Have students write the name of a country on a slip of paper. Put the names in a box and have students draw one. Then have each student find facts about the country on the Internet or in an encyclopedia and write three sentences about it. Have students exchange papers and underline proper nouns and circle common nouns.

ⒺⓁⓁ

On the board write the categories *People, Cities, Months, Clothing,* and *Animals.* Have students use these labels as scaffolding for naming nouns in each category. Ask for proper nouns in the first three categories and common nouns in the last two categories. Under the headings, list the nouns students name.

Watch out for proper nouns of more than one word. The first word and each important word should be capitalized.

No: The local high school band played on Independence day.

Yes: The local high school band played on Independence Day.

Monitor Progress
Check Grammar

If... students have difficulty identifying common and proper nouns,	then... help them find several examples of each in their reading materials.

Test Preparation

✔ Write the letter of the sentence that is written correctly.

1. **A** We saw cranes from florida.

 B We saw Cranes from florida.

 (C) We saw cranes from Florida.

 D We saw Cranes from Florida.

2. **A** There is a zoo in san diego, california.

 (B) There is a zoo in San Diego, California.

 C There is a zoo in san Diego, california.

 D There is a zoo in San Diego, california.

3. **A** We saw doves there on tuesday.

 B We saw Doves there on Tuesday.

 C We saw Doves there on tuesday.

 (D) We saw doves there on Tuesday.

4. **A** Mr. lane showed us pete, a huge parrot.

 B Mr. lane showed us Pete, a huge parrot.

 (C) Mr. Lane showed us Pete, a huge parrot.

 D Mr. Lane showed us Pete, a huge Parrot.

5. **A** Has Joey ever seen a Flamingo?

 B Has joey ever seen a flamingo?

 C Has joey ever seen a Flamingo?

 (D) Has Joey ever seen a flamingo?

Review

☑ Write *C* if the underlined noun is a common noun. Write *P* if the underlined noun is a proper noun.

1. Each region of the <u>United States</u> has unique birds. P
2. Robins and sparrows live in cities like <u>Boston</u>. P
3. <u>Wrens</u> and jays live in forests in the Northeast. C
4. Owls live on the prairies of <u>Nebraska</u>. P
5. Eagles live in the <u>deserts</u> of the Southwest. C
6. Great blue herons fish in the lakes in <u>Texas</u>. P
7. <u>Pelicans</u> fly over the Gulf of Mexico. C
8. Many <u>birds</u> follow the Mississippi River. C

☑ Write the sentences. Capitalize the proper nouns correctly. The number in ( ) tells how many proper nouns are in each sentence.

9. Gray catbirds live in <u>michigan</u>. (1)
10. The painted bunting migrates to <u>mexico</u> each winter. (1)
11. Last year <u>jamal</u> and <u>paul</u> saw birds in <u>louisiana</u>. (3)
12. The ducks had flown from <u>canada</u> in late <u>september</u>. (2)
13. <u>Mr</u>. <u>burns</u> took pictures of roadrunners in <u>arizona</u>. (2)
14. The coast of the <u>pacific</u> <u>ocean</u> is home to many gulls. (1)
15. The rain forests of <u>south</u> <u>america</u> have amazing birds. (1)
16. The toucan lives in <u>brazil</u>. (1)
17. Last <u>valentine's</u> <u>day</u> <u>adam</u> saw a scarlet ibis. (2)
18. The bright red bird was in a swamp near the <u>caribbean</u> <u>sea</u>. (1)

Summarize

Ask students to describe common nouns and proper nouns and tell how they are different.

- A common noun names any person, place, or thing. It is not capitalized.
- A proper noun names a particular person, place, or thing. Each important word in a proper noun is capitalized.

Grammar-Writing Connection

Explain that proper nouns can be used to give more detail than common nouns, making writing more vivid and specific.

Vague: The <u>family</u> spent the <u>holiday</u> on the <u>lake</u>.

Specific: The <u>Browns</u> spent the <u>Fourth of July</u> on <u>Lake Michigan</u>.

Including Necessary Information

- Identify characteristics of a summary.
- Write a summary that includes all necessary information.
- Develop criteria for judging a piece of writing.

TEACH

- Read aloud the information in the box about including necessary information.
- Ask students to tell in their own words what including necessary information means.

Guided Writing

Read aloud the first paragraph in the exercise. Discuss with students the details that are important and those that are unnecessary in a summary of the paragraph.

Independent Writing

After students complete items 2 and 3 in the exercise, have volunteers read their responses to the items. Discuss the merits of each summary.

Monitor Progress

Check Including Necessary Information

If... students need more help with including necessary information,	then... find additional short passages for them to summarize orally. Point out details that are unnecessary in a summary.

 WRITER'S CRAFT

Including Necessary Information

> In a summary, a few sentences tell the main ideas of a story or article. To summarize, **include all necessary information** that readers need to understand what the article is about. Do not include unnecessary supporting details.

 Write one or two sentences summarizing the necessary information in each paragraph.
Possible answers are on page TR35.

1. Millions of years ago, penguins could fly. You can see the long black "wings" on the sides of their bodies. But their wings turned to flippers. Now penguins are excellent swimmers. Their flippers are strong paddles. Penguins' webbed feet also help them swim.

2. Few animals live in the center of Antarctica. But many live in the Antarctic Ocean and along the coast. Many whales go to Antarctica for the summer. The Antarctic fur seal lives on islands near Antarctica. Seals eat fish and squid from the ocean. Many birds, such as gulls and terns, also spend their summers in Antarctica. They nest on land. They get food from the ocean.

3. Antarctica is an unusual continent. About 98% of the continent is covered with an icecap. This is a thick layer of ice and snow. Big sheets of the icecap float in the water off the coast. These are called ice shelves. In summer, parts of the ice shelves break off. They form big, flat icebergs.

84   Writing

RESOURCES

Writing Transparencies 6A, 6B
Writing Rubrics and Anchor Papers p. 14

Summary

A **summary** tells the important ideas and information in an article, or it tells what happens in a story.

Writer describes only the most important events in the story's plot.

Strong verbs *visits*, *fears*, and *creates* make the summary clear and vivid.

The time-order words *after* and *soon* help make the order of events clear.

Summary—Charlotte's Web

Fern Arable wants to save Wilbur, a pig on her family's farm. He becomes her pet. Fern visits Wilbur often, even when he must live at her uncle's farm. Wilbur meets the farm animals, including Charlotte, a spider.

Wilbur fears he may soon be killed by the farmer. Charlotte creates something amazing to save him. The people find "Some Pig" and other messages written on Charlotte's web. Wilbur becomes famous. The animals decide that if Wilbur wins first prize at the County Fair, he will be saved forever. Wilbur wins a special prize thanks to Charlotte's messages. He is saved!

Charlotte is old. After laying many eggs, she dies. The spiders soon hatch. Charlotte's three daughters become Wilbur's friends. Charlotte's grandchildren and great-grandchildren take Charlotte's place as time passes. Yet Wilbur never forgets Charlotte.

Writing **85**

Summary
ANALYZE THE MODEL

Read aloud the model and the callouts to the left of it. Prepare students to write their own summaries.

PROMPT

Write a summary of a story or article. Include only necessary information. Leave out unnecessary details.

Getting Started Students can do any of the following.

- Use an organizer (pp. TR28–TR32).
- List all events in the story or article and then cross out those that aren't necessary.
- Read your summary to a classmate to see if it is clearly written.

Editing/Revising Checklist

☑ Are all the important facts included in my summary?

☑ Can any unnecessary details be deleted?

☑ Have I capitalized all proper nouns?

Self-Evaluation Distribute copies of p. TR26 for students to fill out.

Scoring Rubric Summary

Rubric 4 3 2 1	4	3	2	1
Focus/Ideas	Strong summary; only important information	Good summary; mostly important information	Unfocused; some main ideas and some minor details	Shows lack of understanding of summary form
Organization/ Paragraphs	Important ideas arranged in correct sequence	Sequence of events described mainly in a clear order	Sequence of events not arranged logically	Lacks organization
Voice	Shows understanding of main ideas	Shows understanding of subject	Tries to deal with subject but lacks understanding	Does not understand subject
Word Choice	Uses vivid verbs and time-order words	Uses some vivid verbs and time-order words	Little attempt to use vivid verbs and time-order words	Incorrect or limited word choice
Sentences	Uses simple and compound sentences	Attempts to vary sentence structures	Choppy sentences; lacks variation	Fragments or run-on sentences
Conventions	Excellent control and accuracy	Reasonable control with few errors	Errors that may hinder understanding	Frequent errors that interfere with meaning

For 5- and 6-point rubrics, see Writing Rubrics and Anchor Papers p. 14.

Singular and Plural Nouns

- Distinguish between singular and plural nouns.
- Use singular and plural nouns in writing.
- Become familiar with singular and plural noun assessment on high-stakes tests.

TEACH

Read aloud the definitions, examples, and instruction in the box on p. 86. Explain that even though *-s* is added to form the plural of most nouns, students can decide when *-es* must be added by saying the noun aloud before making it plural. For example, a vowel sound must be added along with *s* in order to say *benches,* indicating that *-es* forms the plural.

Think Aloud **Model** · In the first example, I can tell there is only one weed and one creek. The word *weed* has *a* before it, which means *one.* Neither noun ends in *s.* In the second example, *grasses* ends in *-es* and *trees* ends in *-s.* These endings tell me they are both plural nouns. They name more than one kind of grass and more than one tree.

Singular and Plural Nouns

A **singular noun** names only one person, place, or thing. A **plural noun** names more than one person, place, or thing.

Singular Nouns A tall <u>weed</u> sprouted beside the <u>creek</u>.

Plural Nouns <u>Grasses</u> grew among the <u>trees</u>.

Most nouns add *-s* to form the plural. Add *-es* to a noun that ends in *ch, sh, s, ss,* or *x: benches, wishes, gases, glasses, foxes.* When a noun ends in a consonant and *y,* change the *y* to *i* and then add *-es: cities.*

A Write *S* if the underlined noun is singular. Write *P* if the underlined noun is plural.

1. There are many <u>jobs</u> on the farm. P
2. That job will take you one <u>day</u>. S
3. Daniel picks <u>strawberries</u> with his brother. P
4. The <u>apples</u> are not ripe yet. P
5. Anita plants <u>bushes</u> each fall. P
6. The <u>farmer</u> planted vegetables. S
7. Tomatoes grow on long <u>vines</u>. P
8. Onions and <u>carrots</u> grow under the ground. P
9. Some beans grow on a tall <u>stalk</u>. S
10. A <u>worker</u> is picking crops. S

RESOURCES

Daily Fix-It Lesson 7
See p. TR3.
See also Daily Fix-It Transparency 7.
Grammar Transparency 7

B Write the plural form of the noun in ( ).

1. James worked for Mr. Dixon for five (day) every week. days
2. He planted (flower) in Mr. Dixon's garden. flowers
3. He pulled weeds from the roses and (lily). lilies
4. One day James trimmed tree (branch). branches
5. He cleaned the front and back (porch). porches
6. He took (stone) out of the soil. stones
7. He put them in big (box). boxes
8. James discovered lovely ferns and (moss). mosses
9. Mr. Dixon gave James some (daisy). daisies
10. His mother arranged them in (bunch). bunches
11. He gave them to the (lady) at his church. ladies
12. They put the flowers in tall (vase). vases

C Complete each sentence by adding plural nouns. Write the new sentence. Possible answers:

13. The gardener planted ___ and ___ in the soil.
The gardener planted bushes and flowers in the soil.
14. Insects such as ___ and ___ crawled in the garden.
Insects such as ants and beetles crawled in the garden.
15. Ms. Beasley grows vegetables, including ___ and ___, in her garden. Ms. Beasley grows vegetables, including peas and peppers, in her garden.
16. She needs tools, such as ___ and ___, to work in the garden. She needs tools, such as spades and rakes, to work in the garden.
17. She will make ___ and ___ with the fruits from her garden. She will make jam and pies with the fruits from her garden.
18. Ms. Beasley gives vegetables from her garden to everyone, including ___ and ___. Ms. Beasley gives vegetables from her garden to everyone, including neighbors and relatives.

Grammar **87**

Guided Practice Ⓐ

Work through the exercise with students. Afterwards, have them identify the word clues that show a noun is plural, such as _many jobs._ Also ask them to explain the spellings of the plural nouns in items 3 and 5.

TEACHING TIP

- Point out that although an -s ending on a noun often signals a plural, some singular nouns, such as _gas, iris,_ and _bus,_ end in s. Students should always check a sentence's meaning so that they don't mistake one of these singular nouns for a plural.

Independent Practice Ⓑ and Ⓒ

Have students complete the exercises. For Differentiated Instruction and Extra Practice, see p. TR12.

Differentiated Instruction

Strategic Intervention

Read aloud sentences from Exercise A or B. Ask students to listen for and write each plural noun they hear. Remind them to listen for words that end in s. You may wish to read each sentence several times. Caution: Students may have trouble spelling the plurals for _tomatoes_ and _strawberries._

Advanced

Write these nouns on the board: _city, library, ferry, factory._ Have students write a sentence that defines each noun and uses the noun in its plural form. For example, _Libraries are buildings where books are kept._

ELL

Extend the grammar concept by asking students to write three singular nouns that name items they see in the classroom, such as _desk, book,_ and _floor._ Have them exchange papers with a partner. Partners should say the plural of each noun and use it in an oral sentence.

Don't assume that all nouns that end in s are plural. Some singular nouns also end in s.

Plural noun: Many <u>parents</u> came to the open house.

Singular nouns ending in s: A <u>bus</u> took the <u>class</u> to the museum.

Monitor Progress

Check Grammar

If... students have difficulty distinguishing between singular and plural nouns,	**then...** help them identify examples in their reading materials. Have them explain how they can identify each noun as singular or plural.

Test Preparation

✓ Write the letter of the plural form of each underlined noun.

1. Bob works on <u>ranch</u>.

   A ranchs   **C** ranches
   B ranch   D ranchies

2. He helps his <u>boss</u> each day.

   A bosss   C boss's
   B boss   **D** bosses

3. Bob trains <u>horse</u>.

   A horse   **C** horses
   B horse's D horsies

4. He cares for cows and their <u>baby</u>.

   A babies C babyss
   B babys   D babees

5. Sometimes <u>fox</u> come to the ranch.

   A foxs   C foxis
   B fox's **D** foxes

6. Bob builds <u>fence</u> to keep them out.

   A fencs   C fencies
   B fences D fencess

7. Bob trims the <u>bush</u>.

   A bushs   **C** bushes
   B bushess D bush's

8. He is careful not to get <u>scratch</u>.

   A scratchs   C scratch's
   B scratchess **D** scratches

Review

Write the plural nouns in each sentence. The number in ( ) tells how many plural nouns are in each sentence.

1. Plump <u>grapes</u> grow on the <u>vines</u>. (2)
2. <u>Workers</u> walk beside the <u>plants</u>. (2)
3. They pull <u>grapes</u> from the <u>branches</u> with their <u>fingers</u>. (3)
4. They put <u>pieces</u> of fruit in <u>boxes</u>. (2)
5. They load the <u>crates</u> into <u>trucks</u>. (2)
6. <u>Grocers</u> put <u>displays</u> of fruit in their <u>stores</u>. (3)
7. <u>Customers</u> buy <u>strawberries</u> and <u>cherries</u>. (3)
8. <u>Shoppers</u> also buy <u>blueberries</u> and <u>peaches</u>. (3)
9. <u>Clerks</u> put the <u>bags</u> into the <u>carts</u>. (3)
10. <u>Helpers</u> take the <u>groceries</u> to the <u>cars</u>. (3)

Write the plural form of the noun in ( ).

11. Mark works in the pineapple (field) in Hawaii. fields
12. He picks (pineapple) every day. pineapples
13. Helpers put the fruit into (basket). baskets
14. They go to the fields in (bus). buses
15. The fruit is taken to the factory in (carton). cartons
16. Workers cut the fruit into (slice). slices
17. The fruit is put into (can). cans
18. People put pineapple in fruit (salad). salads
19. They drink pineapple juice from (glass). glasses
20. Chefs use pineapple in many (dish). dishes

Grammar **89**

Summarize

Ask students to explain how they distinguish between singular and plural nouns.

- A singular noun names only one person, place, or thing.
- A plural noun names more than one person, place, or thing. It often ends in -s or -es. The y in nouns ending in a consonant and y must be changed to -i before -es is added.
- Context clues help you determine whether a noun is singular or plural.

Grammar-Writing Connection

Explain that using specific nouns, both singular and plural, makes writing more vivid.

Dull: The <u>place</u> was full of <u>animals</u>.

Vivid: The <u>swamp</u> was full of <u>alligators</u>.

Eliminating Wordiness

TEACH

- Read aloud the information in the box about eliminating wordiness.
- Ask students to tell in their own words what eliminating wordiness is. *(using as few words as possible to state an idea)*

 ### Guided Writing

Read each item in Exercise 1 with students. Discuss the parts of the sentences that are wordy and ask students for suggestions on how to revise them.

 ### Independent Writing

Have volunteers read their responses to Exercise 2. Ask listeners to point out any wordiness.

Monitor Progress

Check Eliminating Wordiness

If... students need more help with eliminating wordiness,	**then...** locate examples of wordiness in students' writing and use them as anonymous examples.

Eliminating Wordiness

Wordiness means using more words than needed.

Wordy	I think the most important thing to remember when you clean your room is to dust each piece of furniture such as the desk, dresser, and night table.
Revised	When you clean your room, dust all the furniture.

Follow these steps to eliminate wordiness:

- Use strong one-word verbs instead of phrases, for example, *remove* instead of *take off.*
- State each idea only once in as few words as possible.
- Delete wordy phrases such as *kind of* and *I think that.*

 Rewrite each sentence to eliminate wordiness. **Possible answers:**

1. It seems to me that the job of babysitting is one of the hardest jobs in the whole wide world.
Babysitting is one of the hardest jobs.
2. Little tiny kids run around like crazy some of the time and it seems like you have to keep your eye on them.
Sometimes kids run wild, and you have to watch them carefully.

 Write a tip about doing a job. Write it in a sentence that is not wordy.

90 Writing

RESOURCES

Writing Transparencies 7A, 7B
Writing Rubrics and Anchor Papers p. 15

Rules

> **Rules** tell what people should do and shouldn't do. Rules are often written in a numbered list.

The rules are written as commands. The first word or phrase in each rule is a verb that tells readers what to do.

Rules include clear details. For example, #4 includes plural nouns that name specific things in a room. ──

Each rule is stated as briefly as possible.

Rules for Cleaning Your Room

1. Pick up toys, clothes, and books from your floor. Put each item in a drawer, in the closet, or on shelves.
2. Make your bed. Pull up the sheet, blanket, and bedspread smoothly. Fluff up the pillow.
3. Remove trash from your desk, floor, and other areas.
4. Straighten up the books, papers, and pencils on your desk.
5. Dust the desk, dresser, and night table.
6. Vacuum the floor.
7. Keep your room neat after you clean it.
8. Don't complain!

Writing **91**

Rules

ANALYZE THE MODEL

Read aloud the model and the callouts to the left of it. Prepare students to write their own rules.

PROMPT

Write a list of rules for a job that you know how to do well. Don't use more words than are necessary.

Getting Started Students can do any of the following.
- Use an organizer (pp. TR28–TR32).
- Visualize themselves doing the job.
- Consider both *dos* and *don'ts*.

Editing/Revising Checklist
- ✓ Have I eliminated any unnecessary words?
- ✓ Is each rule in the form of a command with a strong verb?
- ✓ Have I used the correct forms of plural nouns?

Self-Evaluation Distribute copies of p. TR26 for students to fill out.

Scoring Rubric — Rules

Rubric 4 3 2 1	4	3	2	1
Focus/Ideas	Key aspect of job described in each rule	Topic of each rule reasonably focused	Unfocused, with no clear distinction among rules	Shows lack of understanding of generating rules
Organization/ Paragraphs	Logical sequence	Sequence clear but not imaginative	Sequence of rules confusing	Lacks organization
Voice	Shows understanding of rule format	Shows understanding of topic	Tries to deal with topic but lacks understanding	Does not understand rule format
Word Choice	Uses vivid verbs to get readers' attention	Reasonably strong verbs	Little attempt to use vivid verbs	Incorrect or limited word choice
Sentences	Uses strong, engaging commands	Uses commands with varying degrees of interest	Unsure of use of commands	No attempt to use commands
Conventions	Excellent control and accuracy	Reasonable control with few distracting errors	Clarity diminished by errors	Frequent errors that interfere with meaning

For 5- and 6-point rubrics, see Writing Rubrics and Anchor Papers p. 15.

Irregular Plural Nouns

- Define and identify irregular plural nouns and spell them correctly.
- Use irregular plural nouns in writing.
- Become familiar with irregular plural noun assessment on high-stakes tests.

TEACH

Read aloud the definitions, examples, and instruction in the box on p. 92. Point out that students must depend on a sentence's context to identify plural nouns that are identical to their singular form, such as *sheep*.

Think Aloud **Model** In the first example, I can tell that *ox* and *sheep* are singular because the words *an* and *a* come before them. I can tell that *oxen* and *sheep* are plural in the second example because the words *three* and *some* come before them. I'm familiar with most nouns with irregular plurals, such as *mouse/mice*, because I use them all the time when I speak. Others, such as *ox/oxen*, are less familiar, so I must memorize them.

LESSON 8

Irregular Plural Nouns

A plural noun names more than one person, place, or thing. Most nouns add -s to form the plural. An **irregular plural noun** has a special form for the plural.

Singular Nouns An <u>ox</u> and a <u>sheep</u> live on the farm.

Irregular Plural Nouns Three <u>oxen</u> and some <u>sheep</u> live on the farm.

Some nouns and their irregular plural forms are *child/children, deer/deer, foot/feet, goose/geese, leaf/leaves, life/lives, man/men, mouse/mice, ox/oxen, sheep/sheep, tooth/teeth,* and *woman/women*.

A Write *S* if the underlined noun is singular. Write *P* if the underlined noun is plural.

1. Some <u>children</u> collect pets. P
2. Carrie has four <u>mice</u>. P
3. She has a pet <u>goose</u> in her yard. S
4. Carrie wants some woolly <u>sheep</u>. P
5. She even wants a <u>deer</u>. S
6. We told the <u>woman</u> about our problem. S
7. We could not rake all the <u>leaves</u>. P
8. We can't run with leaves under our <u>feet</u>. P
9. Some <u>men</u> brought machines to school. P
10. The <u>women</u> and men solved the problem. P

92 Grammar

RESOURCES

Daily Fix-It Lesson 8
    See p. TR3.
    See also Daily Fix-It Transparency 8.
Grammar Transparency 8

B Write the plural form of the noun in ( ).

1. At camp, the girls have busy (life). lives
2. They teach the younger (child) songs. children
3. They help the (woman) clean the cabins. women
4. They help the (man) clean the pool. men
5. They rake (leaf). leaves
6. They chase the (mouse) from the tent. mice
7. They feed the (goose) by the lake. geese
8. They brush the (ox) in the barn. oxen
9. They look quietly at the (deer). deer
10. Their (foot) hurt at the end of the day. feet
11. They brush their (tooth) and go to bed. teeth
12. The girls don't need to count (sheep)! sheep

C Write sentences using the plural forms of both nouns.
Possible answers:

13. goose, foot The geese ran around our feet.
14. child, woman Some women played with their children at the park.
15. ox, tooth The oxen had big teeth.
16. leaf, mouse The little mice hid under the leaves.
17. man, life Those men lived useful lives.
18. deer, sheep Deer and sheep have hooves.

Guided Practice A

Work through the exercise with students. Then have them describe context clues that helped them determine whether each noun is singular or plural.

TEACHING TIP

- Help students categorize the irregular plurals into several different groups, such as plurals whose spelling does not change (*deer*), plurals made by changing vowels (*foot/feet*), plurals made by adding letters (*child/children*), and plurals made by changing consonants. (*life/lives*)

Independent Practice B and C

Have students complete the exercises. For Differentiated Instruction and Extra Practice, see p. TR12.

Differentiated Instruction

Strategic Intervention

Make a card for each singular and irregular plural noun listed in the box on p. 92. Have students mix the cards and lay them facedown on a table in a square. Students can then take turns turning over two cards at a time. The goal is to find both the singular and plural forms of a noun. Students continue until all pairs have been found.

Advanced

On a slip of paper, write each of the singular nouns in the box on p. 92. Have students each draw three nouns and write a sentence using the plurals of those nouns. The sentence may be sensible or silly. For example, *The geese and the mice played in the leaves.*

ELL

Find magazine pictures that illustrate one of the irregular plural nouns in the list on p. 92. Give each student a picture. First help students identify the plural noun. Then have them say a sentence about the picture using the plural noun. For example, *The children are happy.* Write the sentence on the board, read it together, and have the student circle the plural noun.

Test Preparation

✓ Write the letter of the plural form of each underlined noun.

1. The <u>woman</u> have a class.

  A woman   **C** womanes

  B womans **(D)** women

2. They teach <u>child</u> about clean rooms.

  A childs   **C** childrens

  (B) children **D** childrens'

3. Don't put your <u>foot</u> on your bed.

  A foot   **(C)** feet

  B foots   **D** feets

4. Put the toothpaste away after brushing your <u>tooth</u>.

  A tooth   **C** tooths

  (B) teeth   **D** teeths

5. Put away your toy army <u>man</u>.

  (A) men   **C** mens

  B man   **D** mans

6. Crumbs under the bed attract <u>mouse</u>.

  A mouse **(C)** mice

  B mouses **D** mices

7. Wipe mud and <u>leaf</u> off your shoes.

  A leafs   **(C)** leaves

  B leaf   **D** leafs'

8. You'll remember these rules all your <u>life</u>.

  (A) lives   **C** life

  B lifes   **D** life's

Review

✐ Write *S* if the underlined noun is singular. Write *P* if the underlined noun is plural.

1. The <u>children</u> saw unusual animals at the farm. P
2. The <u>oxen</u> had huge heads and backs. P
3. Some <u>geese</u> honked by a pond. P
4. A baby <u>deer</u> had big brown eyes. S
5. There were ten <u>sheep</u> with curly fur. P
6. A tiny <u>mouse</u> scampered through the barn. S
7. A horse with big <u>teeth</u> chewed on hay. P
8. Many <u>mice</u> live in the hay. P
9. The <u>woman</u> asked which animal they liked best. S
10. No <u>child</u> could choose a favorite. S
11. They had never seen so many cute animals in their <u>lives</u>. P
12. One <u>goose</u> followed them to the car. S

✐ Write the plural form of the noun in ( ).

13. The (man) solved animals' problems. men
14. The Kellys wanted the (mouse) out of their house. mice
15. Mr. Cox wanted a fence around his (sheep). sheep
16. A farmer didn't want (deer) in his fields. deer
17. The Steins said there were too many (goose). geese
18. Mrs. Henry's (ox) needed a bigger barn. oxen
19. The Clydes' cat could not chew with its (tooth). teeth
20. Bill's guinea pig would not eat its lettuce (leaf). leaves

Grammar **95**

Summarize

Ask students to tell how the plurals of nouns are formed and explain what irregular plural nouns are.

- The plural of many nouns is formed by adding -*s* or -*es* to the singular noun. *(boys; boxes)*
- Some nouns have a special form for the plural, such as *child/children, deer/deer,* and *foot/feet.* These are called irregular plural nouns.
- The spellings of irregular plurals must be memorized.

Grammar-Writing Connection

Explain that students should always use the correct plural forms of nouns so that readers will not become confused or distracted.

Confusing: The <u>woman</u> played against each other in the championship match.

Clear: The <u>women</u> played against each other in the championship match.

Writing Clearly

- Identify characteristics of a problem-solution paragraph.
- Write a problem-solution paragraph clearly.
- Develop criteria for judging a piece of writing.

TEACH

- Read aloud the information in the box about writing clearly.
- Ask students to tell in their own words what it means to write clearly. *(making your message easy to understand by using specific words and words that show how ideas are related)*

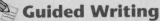

Guided Writing

Read each item in Exercise 1 with students. Ask them to name the words and phrases that are confusing and explain how to make them clear.

Independent Writing

Ask volunteers to read aloud their responses to Exercise 2. Have the class tell whether each sentence is clear and if not, how to improve it.

Monitor Progress

Check Writing Clearly

If... students need more help with writing clearly,	**then...** read anonymous student examples of unclear sentences. Have the class suggest revisions.

 WRITER'S CRAFT

Writing Clearly

Writing clearly means delivering your message so that readers easily understand it.

Unclear	My problem was all the stuff in my closet, and it made me late.
Clear	I had extra clothes, toys, and shoes in my closet. I couldn't find what I needed, so I was late.

Follow these steps to write clearly:

- Use specific, precise words instead of vague or general ones.
- Use words such as *so* and *because* that show how ideas are related.
- Make sure words such as *it* and *they* clearly refer to specific persons or things.

 Rewrite each sentence to make it clearer. **Possible answers:**

1. I like piano lessons better than soccer, and I do it twice a week. I like piano lessons better than soccer, so I take piano twice a week.
2. We need money because the fields and uniforms are old, and they are full of weeds. We need money to replace old uniforms and clean up fields that are full of weeds.
3. The firefighters talk to kids about fire prevention, and they know how to do it. Kids know how to prevent fires because firefighters talk to them about fire prevention.

Write a sentence about a problem you have solved in school. Make sure the sentence states your meaning clearly.

Possible answer: I made a list to help me remember which textbooks to take home with me.

96 Writing

RESOURCES

Writing Transparencies 8A, 8B
Writing Rubrics and Anchor Papers p. 16

Problem-Solution

A **problem-solution** paragraph describes a problem. Then it tells how the problem was solved or how it could be solved.

First part of paragraph describes problem.

Second part of paragraph describes solution. *So* signals change. *First, next,* and *finally* tell order of steps.

Conclusion tells how solution helped writer and looks to future.

My Closet Problem

My closet was a mess! I couldn't find anything in it. I was late for school three times because I couldn't find a matching pair of shoes. Toys, games, shoes, t-shirts, pants, and jackets were jumbled together on the floor and on the shelves. So I called the best organizer I know: my cousin Beth. First, we took everything out of the closet. We gave away all my old clothes. Next, we hung the rest of my clothes on the racks. I put each pair of shoes together on the shelves. Finally, we sorted all my toys and games. I put my skateboard, tennis racket, and baseball bat in the garage. I stacked up all my board games. I put my books on the shelves over my desk. Now I can actually see what I have! From now on, I am keeping my closet neat. I don't want to have to solve this problem again!

Writing **97**

Problem-Solution

ANALYZE THE MODEL

Read aloud the model and the callouts to the left of it. Prepare students to write their own problem-solution paragraphs.

PROMPT

Describe a problem you had or have. Then tell how you solved it or how it could be solved.

Getting Started Students can do any of the following.

- Use an organizer (pp. TR28–TR32).
- Discuss a school or community problem with a group.
- Make a concept web with *Problems I've solved* in the center.

Editing/Revising Checklist

☑ Are the problem and solution described clearly?

☑ Have I used time-order words?

☑ Are irregular plurals correct?

Self-Evaluation Distribute copies of p. TR26 for students to fill out.

Scoring Rubric — Problem-Solution

Rubric 4 3 2 1	4	3	2	1
Focus/Ideas	Clear statement of problem-solution	Fairly clear statement of problem-solution	Problem or solution getting unequal attention	No grasp of problem-solution structure
Organization/ Paragraphs	Problem described fully; solution steps in sequence	Organization good with one or two lapses in sequence	Order of problem-solution confused	Lacks organization
Voice	Shows understanding of problem and how to solve it	Shows some understanding of problem and how to solve it	Tries to deal with problem-solution but unsure of self	Does not understand subject
Word Choice	Effective time-order words and other transitions	Some use of time-order words and other transitions	Few time-order words and other transitions	Incorrect or limited word choice
Sentences	Clear, logical sentences	Reasonably clear sentences	Choppy sentences with lapses in logic	Fragments or run-on sentences
Conventions	Excellent control and accuracy	Reasonable control with few errors	Errors that may prevent understanding	Frequent errors that interfere with meaning

For 5- and 6-point rubrics, see Writing Rubrics and Anchor Papers p. 16.

Singular Possessive Nouns

- Define and identify singular possessive nouns.
- Use singular possessive nouns correctly in writing.
- Become familiar with singular possessive noun assessment on high-stakes tests.

TEACH

Read aloud the instruction and examples in the box on p. 98. Discuss the meaning of ownership or possession, explaining that another way to say the phrase *Jan's dog*, for example, is *the dog that belongs to Jan.*

 Model In the first example, I can tell that *bear* is the subject of the sentence. The sentence tells what the bear did: slept. In the second example, *hare* is the subject of the sentence. The apostrophe + *s* after *bear* shows that the laziness was a trait of his. So *bear's* is a singular possessive noun in this sentence.

LESSON 9

Singular Possessive Nouns

To show that one person, animal, or thing owns something, use a **singular possessive noun**. Add an apostrophe (') and the letter *s* to a singular noun to make it possessive.

Singular Noun   The <u>bear</u> slept all day.
Singular Possessive Noun   The hare did not like the <u>bear's</u> laziness.

A Write the possessive noun in each sentence.

1. The class talked about each person's favorite vegetable. person's
2. Edward likes the carrot's bright color. carrot's
3. Olivia likes broccoli's leafy tops. broccoli's
4. Terrell likes his mom's bean soup. mom's
5. Everyone enjoys the farm's good foods. farm's
6. The farmer's stand has the freshest vegetables. farmer's
7. The corn's sweet flavor makes that soup delicious. corn's
8. What vegetable will be good with tonight's dinner? tonight's
9. The cook's recipes for potatoes are wonderful. cook's
10. Tracy's favorite salad includes lettuce and celery. Tracy's
11. The most important thing is a vegetable's freshness. vegetable's
12. I can almost taste my dad's homemade squash casserole. dad's

98 Grammar

RESOURCES

Daily Fix-It Lesson 9
  See p. TR3.
  See also Daily Fix-It Transparency 9.
Grammar Transparency 9

B Write the singular possessive form of the underlined noun in each sentence.

1. The <u>cat</u> best friend was a pig. cat's
2. The cat visited the <u>pig</u> home each day. pig's
3. The pig rolled around in <u>Farmer Gray</u> muddy yard. Farmer Gray's
4. The cat couldn't believe his <u>friend</u> habit. friend's
5. The cat was the <u>county</u> cleanest animal. county's
6. One day the friends surprised the <u>barnyard</u> other animals. barnyard's
7. The cat rolled in the <u>hog</u> mud, and the pig stayed clean. hog's
8. The <u>farmer</u> wife laughed at the sight of the cat. farmer's
9. I like that <u>story</u> ending. story's
10. The <u>teacher</u> class thought it was funny. teacher's

C Write sentences about events that might happen on a farm. Use the singular possessive form of each noun shown.
Possible answers are on page TR35.

11. horse
12. cow
13. barn
14. worker
15. field
16. tractor
17. hen
18. house

Grammar **99**

PRACTICE

Guided Practice Ⓐ

Work through the exercise with students. Then have them identify the noun that completes each possessive phrase, for example, *vegetable* in *person's favorite vegetable.*

TEACHING TIP

• Emphasize that only nouns can be possessive. Therefore, an apostrophe is never added to a verb or other word ending in s in a sentence. Help students differentiate between possessive nouns ending in apostrophe + s and verbs or plural nouns ending in s.

Independent Practice Ⓑ **and** Ⓒ

Have students complete the exercises. For Differentiated Instruction and Extra Practice, see p. TR12.

Differentiated Instruction

Strategic Intervention

Have students work in small groups. Each student in the group puts a small item, such as a crayon, in a box without letting the others see it. Then one group member pulls out an item and displays it. Each member writes a sentence guessing to whom the item belongs: *That is (Name's) ___.* Group members read their sentences aloud and see who was correct. Continue with the remaining items.

Advanced

Have students write two or three sentences on the subject *my family's favorite ___* about a game, vacation, movie, or something else that the student's family particularly enjoys. Ask students to use at least three singular possessive nouns in their sentences.

ELL

Point out that not all languages have possessive nouns as English does. A speaker of some languages must use a phrase such as *the house of Mr. Bear* to show ownership. Write the following phrases. Have students rewrite them using possessive nouns.

the box of the crayon

the book that belongs to Ms. Park

the tail of the dog

the car of the family

Don't confuse possessive nouns with plural nouns. Like a possessive noun, a plural noun may end in s. But it does not have an apostrophe unless it is possessive.

Possessive noun: The <u>school's</u> playground is large.

Plural noun: The <u>schools</u> have large playgrounds.

Monitor Progress

Check Grammar

If... students have difficulty defining and identifying singular possessive nouns,	**then...** point out some in a reading passage and have students explain who or what owns something and what is owned.

Test Preparation

Write the letter of the correct possessive noun to complete each sentence.

1. A __C__ work never ends.
   A farmer
   B farmers
   C farmer's
   D farmers's

2. The __B__ work begins at sunrise.
   A day
   B day's
   C days
   D days's

3. The __A__ call awakens everyone.
   A rooster's
   B roosters
   C rosters's
   D rooster'

4. The __C__ milk is warm.
   A cows's
   B cows
   C cow's
   D cowses

5. The farmer puts the __D__ eggs in a basket.
   A hen
   B hens
   C hens's
   D hen's

6. The __B__ crop is picked.
   A cornfields
   B cornfield's
   C cornfields's
   D cornfield

Review

☑ Write the possessive noun in each sentence.

1. Each <u>farm's</u> crops are used for different things.
2. <u>Mr. Johnson's</u> fields grow food crops.
3. This <u>field's</u> crop is potatoes.
4. Animal feed grows in <u>Mrs. Long's</u> fields.
5. That <u>animal's</u> favorite crop is grass.
6. Some of our <u>country's</u> crops are used for cloth.
7. Cloth is made from <u>cotton's</u> fibers.
8. Flowers for decorations grow on <u>Ms. Ross's</u> farm.
9. The <u>meadow's</u> wildflowers should not be picked.
10. Ms. Ross likes that <u>rose's</u> color best.

☑ Write the possessive form of the underlined noun in each sentence.

11. <u>Mr. Dean</u> day was not going well.   Mr. Dean's
12. One of the <u>tractor</u> tires was flat. tractor's
13. A <u>cow</u> leg got stuck in a fence. cow's
14. The chicken <u>coop</u> door was broken. coop's
15. The <u>dog</u> bark scared the animals. dog's
16. The <u>truck</u> engine wouldn't start. truck's
17. Some of the <u>roof</u> shingles are missing. roof's
18. The <u>porch</u> light has burned out. porch's
19. The <u>garden</u> plants need water. garden's
20. It was a typical <u>farmer</u> day. farmer's

Summarize

Ask students to tell about singular possessive nouns and explain how to form them.

- A singular possessive noun shows that one person, animal, or thing owns something.
- A singular possessive noun is formed by adding an apostrophe + s to the singular noun.

Grammar-Writing Connection

Explain that using possessive nouns makes writing less wordy.

Wordy: <u>The house of Mr. Bear</u> is on the corner.

Less wordy: <u>Mr. Bear's house</u> is on the corner.

Know Your Purpose

OBJECTIVES

- Identify characteristics of a feature story.
- Write a feature story for a specific purpose.
- Develop criteria for judging a piece of writing.

TEACH

- Read aloud the information in the box about knowing your purpose.
- Ask students to tell in their own words what a writer's purpose is. *(the writer's reason for writing a particular story, such as to inform, to entertain, or to persuade)*

 Guided Writing

Read the paragraphs in the exercise with students. Have them identify the purpose of each paragraph and give examples of word choice and voice that helped them identify the purpose.

 Independent Writing

Read aloud a paragraph from a textbook, a newspaper, and a storybook. Ask students to identify the author's reason, or purpose, for writing each of these.

Monitor Progress

Check Know Your Purpose

If... students need more help with knowing their purpose,	**then...** locate short passages with specific purposes and have students identify those purposes.

Know Your Purpose

> The **purpose** of an article or story is the writer's reason for writing it. A writer's purpose may be to inform, to persuade, or to entertain readers. Knowing your purpose helps you make choices about voice, word choice, and organization.
>
> Here are some kinds of writing that could be done for each purpose:
> **To inform:** newspaper article, how-to article, compare and contrast essay, research report
> **To entertain:** personal narrative, feature article, story, poem
> **To persuade:** editorial, letter to the editor, ad

 Read each paragraph. Write whether its purpose is *to inform, to entertain,* or *to persuade* readers.

1. Everyone should sign up for the park clean-up day next weekend. No one likes a park full of litter. The park is for everyone to enjoy, so everyone should help keep it beautiful. to persuade

2. A fox played a trick. She told the raccoon there were delicious apples under the maple tree. He just had to clear away the fallen leaves. The raccoon raked leaves all day with his paws. But there were no apples. "Thanks," said the fox. Then she disappeared into the cozy hole that the raccoon had uncovered for her. to entertain

102 Writing

RESOURCES

Writing Transparencies 9A, 9B
Writing Rubrics and Anchor Papers p. 17

Feature Story

A **feature story** tells about something interesting that happened to real people. It usually appears in a magazine or newspaper to entertain or inform readers.

Introduction gets readers' attention.

Informal language helps author accomplish purpose.

Direct quotes add interest.

Conclusion lets readers know how Jay's experience changed him.

Lights! Camera! Action!

At 9 years old, Jay Jensen is a movie star. OK, maybe he's not a star. But he has been in a movie with stars.

Last weekend Jay went to the dinosaur museum. He left with his family, thinking about awesome dinosaurs. Outside were bright lights and cameras. A man said to Jay, "Would you like to be an extra in our movie?" Jay's big break would take only an hour. His parents said sure. Jay just had to run up the museum steps behind actors. "It was fun!" said Jay.

Jay's film, *Dinosaur Danger*, hits theaters next summer. Jay doesn't want to become an actor, though. He said, "The director's job is cooler."

Writing **103**

Feature Story
ANALYZE THE MODEL

Read aloud the model and the callouts to the left of it. Prepare students to write their own feature stories.

PROMPT

Write a feature story for your class-mates about an interesting event that happened to some make-believe people.

Getting Started Students can do any of the following.

- Use an organizer (pp. TR28–TR32).
- Share interesting anecdotes with a group.
- Look through magazines for ideas.

Editing/Revising Checklist

☑ Is the purpose of the story clear?

☑ Are the events of the story described vividly?

☑ Have I used singular possessive nouns correctly?

Self-Evaluation Distribute copies of p. TR26 for students to fill out.

Scoring Rubric — Feature Story

Rubric 4 3 2 1	4	3	2	1
Focus/Ideas	Interesting story and characters; clear purpose	Interesting story; purpose fairly clear	Unfocused; no engaging story or characters	Shows no understanding of feature story
Organization/ Paragraphs	Told in clear time order	Clear time order with few lapses	Time order confused	Lacks organization
Voice	Original; shows feelings toward subject	Shows some originality	Little sense of unique voice	No clear voice
Word Choice	Many time-order and descriptive words	Some time-order and descriptive words	Little attempt to use time-order or descriptive words	Incorrect or limited word choice
Sentences	Well-structured, varied sentences	Some variety in sentences	Choppy, illogical sentences	Fragments or run-ons
Conventions	Excellent control and accuracy	Reasonable control with few distracting errors	Many errors that may prevent understanding	Frequent errors that interfere with meaning

For 5- and 6-point rubrics, see Writing Rubrics and Anchor Papers p. 17.

Writing **103**

Plural Possessive Nouns

- Define and identify plural possessive nouns.
- Use plural possessive nouns correctly in writing.
- Become familiar with plural possessive noun assessment on high-stakes tests.

TEACH

Read aloud the definitions, examples, and instruction in the box on p. 104. Emphasize that a plural possessive noun shows ownership by two or more people or things. When using plural possessive nouns in their writing, students should first make the noun plural and then make it possessive.

Think Aloud

Model In the first example, the sentence is about more than one tree. The plural noun *trees* is the subject of the sentence. In the second example, I can tell the word *tree's* is possessive because it has an apostrophe + *s* after the singular noun. In the third example, the word *trees'* sounds the same as the words in the previous two sentences, but it is spelled differently. The apostrophe comes after the *s* at the end of the noun that makes it plural. So I can tell the word shows ownership by more than one tree.

Plural Possessive Nouns

To show that two or more people share or own something, use a **plural possessive noun**.

Plural Noun   The <u>trees</u> grew tall in America.

Singular Possessive Noun   That oak <u>tree's</u> wood is hard.

Plural Possessive Noun   All the <u>trees'</u> wood was strong.

Add an apostrophe (') to plural nouns that end in *-s*, *-es*, or *-ies* to make them possessive. To make plural nouns that do not end in *-s, -es, or -ies* possessive, add an apostrophe and an *s*.

<u>men</u>   <u>men's</u> boots   <u>oxen</u>   <u>oxen's</u> strength

A Write the plural possessive noun in each sentence.

1. The two <u>towns'</u> settlers gathered to celebrate the harvest.
2. The <u>settlers'</u> tables were long boards.
3. The <u>vegetables'</u> flavors were delicious.
4. The <u>cooks'</u> dishes smelled spicy.
5. <u>Men's</u> mouths watered at the smell.
6. The <u>colonies'</u> schools taught reading and arithmetic.
7. <u>Americans'</u> roads were dusty paths.
8. Horses pulled <u>farmers'</u> carts and wagons.
9. The <u>horses'</u> jobs were difficult.
10. <u>Oxen's</u> size made them a better choice for the job.

104 Grammar

RESOURCES

Daily Fix-It Lesson 10
  See p. TR4.
  See also Daily Fix-It Transparency 10.
Grammar Transparency 10

B Write the possessive form of the underlined plural noun in each sentence.

1. Most <u>countries</u> houses have different styles. **countries'**
2. Some <u>Africans</u> homes are mud huts. **Africans'**
3. In England, <u>occupants</u> houses may be very old. **occupants'**
4. <u>Mexicans</u> houses are made to be cool. **Mexicans'**
5. <u>Canadians</u> houses must stay warm. **Canadians'**
6. Coastal <u>residents</u> homes might be on stilts. **residents'**
7. <u>Islanders</u> houses must stand up to wind and rain. **Islanders'**
8. Some <u>Native Americans</u> homes could be moved from place to place. **Native Americans'**
9. Some <u>renters</u> apartments are in tall buildings. **renters'**
10. Are <u>Eskimos</u> houses really made of ice? **Eskimos'**
11. Some <u>sailors</u> homes are their boats. **sailors'**
12. <u>Builders</u> challenges are different in every place. **Builders'**

C Write sentences about different kinds of houses in different places. Use the plural possessive form of each noun in your sentence.
Possible answers are on page TR36.

13. roof
14. city
15. lawn
16. neighborhood
17. family
18. children

Guided Practice Ⓐ

Work through the exercise with students. Ask them to spell the singular possessive noun for selected plural possessive nouns in the sentences. Compare the spellings and discuss how to distinguish singular possessive nouns from plural possessive nouns.

TEACHING TIP

- Point out that whenever an apostrophe appears by itself after a final s, it indicates a plural possessive noun. However, an apostrophe + s may indicate the plural possessive form of a noun with an irregular plural, such as *men's* and *oxen's*.

- Remind students to use a two-step process when spelling a plural possessive noun. First spell the plural noun correctly. Then add an apostrophe if the noun ends in s and an apostrophe + s if it does not end in s.

Independent Practice Ⓑ and Ⓒ

Have students complete the exercises. For Differentiated Instruction and Extra Practice, see p. TR12.

Differentiated Instruction

Strategic Intervention
Make 15 cards, each with a plural noun, a singular possessive noun, or a plural possessive noun written on it. Have a group lay the cards facedown on a table. Students take turns picking a card, reading it aloud, and identifying it as a plural, singular possessive, or plural possessive noun. Group members must agree with the answer. If correct, the player gets a point. Groups play until all words have been identified correctly.

Advanced
Have students write five sentences about the features of specific animals. Each sentence must use a plural possessive noun. For example, *Giraffes' necks are long and thin.* Have students share their sentences in small groups.

ELL
Have students work with more proficient English learners to brainstorm and write on paper three singular nouns that describe features in a house. Possibilities include *floor, bedroom,* and *window.* Have students work with their partners to write the nouns in their plural possessive forms. *(floors', bedrooms', windows')*

Think about how a possessive noun is used in a sentence. Then decide whether it is singular or plural and place the apostrophe correctly.

Plural possessive noun: The <u>houses</u>' kitchens had fireplaces.

Singular possessive noun: The <u>house's</u> kitchen had a fireplace.

Monitor Progress

Check Grammar

If... students have difficulty defining and identifying plural possessive nouns,	**then...** work through the test items with the class, discussing how to make each plural noun possessive.

Test Preparation

☑ Write the letter of the correct plural possessive noun to complete each sentence.

1. Many __B__ efforts are needed to build a house.

   A individuals
   B individuals'
   C individuals's
   D individual's

2. The two __C__ plans are on the table.

   A designer's
   B designers
   C designers'
   D designers's

3. All the __B__ designs are unusual.

   A room's
   B rooms'
   C rooms's
   D rooms

4. The three __D__ tools are in a truck.

   A carpenter's
   B carpenters's
   C carpenters
   D carpenters'

5. The __A__ days are hard and busy.

   A men's
   B mens'
   C mens
   D men

6. The three __B__ talents make the house beautiful.

   A painters
   B painters'
   C painters's
   D painter's

Review

☑ Write the plural possessive noun in each sentence.

1. The colonies' first settlers came from England on ships.
2. The ships' passengers wanted to get rich.
3. The passengers' journey was long and hard.
4. The men's first settlement was in Jamestown.
5. The settlers' hardships almost led to disaster.
6. Captain John Smith's leadership raised the newcomers' spirits.

☑ Write the possessive form of the underlined plural noun in each sentence.

7. The colonists laziness caused some problems. colonists'
8. The nearby Indians leader was Powhatan. Indians'
9. The two groups goal was to get along with one another. groups'
10. Most settlements farms soon produced crops. settlements'
11. The women arrival helped the settlements succeed. women's
12. Fires destroyed many folks homes in the late 1600s. folks'
13. The Virginians new home was Williamsburg. Virginians'
14. Both towns histories are fascinating. towns'
15. Many buildings ruins still stand in Jamestown. buildings'
16. They teach us about Americans struggles in the past. Americans'
17. We can read the leaders letters and journals. leaders'
18. They tell about many children deaths. children's

Summarize

Ask students to explain what a plural possessive noun shows and how to form it.

- A plural possessive noun shows ownership by two or more people or things.
- To form the possessive of a plural noun ending in s, add an apostrophe. To form the possessive of a noun with an irregular plural, add an apostrophe + s.

Grammar-Writing Connection

Explain that using plural possessive nouns can make writing less wordy.

Wordy: The houses of the first Americans were very simple.

Less wordy: The first Americans' houses were very simple.

Use Precise Words

- Identify characteristics of an explanatory paragraph.
- Write an explanatory paragraph using precise words.
- Develop criteria for judging a piece of writing.

TEACH

- Read aloud the information in the box about using precise words.
- Ask students to tell in their own words what precise words are. *(words that tell a writer's exact meaning)*

Guided Writing

Read the sentences in Exercise 1 with students. Ask them to suggest precise words for the underlined words in each sentence. Point out that there is more than one possible answer.

Independent Writing

Have volunteers read aloud their responses to Exercise 2. Ask the class to point out examples of precise words in each response and to suggest additional words.

Monitor Progress

Check Use Precise Words

If... students need more help with using precise words,	**then...** read aloud passages with especially precise words and have students identify the words.

 WRITER'S CRAFT

Use Precise Words

> **Precise words** tell a writer's exact meaning. For example, the words *hut, shack, lodge, cabin,* and *mansion* give readers a better picture than *house.* Using precise words can also help you use fewer words.
>
> | **Wordy** | The cow <u>made a loud, angry sound</u>. |
> | --- | --- |
> | **Precise** | The cow <u>bellowed</u>. |

 Write the sentences. Replace the underlined words with one precise word. **Possible answers:**

1. The girls <u>laughed in a high, happy, breathless way</u>. The girls giggled.
2. John and Holly <u>walked in a slow and relaxed way</u> around the mall. John and Holly strolled around the mall.
3. The pig <u>made a sharp, shrill noise</u>. The pig squealed.
4. Suddenly a child <u>let out a loud, piercing cry</u>. Suddenly a child shrieked.
5. Across the street from the cabin was a <u>body of water that was smaller and calmer than a lake</u>. Across the street from the cabin was a pond.
6. For the holiday, the family had a <u>big meal with many different dishes</u>. For the holiday, the family had a feast.

 Write several sentences about an animal. Use precise words to tell about things the animal does. Possible answer is on page TR36.

RESOURCES

Writing Transparencies 9A, 9B
Writing Rubrics and Anchor Papers p. 18

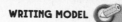

Writing for Tests

Prompt Suppose you are introducing a new student to your school. What <u>important facts about your school</u> would you explain to him or her? Write an <u>explanatory paragraph</u> to a <u>new student</u> telling what he or she should know.

Topic sentence that tells what the paragraph is about.

Words and phrases show the order of events during the day.

Conclusion shows that the paragraph is finished.

Life at McKinley School

The third-grade class at McKinley School is a great place to learn! At 9:00 each morning Mr. Chase, the principal, makes announcements. Then third graders have reading and spelling. At noon, we go to lunch. All the classes' lunch periods are at different times. You can bring your lunch, or you can buy it. (On Wednesdays, the lunchroom serves spaghetti. It's great!) After lunch we have social studies and then physical education. Then we have math and science. In late afternoon, we work on projects, such as the science fair. Sometimes we have a field trip, like to the art museum. Finally, Ms. Perez reviews our homework assignments. It's the end of another educational day at McKinley School.

Writing **109**

Writing for Tests

ANALYZE THE MODEL

Read aloud the model and the callouts to the left of it. Prepare students to write their own explanatory paragraphs.

PROMPT

Write an explanatory paragraph to a new student. Tell facts about your school that he or she should know.

Getting Started Students should do the following.

- Read the prompt and develop a plan for what they want to say.
- Support their ideas with facts, examples, and details.
- Check their writing for errors.

Editing/Revising Checklist

☑ Do precise words create pictures for readers?

☑ Are ideas supported with details?

☑ Have I used plural possessive nouns correctly?

Self-Evaluation Distribute copies of p. TR26 for students to fill out.

Scoring Rubric — Writing for Tests

Rubric 4 3 2 1	4	3	2	1
Focus/Ideas	Paragraph with clear explanation and well-chosen supporting details	Paragraph fairly clear with some details	Paragraph with few details and/or no focus	Paragraph lacking clarity and development
Organization/ Paragraphs	Engaging topic sentence and conclusion	Informative topic sentence and conclusion	Attempts to include topic sentence and conclusion	No attempt to include topic sentence and conclusion
Voice	Sense of writer's personality clearly conveyed	Writer engaged with subject	Weak voice	Writer not engaged with subject
Word Choice	Sense of writer's personality clearly conveyed	Shows attempt to use precise words	Vague words used instead of precise ones	Uses inadequate or incorrect words
Sentences	Well-crafted sentences; some compound	Fairly well crafted, with attempt at sentence variety	Simple sentences only; no variety	Fragments or incoherent sentences
Conventions	Excellent control and accuracy	Few errors	Errors that may prevent understanding	Serious errors that interfere with meaning

For 5- and 6-point rubrics, see Writing Rubrics and Anchor Papers p. 18.

Action and Linking Verbs

- Define and identify action verbs and linking verbs.
- Use action and linking verbs correctly in writing.
- Become familiar with action and linking verb assessment on high-stakes tests.

TEACH

Read aloud the definitions and examples in the box on p. 110. Point out that the verb is part of the predicate of a sentence, which is the part that tells what the subject is or does.

Think Aloud

Model In the first two examples, it is easy to recognize the verbs. The word *grow* shows what the roses do. The word *have* also shows a kind of action. In the third example, I notice that the complete predicate tells what the subject, *rose*, is like. The word *is* links the subject to the words in the predicate that describe it. So it makes sense that the word *is* is called a linking verb.

LESSON 11

Action and Linking Verbs

A **verb** is a word that tells what someone or something is or does. **Action verbs** are words that show action. **Linking verbs,** such as *am, is, are, was,* and *were,* do not show action. They link a subject to a word or words in the predicate.

Action Verb	Roses <u>grow</u> on bushes in the garden. They <u>have</u> soft petals.
Linking Verb	Each rose <u>is</u> a different color.

A Write the verb in each sentence.

1. We see many wildflowers on our trips. see
2. Wildflowers have wonderful names. have
3. My favorites are bluebonnets. are
4. Queen Anne's Lace is a soft white flower. is
5. My sister loves little yellow buttercups. loves
6. Wildflowers wilt on a hot day. wilt
7. Once I picked a fairy slipper. picked
8. Clover is usually purple. is
9. Tina steps on a lily by mistake. steps
10. Forests are full of violets and other wildflowers. are

110 Grammar

RESOURCES

Daily Fix-It Lesson 11
　　See p. TR4.
　　See also Daily Fix-It Transparency 11.
Grammar Transparency 11

B Write the verb in each sentence. Write *A* after an action verb. Write *L* after a linking verb.

1. Some flowers grow from bulbs. grow; A
2. A bulb is an underground stem. is; L
3. Gardeners plant some bulbs in the fall. plant; A
4. Tulips come from bulbs. come; A
5. Flowers from bulbs bloom each year. bloom; A
6. Other flowers start as seeds. start; A
7. They are annuals. are; L
8. My favorite annual is a snapdragon. is; L
9. It has many little blossoms. has; A
10. Petunias are annuals also. are; L

C Add a verb to complete each sentence. Write the sentence.
Possible answers:
11. A garden ____ a peaceful place to relax.
A garden is a peaceful place to relax.
12. Butterflies ____ around the flowers.
Butterflies flutter around the flowers.
13. Leaves ____ in the breeze. Leaves blow in the breeze.
14. The flowers ____ colorful and fragrant.
The flowers are colorful and fragrant.
15. Bees ____ noisily around the flowers and vegetables.
Bees buzz noisily around the flowers and vegetables.

Guided Practice Ⓐ

Work through the exercise with students. Then have volunteers explain how they identified each verb.

TEACHING TIP

- Point out that the verb is a necessary part of the predicate of a sentence, telling what the subject is or does. Explain that students can recognize an action verb because it describes an action that could be pantomimed. Have students act out the action verbs in sentences 1, 5, 6, 7, and 9 in Exercise A.

Independent Practice Ⓑ and Ⓒ

Have students complete the exercises. For Differentiated Instruction and Extra Practice, see p. TR13.

Differentiated Instruction

Strategic Intervention

Have small groups take turns identifying the verb in each sentence in a simple reading passage. After a verb is identified, have students use gestures to act out the action or identify the linking verb that connects the subject of the sentence with other words in the sentence. After you have monitored several correct verb identifications, allow the groups to continue on their own.

Advanced

Ask students to write three sentences that use linking verbs to describe a garden. Have students exchange papers with a partner. Partners should rewrite each sentence using an action verb. For example, *A tulip is bright yellow and orange* could be revised to *A tulip blooms in bright yellow and orange.*

ELL

Work with students to brainstorm verbs that tell about actions people do in a yard or garden, such as *mow, rake,* and *dig*. Write the verbs on the board and have students pantomime the actions. Use this activity as scaffolding for writing sentences with these verbs.

Test Preparation

Write the letter of the word that is a verb.

1. You find flowers in many places.
   - (A) find
   - B in
   - C many
   - D flowers

2. Poppies bloom in the desert.
   - A Poppies
   - (B) bloom
   - C in
   - D desert

3. A cactus has pretty flowers.
   - A cactus
   - (B) has
   - C pretty
   - D flowers

4. Many plants are in the mountains.
   - A plants
   - B Many
   - C mountains
   - (D) are

5. A sunflower grows on the prairie.
   - A sunflower
   - B prairie
   - (C) grows
   - D on

6. Water lilies live in the forest.
   - A Water
   - B lilies
   - (C) live
   - D forest

112 Grammar

Review

Write the verb in each sentence.

1. Alex <u>wants</u> vegetables in his garden.
2. He <u>plants</u> many different seeds.
3. He <u>waters</u> the plants each day.
4. The garden <u>is</u> soon full of vegetables.
5. Carrots <u>are</u> Alex's favorite vegetable.
6. The carrots <u>have</u> bushy green tops.
7. Rabbits <u>like</u> the carrot plants.
8. Those plants <u>are</u> tomatoes.
9. Alex <u>weeds</u> the garden often.
10. The garden <u>is</u> a big success.

Write the verb in each sentence. Write *A* after an action verb. Write *L* after a linking verb.

11. Herbs <u>bloom</u> in Shawna's garden. A
12. Parsley and rosemary <u>are</u> herbs. L
13. The garden <u>has</u> mint and sage too. A
14. Shawna's mom <u>cooks</u> with the herbs. A
15. She <u>puts</u> parsley in the soup. A
16. The parsley <u>is</u> fresh and green. L
17. Shawna <u>saves</u> the mint for tea. A
18. The mint <u>is</u> cool and spicy. L
19. Shawna <u>tastes</u> sage in the chicken. A
20. The herbs <u>are</u> delicious. L

Grammar **113**

Summarize

Ask students to tell about action verbs and linking verbs.

- A verb is a word that tells what someone or something does or is.
- An action verb shows action.
- A linking verb links a subject to words in the predicate that tell about the subject.

Grammar-Writing Connection

Explain that strong action verbs make writing vivid and lively.

Dull: The vine <u>goes</u> along the garden wall.

More vivid: The vine <u>creeps</u> along the garden wall.

Sensory Details

OBJECTIVES

- Identify characteristics of a journal entry.
- Write a journal entry with sensory details.
- Develop criteria for judging a piece of writing.

TEACH

- Read aloud the information about sensory details in the box.
- Ask students to tell in their own words what sensory details are. *(details that describe how something looks, sounds, feels, tastes, or smells)*

Guided Writing

Read each description in Exercise 1 with students. Have them point out specific words that appeal to specific senses in the descriptions.

Independent Writing

Ask volunteers to read aloud their responses to Exercise 2. Have listeners identify the sense to which each sentence appeals.

Monitor Progress

Check Sensory Details

If... students need more help with sensory details,	then... have them find and share passages in favorite stories that appeal to specific senses.

Sensory Details

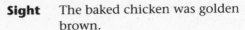

> **Sensory details** describe the way something looks, sounds, feels, tastes, or smells.
>
> | **Sight** | The baked chicken was golden brown. |
> |---|---|
> | **Sound** | Juices in the pan were hissing and popping. |
> | **Smell** | The sauce smelled like ripe plums. |
> | **Taste** | I bit into the warm, tender meat. |
> | **Touch** | The sauce made my fingers sticky. |

 Read each description. Write whether it appeals mainly to the sense of *sight*, *sound*, *smell*, *taste*, or *touch*.

1. The air is perfumed with the sweetness of roses in bloom and recently mown grass. smell
2. I am awakened by the soft chirps of robins, the loud honks of geese, and the rowdy cries of crows. sound
3. The moon is a big golden pumpkin in the autumn sky. sight
4. The chill stings my nose and hands and creeps under my coat. touch
5. I love salty pretzels dipped in mustard sauce. taste
6. A siren screamed through the darkness. sound

 Write three sentences. Each sentence should appeal to a different sense. Possible answer: The sky looked black and heavy. The wind howled through the trees. Raindrops thumped on my head.

114 Writing

RESOURCES

Writing Transparencies 11A, 11B
Writing Rubrics and Anchor Papers p. 19

Journal Entry

> A person writes a **journal entry** to describe an idea, feeling, or experience he or she has had.

First sentence tells what the entry is about.

Color words create details that appeal to the sense of sight.

Vivid words create sensory details.

Comparison creates a vivid sensory detail.

My Favorite Place

I love the beach on a summer day. I see white sand, dark blue water, and light blue sky. The sea gulls make sharp cries overhead, and the ocean roars in the background. I smell the salty air and suntan lotion on the people around me. The sand feels warm and scratchy under my bare feet, and the ocean breeze feels fresh on my face. When I finally get the nerve to go in the water, it feels like ice, and the waves startle me. But then I get used to it. The water feels refreshing, and the waves have a nice rhythm. The beach is my favorite place.

Writing **115**

Journal Entry
ANALYZE THE MODEL

Read aloud the model and the callouts to the left of it. Prepare students to write their own journal entries.

PROMPT

Write a journal entry that describes a place where you enjoy nature. Use details that appeal to the senses.

Getting Started Students can do any of the following.

- Use an organizer (pp. TR28–TR32).
- Make a concept web with *outdoor places* in the center.
- Close their eyes and visualize a place.

Editing/Revising Checklist

✓ Does my writing appeal to different senses?

✓ Do my sensory details make the place come alive?

✓ Have I used action and linking verbs correctly?

Self-Evaluation Distribute copies of p. TR26 for students to fill out.

Scoring Rubric   Journal Entry

Rubric 4 3 2 1	4	3	2	1
Focus/Ideas	Journal entry that vividly describes place	Place well described in journal entry	Journal entry with weak description of place	Not a journal entry; no description of place
Organization/ Paragraphs	Consistent spatial or other organization	Organization logical	Illogical or faulty organization	Lacks organization
Voice	Shows original thoughts and feelings	Communicates feelings about place	Little sense of individual emotions	No sense of individual voice
Word Choice	Effective sensory words	Some use of sensory words	Limited attempt to use sensory words	Incorrect or severely limited word choice
Sentences	Clear, interesting sentences	Reasonably clear sentences	Choppy sentences with lapses in logic	Fragments or run-on sentences
Conventions	Excellent control and accuracy	Reasonable control with few distracting errors	Errors that may hinder understanding	Frequent errors that interfere with meaning

For 5- and 6-point rubrics, see Writing Rubrics and Anchor Papers p. 19.

Main and Helping Verbs

OBJECTIVES

- Define and identify main verbs and helping verbs.
- Use main and helping verbs correctly in writing.
- Become familiar with main and helping verb assessment on high-stakes tests.

TEACH

Read aloud the definitions, examples, and instruction in the box on p. 116. Point out that students often use verb phrases in speaking because helping verbs make the time of an action more specific.

Think Aloud

Model When I read the first example, I know that the action described is going on right now. The verb phrase *are telling* gives this information. It is more specific than if the sentence used the action verb alone and said, *The people tell stories*. The last two examples are similar. The first tells me that an action took place in the past, and the second tells me that an action will take place in the future.

Main and Helping Verbs

A **verb phrase** is a verb that has more than one word. The **main verb** shows action. A **helping verb** shows the time of the action. In the following sentence, *telling* is the main verb, and *are* is the helping verb.

The people are telling stories.

The helping verbs *am, is,* and *are* show present time. *Was* and *were* show past time. *Will* shows future time. The helping verbs *has, have,* and *had* show that an action happened in the past. In the following sentences, *had* and *will* are helping verbs.

He had told that story before. He will tell that story again.

A Write the verb phrase in each sentence.

1. The Native Americans <u>had told</u> interesting legends.
2. They <u>were explaining</u> the world around them.
3. I <u>have heard</u> legends about the sun and the moon.
4. In some stories, animals <u>are talking</u> like people.
5. Someday I <u>will entertain</u> you with the stories.
6. I <u>am writing</u> a legend.
7. I <u>have set</u> the story in a forest.
8. The flowers <u>are talking</u> to the trees.
9. The huge trees <u>will care</u> for the little flowers.
10. You <u>will hear</u> my story soon.

116 Grammar

RESOURCES

Daily Fix-It Lesson 12
   See p. TR4.
   See also Daily Fix-It Transparency 12.
Grammar Transparency 12

B Look at the underlined verb in each sentence. Write *M* if it is a main verb. Write *H* if it is a helping verb.

1. Those Native Americans were <u>living</u> in a rich region. M
2. The land <u>was</u> covered with trees. H
3. The women are <u>picking</u> berries. M
4. The men <u>are</u> gathering for a feast. H
5. The host <u>will</u> serve good food. H
6. The people had <u>created</u> beautiful copper shields. M
7. They <u>were</u> fishing for salmon. H
8. Some boys were <u>cutting</u> redwood trees. M
9. They <u>have</u> painted colorful designs on the wood. H
10. Their canoes will <u>hold</u> many men. M
11. The men are <u>paddling</u> the canoes up the river. M
12. One woman <u>has</u> found some wild blueberries. H

C Add a verb phrase with a main verb and a helping verb to complete each sentence. Write the sentence.
Possible answers:
13. People in the village ____ their resources wisely.
    People in the village were using their resources wisely.
14. They ____ homes and canoes from wood.
    They are making homes and canoes from wood.
15. The people ____ fish from the ocean.
    The people were eating fish from the ocean.
16. Men and boys ____ deer and moose in the woods.
    Men and boys had hunted deer and moose in the woods.
17. Craftspeople ____ beautiful blankets and masks.
    Craftspeople have created beautiful blankets and masks.
18. Villagers always ____ the land and the ocean.
    Villagers always will respect the land and the ocean.

Grammar **117**

PRACTICE

Guided Practice A

Work through the exercise with students. Then determine if they understand the concept by asking them to tell whether the helping verb in each sentence shows present, past, or future time.

TEACHING TIP

- Tell students that when identifying a verb phrase in a sentence, they should first look for an action verb. They should then check to see if there are helping verbs that make the action verb more specific.

Independent Practice B and C

Have students complete the exercises. For Differentiated Instruction and Extra Practice, see p. TR13.

Differentiated Instruction

Strategic Intervention

Write each of these helping verbs on a card: *am, is, are, was, were, has, have, had,* and *will.* Mix the cards and let students choose one. Have each student write a sentence about a game or sport, using a verb phrase with the helping verb on the card. Ask students to read their sentences aloud and identify the main verb, the helping verb, and the time the sentence describes.

Advanced

Have students write a short journal entry describing how their feelings about something such as a sport or extracurricular activity have changed recently. Ask students to use two or more sentences with verb phrases. For example, *I had always disliked piano lessons. Now I will practice more often.*

ELL

Display photos that show one or more people or animals in action. Help students think of a sentence that describes the action in each picture. Encourage them to use verb phrases. (*The kittens are playing with yarn.*) Write the sentences next to the pictures. Then read the sentences together and have volunteers underline the verb phrases.

Tell students that sometimes one or more words come between a main verb and a helping verb.

Example: Hummingbirds <u>are</u> always <u>moving</u> their wings.

In this sentence, *moving* is the main verb, and *are* is the helping verb. The word *always* is not part of the verb.

Monitor Progress

Check Grammar

If... students have difficulty identifying main verbs and helping verbs,	**then...** work through the test items with the class and have volunteers explain how they identified each main verb and distinguished it from a helping verb.

Test Preparation

Write the letter that shows the main verb in each sentence.

1. The villagers had held a festival.
   - **A** had
   - **B** had held
   - **C** villagers had
   - Ⓓ held

2. They were celebrating a good harvest.
   - **A** were
   - Ⓑ celebrating
   - **C** were celebrating
   - **D** they

3. They have danced around a campfire.
   - **A** have
   - **B** have danced
   - Ⓒ danced
   - **D** around

4. They are eating a delicious feast.
   - **A** They
   - **B** are
   - Ⓒ eating
   - **D** feast

5. They will have another festival next year.
   - Ⓐ have
   - **B** will have
   - **C** will
   - **D** They

6. My grandparents had attended the festival several years ago.
   - **A** had attended
   - Ⓑ attended
   - **C** had
   - **D** My

Review

⊘ Write the verb phrase in each sentence.

1. The Native Americans on the plains <u>were hunting</u> buffalo.
2. The hunters <u>are wearing</u> deerskin leggings.
3. The women <u>had planted</u> squash.
4. They <u>will grind</u> corn for cornmeal.
5. The children <u>are sleeping</u> in a log lodge.
6. Other Indians <u>were living</u> in the Southwest.
7. They <u>had built</u> homes of adobe bricks.
8. The girls <u>have displayed</u> their dolls.
9. The boys <u>are rolling</u> a hoop.
10. The children <u>will play</u> all day.

⊘ Look at the underlined verb in each sentence. Write *M* if it is a main verb. Write *H* if it is a helping verb.

11. The Pueblo people had <u>woven</u> beautiful cloth. M
12. They <u>have</u> shaped pottery. H
13. The artists <u>are</u> painting the pots with colorful designs. H
14. The Navajo were <u>stitching</u> colorful blankets. M
15. They are <u>creating</u> silver jewelry. M
16. The Pomo people <u>were</u> making baskets. H
17. They <u>had</u> decorated them with feathers. H
18. The baskets <u>will</u> hold water. H
19. That drum was <u>crafted</u> by an Arapaho. M
20. Who was <u>wearing</u> that beaded belt? M

Summarize

Ask students to describe verb phrases and explain how to identify them.

- A verb phrase consists of a main verb and one or more helping verbs.
- Helping verbs help specify the time of an action shown by a main verb. Some common helping verbs are *is, are, has, have,* and *will.*

Grammar-Writing Connection

Explain that describing the precise time of an action makes writing clearer and more specific. Helping verbs express time.

Specific: The men <u>have seen</u> bears many times before.

Strong Verbs

- Identify characteristics of a skit.
- Write a skit using strong verbs.
- Develop criteria for judging a piece of writing.

TEACH

- Read aloud the information about strong verbs in the box.
- Ask students to tell in their own words what strong verbs are. *(verbs that tell exactly what the action is)*

Guided Writing

Read each item in Exercise 1 with students. Ask for several suggestions for verbs and have students discuss which are the most vivid and precise.

Independent Writing

Have volunteers read aloud their responses to Exercise 2. Have the class identify the strong verb in each response.

Monitor Progress

Check Strong Verbs

If... students need more help with strong verbs,	**then...** locate a reading passage with especially strong verbs and have students identify them.

 WRITER'S CRAFT

Strong Verbs

> **Strong verbs** are verbs that describe an action precisely. Here are some strong verbs that might be used in place of *run*:
>
> scramble   rush   sprint   gallop   trot

 Write each sentence. Replace the underlined verb with a verb that is more vivid and precise. You may need to add or take out other words.
Possible answers:

1. The coyote <u>walked</u> slyly toward the people.
   The coyote strolled slyly toward the people.
2. The coyote <u>laughed</u> at his trick.
   The coyote chuckled at his trick.
3. The other animals <u>spoke</u> to the coyote.
   The other animals scolded the coyote.
4. The coyote <u>talked</u> about how smart he was.
   The coyote bragged about how smart he was.
5. The lazy coyote <u>lay</u> against a tree.
   The lazy coyote lounged against a tree.
6. The coyote <u>took</u> a nap in the warm sun.
   The coyote dozed in the warm sun.
7. When he woke up, he <u>wanted</u> food.
   When he woke up, he demanded food.
8. The other animals <u>said</u> that he should find his own food. The other animals shouted that he should find his own food.

 Write a sentence about a tricky coyote or another clever animal. Use a strong verb.
Possible answer: The coyote fooled the beaver with this clever plan.

120 Writing

RESOURCES

Writing Transparencies 12A, 12B
Writing Rubrics and Anchor Papers p. 20

Skit

A **skit** is a short play with a few characters. The plot, or events, of a skit are told through dialogue. Dialogue consists of the words the characters say to one another.

How Coyote Stole Fire

NARRATOR: Long ago, people had no fire.

COYOTE: People get cold in winter. The Fire Beings have fire. But they will not share it. I will go take it.

NARRATOR: Coyote went into the hills. He spied on the Fire Beings, but they guarded fire all the time. They didn't want others to have it.

COYOTE: *(He hides behind a tree.)* I have been here all day. Now it is late at night. The Fire Being who is guarding the fire is asleep. *(He grabs fire from the Fire Being and runs; the Fire Being chases him. The fire passes from Coyote to Beaver, Squirrel, and Chipmunk; all are chased by Fire Being. The fire is passed to Tree, and Fire Being cannot get it. Fire Being leaves.)*

NARRATOR: I will show how to get fire from Tree. *(Rubbing two branches together, he starts a fire. The people look happy.)*

A character explains the problem.

Skits are often read and not performed. Strong verbs help readers picture the action in their minds.

Narrator provides the conclusion.

Writing **121**

Skit

ANALYZE THE MODEL

Read aloud the model and the callouts to the left of it. Prepare students to write their own skits.

PROMPT

Write a skit that gives a fanciful explanation for something in nature. Use strong verbs.

Getting Started Students can do any of the following.

- Use an organizer (pp. 28–32).
- Find Native American legends in the library or on the Internet to use in their skit.
- List natural events that they could explain and choose one.

Editing/Revising Checklist

☑ Does the skit have characters and a plot?

☑ Does dialogue help tell the story?

☑ Have I used main and helping verbs correctly?

Self-Evaluation Distribute copies of p. TR26 for students to fill out.

Scoring Rubric Skit

Rubric 4 3 2 1	4	3	2	1
Focus/Ideas	Skit with focus on dramatic telling of nature story	Skit with fairly sharp dramatic focus	Unfocused skit or one not focused on natural event	Shows lack of understanding of skit or focus
Organization/ Paragraphs	Excellent control of time order	Good control of time order	Time order confused	Lacks organization
Voice	Highly entertaining voice	Shows some engaging traits	Little sense of engaging voice	No sense of engaging voice
Word Choice	Strong verbs and time-order words	Some use of strong verbs and time-order words	Limited attempt to use strong verbs and time-order words	Incorrect or limited word choice
Sentences	Suitable sentences for dramatic style	Some sentences suitable for dramatic style	Choppy sentences with lapses in logic	Fragments or run-on sentences
Conventions	Good control of drama's conventions	Reasonable control of drama's conventions	Errors that may hinder understanding	Frequent errors that interfere with meaning

For 5- and 6-point rubrics, see Writing Rubrics and Anchor Papers p. 20.

Subject-Verb Agreement

OBJECTIVES

- Define subject-verb agreement.
- Make sure verbs agree with subjects in writing.
- Become familiar with subject-verb agreement assessment on high-stakes tests.

TEACH

Read aloud the definition, examples, and instruction in the box on p. 122. Point out that action verbs must agree with their subjects only in present tense. However, forms of the verb *be* must agree with their subjects in both present and past tenses.

Think Aloud **Model** In the first example, the subject is a singular noun, so the action verb *set* ends in *-s*. In the second example, the subject is a plural noun, so the action verb *play* does not end in *-s*. In the third example, the subject is plural because the word *and* connects two different nouns. So the action verb *sit* does not end in *-s*. In the examples using the verb *be*, I know that *is* and *was* always agree with singular nouns while *are* and *were* always agree with plural nouns.

LESSON 13

Subject-Verb Agreement

The subject and the verb in a sentence must work together, or **agree**.

To make most present tense verbs agree with singular nouns or *he, she,* or *it,* add -s. If the subject is a plural noun or *I, you, we,* or *they,* the present tense verb does not end in -s.

Singular Subject	The <u>sun</u> <u>sets</u> today.
Plural Subject	The <u>girls</u> <u>play</u> outside.
Plural Subject	<u>A boy and a dog</u> <u>sit</u> there.

A form of *be* in a sentence also must agree with the subject. Use *is* or *was* to agree with singular nouns. Use *are* or *were* to agree with plural nouns.

Singular Subject	The <u>moon</u> <u>is</u> <u>shining</u> brightly. The <u>moon</u> <u>is</u> full.
Plural Subject	<u>Fireflies</u> <u>are</u> <u>lighting</u> the sky. <u>They</u> <u>were</u> everywhere.

A Write *C* next to each sentence that is correct.

1. Two deer is standing in the clearing.
   Two deer are standing in the clearing.
2. David steps on a branch. C
3. Both deer scampers away. Both deer scamper away.
4. Their white tails lift like flags. C
5. These animals are graceful. C

122 Grammar

RESOURCES

Daily Fix-It Lesson 13
   See p. TR5.
   See also Daily Fix-It Transparency 13.
Grammar Transparency 13

B Choose the verb in ( ) that agrees with the subject. Write the sentence.

1. Some animals (<u>stay</u>, stays) awake at night.
2. Bats (is, <u>are</u>) flying around the treetops.
3. Raccoons (<u>are</u>, is) prowling in the yard.
4. In the wild, a wolf (howl, <u>howls</u>).
5. An owl (hoot, <u>hoots</u>) in the forest.
6. Beavers (works, <u>work</u>) at night.
7. A moth and a firefly (is, <u>are</u>) fluttering in the dark.
8. The neighbors' cat (cry, <u>cries</u>) out at midnight.
9. A bullfrog (<u>is</u>, are) croaking at the pond.
10. Many animals (is, <u>are</u>) night creatures.

C Write sentences. Use each numbered phrase as a subject, along with a verb from the box. Make each verb agree with its subject. You may use the same verb more than once.

bark	spin	crawl	sway	glow

Possible answers:

11. The stars and the moon
12. A little snake
13. A neighborhood dog
14. The tree branches
15. A spider

11. The stars and the moon glow brightly.
12. A little snake crawls through the garden.
13. A neighborhood dog barks for no reason.
14. The tree branches sway in the breeze.
15. A spider spins a web on the backyard fence.

Grammar **123**

PRACTICE

Guided Practice Ⓐ

Work through the exercise with students. Then have them explain how to revise each sentence that is incorrect.

TEACHING TIP

- Point out that students must make forms of the verb *be* agree with subjects whether they are used as main verbs or helping verbs. Explain that students should memorize that *is* and *was* always agree with singular subjects while *are* and *were* always agree with plural subjects.

Independent Practice Ⓑ **and** Ⓒ

Have students complete the exercises. For Differentiated Instruction and Extra Practice, see p. TR13.

Differentiated Instruction

Strategic Intervention

Have students name specific insects. List the names on the board as singular nouns. Then have students name specific birds. List these names as plural nouns. For each word on the first list, have students make up and say a sentence using *is*. For example, *A moth is white.* For each word on the second list, have students make up and say a sentence using *are*. For example, *Wrens are tiny.*

Advanced

Have groups of students think of verbs that describe the action of fireworks, such as *burst, explode, glow,* and *sparkle.* List the words on the board. Then each student can write sentences using three of the verbs to describe summer details other than fireworks. For example, *The butterfly glows in the sun.* Have students exchange papers, mark the subject and verb of each sentence, and check that they agree.

ELL

To build on the concept of the lesson topic, write animals' names, such as *frog, bat, raccoon, snake, spider,* and *beaver,* in one column and their plural forms in another column. Read the words aloud with students. Ask them to think of sentences that describe one of the animals, using both forms of the animal's name. Model the process: *A frog hops. Frogs hop.* Write the sentences on the board and discuss how the subject and verb agree. Continue with students' sentences.

Remind students that the form of *be* in a sentence must agree with the subject. Use *is* or *was* to agree with singular nouns. Use *are* or *were* to agree with plural nouns.

Examples: The <u>moon</u> <u>is</u> bright tonight.
The <u>stars</u> <u>are</u> shining.

Monitor Progress

Check Grammar

If... students have difficulty with subject-verb agreement,	then... work through the test items, reminding students what to look for that can help them choose the correct verb for each sentence.

Test Preparation

✓ Write the letter of the verb that completes each sentence.

1. Animals __D__ all their senses at night.

   A uses   **C** useing

   B using   **D** use

2. Some animals __C__ well in the dark.

   A seen   **C** see

   B seeing   **D** sees

3. Wolves __B__ other animals.

   A smelling   **C** smells

   B smell   **D** smelles

4. The deer and the elk __B__ hearing footsteps.

   A is   **C** am

   B are   **D** be

5. My cat __A__ tiny insects.

   A hears   **C** hear

   B hearing   **D** heares

6. The cat __C__ using its bright eyes also.

   A are   **C** was

   B am   **D** were

7. A raccoon __B__ for food.

   A sniff   **C** sniffing

   B sniffs   **D** sniffs'

8. The bats __A__ hearing echoes.

   A are   **C** is

   B was   **D** am

9. Owls __D__ huge eyes.

   A has   **C** having

   B hadnt   **D** have

10. Animals' senses __C__ them.

   A helping   **C** help

   B helps   **D** helpes

Review

Write the sentence from each pair that is correct.

1. The girls is camping in the woods.
   <u>The girls are camping in the woods.</u>

2. The campers hear many sounds.
   <u>The campers hears many sounds.</u>

3. Some birds call at night.
   <u>Some birds calls at night.</u>

4. <u>A small animal is scampering in the bushes.</u>
   A small animal are scampering in the bushes.

5. Coyotes was howling in the distance.
   <u>Coyotes were howling in the distance.</u>

Choose the verb in ( ) that agrees with the subject. Write the sentence.

6. The desert (<u>is</u>, are) alive at night.

7. Desert animals (<u>sleep</u>, sleeps) during the hot day.

8. Snakes (<u>slither</u>, slithers) out of holes at night.

9. Mice (runs, <u>run</u>) across the dry ground.

10. A fox (<u>is</u>, are) looking for food.

11. Jackrabbits (<u>hop</u>, hops) around the cactus.

12. Two little rats (was, <u>were</u>) hiding from the wolves.

13. A lizard and a toad (is, <u>are</u>) sitting under a rock.

14. A big owl (watch, <u>watches</u>) the animals.

15. A cool breeze (blow, <u>blows</u>) through the desert.

Grammar **125**

Putting Ideas in Order

OBJECTIVES

- Identify characteristics of a friendly letter.
- Write a friendly letter, putting ideas in order.
- Develop criteria for judging a piece of writing.

TEACH

- Read aloud the information in the box about putting ideas in order.
- Ask students to tell in their own words what putting ideas in order means. *(using the best order for the type of writing, such as time order for a narrative)*

 Guided Writing

Read Exercise 1 with the class. Ask students to point out words that helped them determine the type of order used.

 Independent Writing

Have volunteers read their responses to Exercise 2 aloud. Have students tell how they used space order in their descriptions.

Monitor Progress

Check Putting Ideas in Order

If... students need more help with putting ideas in order,	**then...** locate passages written in different orders and have students identify the orders.

 WRITER'S CRAFT

Putting Ideas in Order

You can **put your ideas in order** in several different ways:

- To describe an event, use time order.
- To describe a place or a thing, use space order. For example, go from top to bottom or from left to right.
- To compare and contrast two things, describe their likenesses. Then describe their differences.
- To explain causes and effects, describe the causes. Then explain the effects of the causes.

 Read the paragraph. Write whether the paragraph is in *time order*, *space order*, *comparison-contrast order*, or *cause-effect order*.

Garden flowers and wildflowers are both beautiful and colorful. However, garden flowers grow in small areas. They need to be weeded and watered by people. On the other hand, wildflowers often grow in big fields or forests. They just need sunlight and rain to keep growing.
comparison-contrast order

 Write a short description of a place. Use space order.

Possible answer: On the left side of the garden are tall lilies. In the middle are roses. On the right are daisies.

RESOURCES

Writing Transparencies 13A, 13B
Writing Rubrics and Anchor Papers p. 21

Friendly Letter

A **friendly letter** is written by a person to a friend or family member. The letter expresses the writer's experiences and feelings. A friendly letter begins with a greeting and ends with a closing.

A Thunderstorm

July 2, _____

First sentence tells what the topic is.

Dear Luisa,

We had the most amazing storm yesterday! It was much worse than the one we had at camp last year. It was a hot, muggy afternoon, and I was reading a book on our porch. Suddenly black clouds formed in the sky. I saw a zigzag of lightning. Soon I heard a loud crash of thunder, and I ran inside. A few fat raindrops fell on the porch. Before long, rain was pouring out of the sky. The wind battered the trees and bushes. The downpour went on for ten minutes.

Then suddenly the storm ended. In another ten minutes, the sun reappeared. Soon the only signs of the storm were the puddles on my porch. I know you love nature, so I just had to tell you about this awesome summer storm.

Your friend,
Maya

Writer describes events in sequence.

Writer uses time-order words and vivid descriptive words.

Last sentence sums up letter. Closing indicates friendly letter.

Writing **127**

Friendly Letter
ANALYZE THE MODEL

Read aloud the model and the callouts to the left of it. Prepare students to write their own friendly letters.

PROMPT

Write a letter to a friend. Describe an interesting outdoor sight or event.

Getting Started Students can do any of the following.

- Use on organizer (pp. TR28–TR32).
- Close their eyes and think of an outdoor place.
- Talk with a partner about unusual events in nature.

Editing/Revising Checklist

- ✓ Are my ideas in a logical order?
- ✓ Does my letter express my feelings?
- ✓ Do my subjects and verbs agree?

Self-Evaluation Distribute copies of p. TR26 for students to fill out.

Scoring Rubric — Friendly Letter

Rubric 4 3 2 1	4	3	2	1
Focus/Ideas	Letter with vivid description of experience	Letter with good description of experience	Unfocused letter; little description or sense of experience	No letter or description; lacks focus and development
Organization/ Paragraphs	Appropriate order chosen and developed	Reasonable order chosen	Order confused or inappropriate	Lacks organization
Voice	Informal, conversational, engaging voice	Fairly engaging, informal voice	Voice not fitting subject or not engaging	Individual voice not communicated
Word Choice	*I* and vivid descriptive words used	Consistent use of *I;* some vivid words	*I* used inconsistently; no vivid words	Incorrect or limited word choice
Sentences	Clear, logical sentences	Reasonably clear sentences	Choppy sentences with lapses in logic	Fragments or run-on sentences
Conventions	Uses letter conventions correctly	Letter conventions used with accuracy	Letter conventions not used correctly	No evidence of letter conventions

For 5- and 6-point rubrics, see Writing Rubrics and Anchor Papers p. 21.

Present, Past, and Future Tenses

OBJECTIVES

- Define and identify present, past, and future tenses.
- Use present, past, and future tenses correctly in writing.
- Become familiar with verb tense assessment on high-stakes tests.

TEACH

Read aloud the definition, examples, and instruction in the box on p. 128. Remind students that present tense verbs that agree with a plural subject usually do not end in -s. For example, *The boys jump on the trampoline.*

Think Aloud

Model The present, past, and future tenses are easy to recognize. In the first example, I recognize the present tense: the verb *jump* only has to have -s added to agree with the singular subject *fish.* In the second example, -ed has been added to the verb, and that ending always indicates past tense. In the third example, the helping verb *will* has been used with the verb; that word always indicates the future tense.

Present, Past, and Future Tenses

Verbs can show when an action happens. This is called **tense**. Different verb tenses have different forms. Many present tense verbs end in -s. Form the past tense of many verbs by adding -ed. Add the helping verb *will* to a verb to show future tense.

Present Tense	A fish <u>jumps</u> out of the pond.
Past Tense	The boy <u>pulled</u> the fish in on a line.
Future Tense	The boy <u>will toss</u> the fish back.

- When a verb ends with *e*, drop the *e* before adding -ed: *close closed*
- When a one-syllable verb ends with one vowel followed by one consonant, double the final consonant before adding -ed: *hop hopped*
- When a verb ends with a consonant followed by *y*, change the *y* to *i* before adding -ed: *cry cried*

A Tell the tense of the underlined verb in each sentence. Write *present, past,* or *future.*

1. A whale <u>calls</u> to other whales. present
2. The whale <u>will use</u> the sound's echo. future
3. A whale's tail <u>moves</u> up and down. present
4. The whale <u>will glide</u> through the water. future
5. The whale <u>breathed</u> through the blowhole on its head. past
6. Ice <u>trapped</u> the whales in the bay. past

128 Grammar

RESOURCES

Daily Fix-It Lesson 14
   See p. TR5.
   See also Daily Fix-It Transparency 14.
Grammar Transparency 14

B Choose the verb in ( ) that completes each sentence. Use the tense that follows the sentence. Write the sentence.

1. Many different kinds of whales (lived, <u>live</u>) in the oceans. (present)

2. The gentle waves (carry, <u>carried</u>) the whales with them. (past)

3. You (<u>will discover</u>, discovered) gray whales in the North Pacific. (future)

4. Greenland whales (will measure, <u>measure</u>) up to 60 feet long. (present)

5. The size of a blue whale (surprised, <u>will surprise</u>) you. (future)

6. The humpback whale (uses, <u>used</u>) long flippers. (past)

7. Many humpback whales (stay, <u>will stay</u>) near the coast. (future)

C Choose a verb from the word bank to complete each sentence. Use each verb in the tense shown.

collect	hurry	provide	tap	travel

Possible answers:

8. A baby whale ____ along near its mother. (past)
A baby whale hurried along near its mother.

9. A mother whale gently ____ her baby's body. (past)
A mother whale gently tapped her baby's body.

10. Warm waters ____ a nice home for the babies. (past)
Warm waters provided a nice home for the babies.

11. The whales ____ to cold waters in summer. (present)
The whales travel to cold waters in summer.

12. They ____ much food there. (future)
They will collect much food there.

Guided Practice A

Work through the exercise with students. Then ask volunteers to explain how they recognized each tense.

TEACHING TIP

- Point out that in a narrative, different verb tenses may be used. For example, a character may think about the future and use the future tense. However, a story should be written in either the present or past tense.

Independent Practice B and C

Have students complete the exercises. For Differentiated Instruction and Extra Practice, see p. TR13.

Differentiated Instruction

Strategic Intervention

Write *present, past,* and *future* on three slips of paper. Have students take turns choosing a tense. They should make up and say a sentence about hobbies and after-school activities using the tense specified. For example, *I painted a picture yesterday. I play the piano every day. We will practice soccer each week.* Have other students identify the tense used.

Advanced

Have students think of a topic for a short narrative, such as a recent outing. Ask them to write three or four sentences on the topic using past tense. Then have students rewrite their narratives, changing the tense first to present and then to future.

ELL

With students, brainstorm vivid action verbs that describe activities people can do outdoors, such as *ski, hike,* and *climb.* Write the verbs on the board. Pair students of different abilities. Have the partners choose one verb and use it in a present tense sentence, a past tense sentence, and a future tense sentence. Let students read their sentences aloud.

Remind students that they may be asked to identify the tense of a verb in a sentence. Remember that a verb that has no ending or that ends with -s and has no helping verb is a present tense verb. A verb with -ed is a past tense verb. A verb with the helping verb *will* is a future tense verb.

Present: Whales <u>swim</u> near the boat.

Past: They <u>bumped</u> into the side.

Future: They <u>will stay</u> away next time.

Test Preparation

Write the letter of the verb that completes each sentence. Use the tense in ( ).

1. We __B__ some whales off the coast. (past)

   A view

   B viewed

   C will view

   D views

2. A whale __C__ its tail out of the water. (past)

   A flips

   B will flip

   C flipped

   D fliped

3. The whale __A__ the water with its tail. (present)

   A slaps

   B slapping

   C slapped

   D slap

4. The whale's tail __C__ very loud. (future)

   A sound

   B sounded

   C will sound

   D sounding

5. Sometimes whales __A__ their heads through the water. (future)

   A will poke

   B poke

   C poking

   D pokes

6. The whales __B__ with an unusual sound. (past)

   A crying

   B cried

   C cryed

   D cry

Review

✓ Tell the tense of the underlined verb in each sentence. Write *present, past,* or *future.*

1. Scientists <u>classified</u> dolphins as whales. past
2. Dolphins <u>will learn</u> quickly. future
3. People <u>call</u> a group of dolphins a school. present
4. A school of dolphins <u>followed</u> a ship. past
5. The animals <u>turn</u> flips in the ocean. present

✓ Choose the verb in ( ) that completes each sentence. Use the tense that follows the sentence. Write the sentence.

6. Dolphins (<u>performed</u>, perform) in the show. (past)
7. They (invent, <u>will invent</u>) their own tricks. (future)
8. A dolphin (tosses, <u>tossed</u>) a ball through a hoop. (past)
9. Two dolphins (<u>jump</u>, will jump) over a net. (present)
10. Dolphins (produce, <u>will produce</u>) whistles and clicks. (future)
11. The sounds (<u>echo</u>, echoed) off objects in the water. (present)
12. Dolphins' good vision (<u>helps</u>, helped) them too. (present)
13. The ancient Greeks (<u>liked</u>, like) dolphins. (past)
14. The people (<u>painted</u>, will paint) dolphins on their pottery. (past)
15. Sailors still (<u>consider</u>, will consider) dolphins good luck. (present)

Grammar **131**

Summarize

Ask students to tell what they have learned about present, past, and future tenses and how to form them.

- Add *-s* to form a present tense verb to agree with a singular subject.
- Add *-ed* to many verbs to form the past tense.
- Use the helping verb *will* to form the future tense.

Grammar-Writing Connection

Explain to students that using present, past, and future tenses in writing tells readers exactly when an action happened.

Future tense: The whales <u>will return</u> to warm water in the winter.

By using the future tense in this sentence, the writer tells readers that the action will happen in the future.

Answer the 5Ws and *How*

- Read aloud the information in the box about answering the 5 Ws and *how*.
- Ask students to tell in their own words what answering the 5 Ws and *how* means. *(telling who, what, when, where, why, and how about an event)*

 ## Guided Writing

Read each question in Exercise 1 with the class. Have students read the sentence(s) that answer each question.

 ## Independent Writing

Ask students to write a lead sentence as the beginning of a news story about a special school event. Have them include answers to as many of the 5 Ws and *how* as possible.

Monitor Progress

Check Answer the 5 Ws and *How*

If... students need more help with answering the 5 Ws and *how*,	then... locate news stories in student news magazines and have students point out answers to the 5 Ws and *how*.

 WRITER'S CRAFT

Answer the 5 Ws and How

> A good news story answers the questions **who, what, where, when,** and **why** about an event. It might also answer the question **how** about the event.

 Read the news story. Answer the questions.

Lunch Guest

A Boulder family had an unexpected lunch guest yesterday. At approximately 12:45 P.M. Charles, Ava, and Alex Martin were eating lunch on their back deck. They suddenly remembered that Alex had soccer practice and rushed inside, leaving their uneaten food on the table. Just as they were about to leave, Mr. Martin decided to bring in the food. "I didn't want to attract any squirrels or raccoons," Mr. Martin said. "Little did I know what had already shown up." When he went outside, Mr. Martin found a huge black bear enjoying the family's chicken salad and apple pie. Mr. Martin went indoors and called the fire department. However, the bear—and the food—were gone before help arrived.

1. *Who* was involved in the event?
   the Martin family
2. *What* happened?
3. *Where* did the event happen?
   at the Martin family's home in Boulder
4. *When* did the event happen?
   yesterday afternoon at 12:45
5. *Why* was the bear able to steal the food?
   The Martins had gone inside.

2. A black bear came to the family's deck and ate some leftover food.

132 Writing

RESOURCES

Writing Transparencies 14A, 14B
Writing Rubrics and Anchor Papers p. 22

News Story

A **news story** describes an interesting recent event. It answers the questions *who, what, where, when,* and *why* about the event. These questions are called the 5 Ws. The news story often also answers the question *how* about the event.

Saving Whales

First sentence provides an interesting lead.

Thousands of whales in the Northern Hemisphere owe their lives to a young girl. On April 18, a herd of whales became stranded near a shore of the Antarctic Ocean. The Edir Konek family of Pontak heard strange sounds and discovered the group of whales stuck in the bay. After discovering that the path to the ocean was covered with ice, the Koneks called an icebreaker to save the whales.

News story answers the 5 Ws and *how.*

Captain George Turner and his crew arrived. Time was running out for the whales when young Glashka Konek had an idea. "I suggested the crew play music for the whales," Glashka said. "I thought it would calm the whales and get them to move." Turner's crew tried many kinds of music, but the whales would not budge. Then Captain Turner played classical music.

Last sentence provides a conclusion.

The whales followed the boat and were saved.

Writing **133**

News Story

ANALYZE THE MODEL

Read aloud the model and the callouts to the left of it. Prepare students to write their own news stories.

PROMPT

Write a news story about an event in nature. Answer the 5 Ws and *how* about the event.

Getting Started Students can do any of the following.

- Use an organizer (pp. TR28–TR32).
- Read a newspaper or magazine to find ideas for nature stories.
- Look through books about nature.

Editing/Revising Checklist

✓ Does the news story tell about an event in time order?

✓ Does the story answer the 5 Ws and *how?*

✓ Have I used the correct tense throughout my news story?

Self-Evaluation Distribute copies of p. TR26 for students to fill out.

Scoring Rubric New Story

Rubric 4 3 2 1	4	3	2	1
Focus/Ideas	News story with tight focus on details	New story with fairly clear focus	Unfocused news story; facts unclear	Shows lack of understanding of news story
Organization/ Paragraphs	Clear time order	Organization good with one or two lapses in sequence	Order of story confused	Lacks organization
Voice	Knowledgeable, factual voice	Shows knowledge of facts	Tries to deal with facts but unsure of self	Voice not trustworthy
Word Choice	Effective time-order words; no wordiness	Some use of time-order words; little wordiness	Little attempt to use time-order words; some wordiness	Incorrect or limited word choice
Sentences	Clear sentences in variety of lengths	Clear sentences	Choppy sentences with no variety	Fragments or run-on sentences
Conventions	Excellent control and accuracy	Reasonable control with few errors	Errors that may hinder understanding	Frequent errors that interfere with meaning

For 5- and 6-point rubrics, see *Writing Rubrics and Anchor Papers* p. 22.

Irregular Verbs

OBJECTIVES

- Define and identify irregular verbs.
- Use irregular verbs correctly in writing.
- Become familiar with irregular verb assessment on high-stakes tests.

TEACH

Read aloud the instruction and examples in the box on p. 134. Explain that the tenses of irregular verbs must be memorized because they do not follow a pattern.

Think Aloud **Model** As I look at the list of irregular verbs and their tenses, I see that I'm familiar with most of them because we use them in everyday speech. So I don't have to think, "*See* is an irregular verb" before I use the past tense, *saw*, correctly. But I also know that some people tend to use certain irregular verb forms incorrectly. So, for example, if I knew that I have used *seen* instead of *saw* for the past tense, I would work on that and memorize the correct tenses of the verb *see*.

LESSON 15

Irregular Verbs

Usually you add *-ed* to a verb to show past tense. **Irregular verbs** do not follow this rule. These verbs change to other words to show past tense.

Present Tense	We <u>see</u> a volcano.
Past Tense	We <u>saw</u> a volcano.
Past with *has*, *have*, or *had*	We <u>have seen</u> a volcano.

Verb	Past Tense	Past with *has*, *have*, or *had*
begin	began	(has, have, had) begun
do	did	(has, have, had) done
find	found	(has, have, had) found
give	gave	(has, have, had) given
go	went	(has, have, had) gone
run	ran	(has, have, had) run
see	saw	(has, have, had) seen
take	took	(has, have, had) taken
think	thought	(has, have, had) thought
wear	wore	(has, have, had) worn

A Write the correct form of the irregular verb in ( ).

1. That island (begun, began) as a volcano. began
2. A volcano in the ocean (gone, went) off. went
3. Lava has (run, ran) into the ocean. run
4. We have (taken, took) a trip to that island. taken

134 Grammar

RESOURCES

Daily Fix-It Lesson 15
See p. TR5.
See also Daily Fix-It Transparency 15.
Grammar Transparency 15

B Write each sentence. Use the correct past form of the verb in ( ).

1. We (see) the world's largest volcano in Hawaii. **saw**
2. We had (go) to the big island of Hawaii for a vacation. **gone**
3. My uncle (take) us to Mauna Loa for the day. **took**
4. We (find) a nice hiking trail on the volcano's slope. **found**
5. I had (wear) a warm sweater, and I was glad. **worn**
6. The next day, we (go) to another volcano in Hawaii. **went**
7. Kilauea (begin) erupting. **began**
8. Bright red lava had (run) down the volcano. **run**
9. Now I have (see) two volcanoes. **seen**
10. I (do) a report on the volcanoes after my trip. **did**

C Use verbs from the chart to complete the sentences. Write the sentences. **Possible answers:**

11. Yesterday lava ____ down the volcano.
    Yesterday lava ran down the volcano.
12. The eruption had ____ a month ago.
    The eruption had begun a month ago.
13. I ____ Mount St. Helens last spring.
    I saw Mount St. Helens last spring.
14. The sunshine that day ____ the volcano a cheerful look. The sunshine that day gave the volcano a cheerful look.
15. I always had ____ volcanoes were scary.
    I always had thought volcanoes were scary.

Guided Practice Ⓐ

Work through the exercise with students. Show them how they can refer to the chart to help them find the correct verb forms.

TEACHING TiP

• Take note of irregular verb forms that students tend to use incorrectly. For example, some students may say "I had gave" or "I had took." Call these errors to students' attention and provide additional exercises.

Independent Practice Ⓑ and Ⓒ

Have students complete the exercises. For Differentiated Instruction and Extra Practice, see p. TR13.

Differentiated Instruction

Strategic Intervention

Write each irregular verb in the chart on p. 134 on a separate card. Place cards facedown and have students choose one. Point to each student and name a tense: present, past, or past with *has, have,* or *had.* Students should write a sentence using their chosen verb in their assigned tense. Have students read their sentences aloud. The rest of the class can discuss whether the verb is used correctly.

Advanced

Challenge students to write a paragraph using as many of the irregular verbs in the chart on p. 134 as possible. Tell them to use each of the three tenses at least once. Have students read their paragraphs aloud in small groups.

ELL

Build on the lesson concept. Using only a few of the irregular verbs at a time, write all three forms for each verb, one form per card. Give each student a card. Have students find those who have the verb forms that belong with their verb form. They may then write the forms for their verb on the board.

Remind students that they may be asked to identify the correct past tense of an irregular verb. Learn which verbs are irregular and practice using their past tense.

The volcano <u>began</u> an eruption.

The volcano <u>has done</u> this before.

Rocks <u>have gone</u> far into the air.

Monitor Progress

Check Grammar

If... students have difficulty identifying and using irregular verbs,	**then...** discuss how they can find the correct answer for each test item using the chart on p. 134.

Test Preparation

✓ Write the letter of the verb that completes each sentence.

1. We __C__ many natural wonders in Hawaii.
   A finding   **C** found
   B finded   **D** founded

2. We __A__ two active volcanoes.
   A saw   **C** seed
   B sawn   **D** seen

3. We had __B__ to a rain forest.
   A go   **C** went
   B gone   **D** going

4. We have __A__ into big ocean waves.
   A run   **C** ran
   B running   **D** runned

5. Our teacher has __D__ a talk about Hawaii's formation.
   A gave   **C** giving
   B give   **D** given

6. It __B__ as five volcanoes.
   A begun   **C** begin
   B began   **D** beginning

7. We have __C__ a tour of a pineapple farm.
   A took   **C** taken
   B taking   **D** taked

8. Katie has __C__ many wonderful places.
   A saw   **C** seen
   B see   **D** seeing

136 Grammar

Review

☑ Write the correct form of the irregular verb in ( ) to complete each sentence.

1. I (<u>did</u>, done) a report about a volcano in Mexico.
2. It (begun, <u>began</u>) in 1943.
3. Lava had (<u>run</u>, ran) out of a crack in a farmer's cornfield.
4. After six days, the farmer had (find, <u>found</u>) a 500-foot volcano in his field.
5. That must have (gave, <u>given</u>) him quite a scare!

☑ Write each sentence. Use the correct past form of the verb in ( ).

6. I (think) Krakatoa was an incredible volcano. thought
7. It (give) an unbelievable boom when it erupted in 1883. gave
8. The volcano (do) a great amount of damage. did
9. My family has (take) a trip to Lassen Peak in California. taken
10. That volcano had (begin) erupting in May 1914. begun
11. A year later, an explosion (go) off and ruined a nearby forest. went
12. We (see) strange lava formations near Lassen Peak. saw
13. Mount Katmai in Alaska had (go) off in 1912. gone
14. Lava and ash (run) for 15 miles and formed a valley. ran
15. I always have (find) volcanoes interesting. found

Grammar **137**

Summarize

Ask students to describe irregular verbs.

- An irregular verb is a verb that does not add -ed to form the past tense.
- Irregular verbs change to other words to show the past tense.
- Forms of irregular verbs must be memorized.

Grammar-Writing Connection

Explain that using a variety of verbs makes writing lively. Some verbs that writers use are irregular verbs.

Irregular verbs: I <u>found</u> hard lava and <u>took</u> photographs.

Compare/ Contrast Words

TEACH

- Read aloud the instruction about compare/contrast words in the box.
- Ask students to tell in their own words what compare/contrast words are. (words such as *also* and *but* that signal how two things are alike and different)

Guided Writing

Read the first five items in the exercise with the class. Have students explain how they decided which word to use in each sentence.

Independent Writing

Ask volunteers to read their responses to item 6 aloud. Have students identify the compare/contrast word the writer used in the sentence and discuss why it is a good choice.

Monitor Progress

Check Compare/Contrast Words

If... students need more help with compare/contrast words,	then... have them locate some in their reading materials and explain why they are useful.

 WRITER'S CRAFT

Compare/Contrast Words

When you compare or contrast two things, use words that signal how the two things are alike and different.

Alike	Spring is a warm season. Summer is <u>also</u> warm.
Different	Spring is often rainy, <u>but</u> summer is usually dry.

 Use a word or words from the box to signal a likeness or difference in each pair of sentences. Write the sentences as two sentences or combine them into a compound sentence. Write a final sentence that compares or contrasts two insects.

and	also	as well
but	however	on the other hand

Possible answers:

1. Leaves are green in summer. They turn red in autumn.
   Leaves are green in summer, but they turn red in autumn.
2. Oak trees lose their leaves in winter. Pine trees keep their leaves all year. Oak trees lose their leaves in winter. However, pine trees keep their leaves all year.
3. Tulips bloom in spring. Lilies bloom in spring.
   Tulips bloom in spring. Lilies bloom in spring as well.
4. Redwood trees grow very tall. Sequoias grow taller.
   Redwood trees grow very tall, but sequoias grow taller.
5. The plants in your garden need water every day in summer. Trees need water. The plants in your garden need water every day in summer. Trees need water also.
6. (Your sentence) An ant crawls, but a bee flies.

138 Writing

RESOURCES

Writing Transparencies 15A, 15B
Writing Rubrics and Anchor Papers p. 23

Writing for Tests

WRITING MODEL

Prompt Think about <u>two things in nature</u>. They might be two birds, two trees, or two seasons. Write a <u>compare/contrast paragraph</u> for a nature magazine that tells how the two things are <u>alike</u> and <u>different</u>. Use <u>compare/contrast words</u> to signal similarities and differences.

Two Beautiful Blossoms

Both and *also* signal similarities.

Roses and tulips are both beautiful flowers. They grow in a variety of bright colors, such as yellow, red, and pink. Tulips look pretty in vases. Roses also make lovely flower arrangements. Tulips usually bloom in early spring. However, roses often bloom in the middle of summer. Tulips grow on long smooth stalks, while roses have thorny stems. Tulips grow in the ground, but roses grow on bushes. Although these two flowers are different in some ways, both are sure to brighten your day.

However, while, and *but* signal differences.

The final sentence sums up the paragraph.

Writing **139**

Writing for Tests

ANALYZE THE MODEL

Read aloud the model and the callouts to the left of it. Prepare students to write their own compare/contrast paragraphs.

PROMPT

Write a compare/contrast paragraph that tells how two things in nature are alike and different.

Getting Started Students should do the following.

- Read the prompt and develop a plan for what they want to say.
- Support their ideas with facts, examples, and details.
- Check their writing for errors.

Editing/Revising Checklist

☑ Does my paragraph compare and contrast two things?

☑ Are compare/contrast words used?

☑ Have I formed the past tense of irregular verbs correctly?

Self-Evaluation Distribute copies of p. TR26 for students to fill out.

Scoring Rubric — Writing for Tests

Rubric 4 3 2 1	4	3	2	1
Focus/Ideas	Focused paragraph; many compare/contrast details	Fairly focused paragraph; some compare/contrast details	Paragraph not focused on topic; few compare/contrast details	Not a paragraph; no development of compare/contrast details
Organization/ Paragraphs	Compare/contrast details organized clearly	Some attempt to organize compare/contrast details	Details not clearly organized	No organization of details
Voice	Clearly aware of purpose and audience	Recognizes purpose and audience	Writer vague and uninvolved with topic	Writer not involved with topic
Word Choice	Clear and appropriate use of signal words	Uses some appropriate signal words	Little use of signal words	No use of signal words
Sentences	Varied, well-constructed sentences	Sentences well constructed; some variety	Little variety; some sentences poorly constructed	Lacks variety; fragments and run-on sentences
Conventions	Excellent control and accuracy	Reasonable control with few errors	Errors that may hinder understanding	Frequent errors that interfere with meaning

For 5- and 6-point rubrics, see *Writing Rubrics and Anchor Papers* p. 23.

Singular and Plural Pronouns

- Define and identify singular and plural pronouns.
- Use singular and plural pronouns correctly in writing.
- Become familiar with singular and plural pronoun assessment on high-stakes tests.

TEACH

Read aloud the definitions, examples and instruction in the box on p. 140. Point out to students that they use pronouns frequently in speech and in writing instead of repeating nouns over and over.

Model I recognize both singular and plural pronouns because I often use them in place of nouns when I'm writing and speaking. One way I can check to make sure a word is a pronoun is to ask *what* or *who*. In the second example, *It took off,* I could ask *What took off?* The answer is the plane. *Plane* is the noun that the pronoun *it* takes the place of.

LESSON 16

Singular and Plural Pronouns

Pronouns are words that take the place of nouns. Pronouns that take the place of singular nouns are **singular pronouns**. *I, me, he, she, him, her,* and *it* are singular pronouns.

The <u>plane</u> took off. <u>It</u> took off.

Pronouns that take the place of plural nouns are **plural pronouns**. *We, us, they,* and *them* are plural pronouns.

The <u>wheels</u> lifted up. <u>They</u> lifted up.

You can be used as a singular and a plural pronoun.

<u>Children</u>, do <u>you</u> know the story of Icarus?
<u>Icarus</u>, <u>you</u> must not fly too high.

A Write the pronoun in each sentence.

1. Mr. Lewis told us an old story. us
2. It was about a boy with wings. It
3. The boy's dad told him not to fly too high. him
4. He went too close to the sun. He
5. The sun heated the wings, and they melted. they
6. Did you learn a lesson from the story? you
7. He drew a flying machine in 1500. He
8. They have designed machines with all kinds of wings. They

140 Grammar

RESOURCES

Daily Fix-It Lesson 16
  See p. TR6.
  See also Daily Fix-It Transparency 16.
Grammar Transparency 16

B Write *S* if the underlined pronoun is singular. Write *P* if it is plural.

1. Orville Wright and <u>he</u> built the first successful airplane over a century ago. s

2. <u>They</u> flew the plane in 1903. P

3. A woman watched from afar, and <u>she</u> was amazed. s

4. Louis Bleriot built a plane and flew <u>it</u> from France to England. s

5. Early planes were unlike those that carry <u>us</u>. P

6. Ben, <u>you</u> would like the Wright brothers' glider. s

7. <u>It</u> had two wings, one atop the other. s

8. Companies held air races and from <u>them</u> developed better airplanes. P

9. <u>I</u> am interested in old airplanes. s

C Revise each pair of sentences. Replace the underlined words with one of these pronouns: *she, he, they.*
Answers on page TR36

10. The government sold planes from World War I. <u>The planes</u> were made of wood and cloth.

11. Charles Lindbergh flew nonstop across the Atlantic Ocean. <u>Lindbergh</u> was the first to do this alone.

12. Amelia Earhart flew across the Atlantic Ocean nonstop. <u>Earhart</u> flew in a plane called *Friendship*.

Grammar **141**

Guided Practice (A)

Work through the exercise with students. Then to check their understanding of the concept, have them identify whether each pronoun is singular or plural.

TEACHING TIP

- Explain that a pronoun must agree with the noun it replaces. The third-person noun *girl* must be replaced by the third-person pronoun *she;* the pronoun *I* or *you* would not agree. The pronoun must also have the same number. The singular noun *girl* agrees with the singular pronoun *she,* not a plural pronoun such as *they.*

Independent Practice **B** and **C**

Have students complete the exercises. For Differentiated Instruction and Extra Practice, see p. TR14.

Differentiated Instruction

Strategic Intervention

Have students write each pronoun on a self-stick note. On chart paper, write sentences, underlining the nouns that can be replaced by pronouns. For example, *Ed rows the boat. Children play with the toys.* Have students come to the chart and stick the note with the correct pronoun over the underlined word or words in a sentence. Together read both versions of the sentences.

Advanced

Challenge students to write a paragraph of three or four sentences about traveling. Tell them that they cannot use the pronouns *I, me, he, she, him, her,* and *it* to replace nouns. Have students exchange papers with a partner. Partners rewrite the paragraph using pronouns to make the writing less wordy and awkward.

ELL

Explain that in many languages, pronouns similar to *he* and *she* in English are used for things. In English, these pronouns are used only for people, and the pronouns *it, they,* and *them* are used for things. Display pictures of a girl, a boy, a clock, and apples. Have students say sentences about the pictures first in their home language and then in English. Make sure they use the correct pronouns.

Test Preparation

Write the letter of the pronoun that can replace the underlined word or words.

1. <u>People</u> were fascinated by flying.
   - **A** He
   - **C** They
   - **B** She
   - **D** I

2. A four-engine plane was flown by <u>a Russian inventor</u>.
   - **A** we
   - **C** them
   - **B** him
   - **D** you

3. <u>Richard Byrd</u> flew across the North Pole.
   - **A** They
   - **C** We
   - **B** She
   - **D** He

4. <u>Lindbergh's plane</u> was the *Spirit of St. Louis*.
   - **A** It
   - **C** They
   - **B** He
   - **D** Them

5. <u>Herndon and Pangborn</u> flew across the Pacific.
   - **A** We
   - **C** They
   - **B** He
   - **D** Us

6. <u>Amelia Earhart</u> tried to fly around the world.
   - **A** He
   - **C** They
   - **B** She
   - **D** Us

7. Many speed records were set by <u>Jacqueline Cochran</u>.
   - **A** us
   - **C** her
   - **B** them
   - **D** me

8. Courage was needed in <u>early flights</u>.
   - **A** them
   - **C** him
   - **B** it
   - **D** her

Review

✓ Write the pronoun in each sentence.

1. <u>We</u> flew a kite outside.
2. <u>It</u> was in the shape of a box.
3. Dad and <u>I</u> made the kite carefully.
4. The wind was blowing all around <u>us</u>.
5. Dad let the kite go, and <u>it</u> soared above the trees.
6. Darcy came along, and <u>she</u> wanted to hold the kite.
7. Dad handed the string to <u>her</u>.
8. Tyler was there, and Darcy handed the string to <u>him</u>.
9. <u>They</u> ran around the field with the kite.
10. The kite entertained <u>them</u> all afternoon.

✓ Write *S* if the underlined pronoun is singular. Write *P* if it is plural.

11. Students, did <u>you</u> know that a kite is an aircraft? P
12. The Chinese made <u>them</u> thousands of years ago. P
13. Benjamin Franklin made a kite and flew <u>it</u> during a storm. S
14. <u>He</u> learned about electricity from the kite. S
15. The Wright brothers made kites and studied <u>them</u>. P
16. <u>They</u> learned about wings from the kites. P
17. Lorraine's father gives <u>her</u> a new kite every spring. S
18. <u>We</u> can make our own kites. P
19. Joanna is an artist, and <u>she</u> builds beautiful kites. S
20. <u>I</u> like kites because they are fun. S

Grammar **143**

Vivid Words

OBJECTIVES

- Identify characteristics of a poem.
- Write a poem, using vivid words.
- Develop criteria for judging a piece of writing.

TEACH

- Read aloud the information about vivid words in the box.
- Ask students to tell in their own words what vivid words are. *(words that help readers see, hear, touch, taste, or smell what is described)*

Guided Writing

Read each item in Exercise 1 with the class. Discuss different word choices for each sentence with students and have them tell why some choices are better than others.

Independent Writing

Ask volunteers read aloud their responses to Exercise 2. Have listeners identify the vivid words.

Monitor Progress

Check Vivid Words

If... students need more help with vivid words,	**then...** have them use thesauruses to look up more vivid synonyms for words such as *dim, bad, old,* and *many.*

 WRITER'S CRAFT

Vivid Words

> **Vivid words** help readers see, hear, touch, taste, or smell what the writer describes. Vivid words include verbs such as *swirl*, nouns such as *whirlwind*, and adjectives such as *slick*.

 Replace the underlined word or words with a more vivid word from the box or your own word.

fierce	crashed	clutched	howled	fluttered
wailed	whispered	fluffy	ripped	stroked

Possible answers:

1. The breeze blew <u>full</u> clouds across the sky.
   The breeze blew fluffy clouds across the sky.
2. Trees' leaves <u>moved</u> in the breeze.
   Trees' leaves fluttered in the breeze.
3. Suddenly the wind became <u>bad</u>.
   Suddenly the wind became fierce.
4. It <u>took</u> the petals off the wildflowers.
   It ripped the petals off the wildflowers.
5. The wind <u>made a big noise</u> through the trees.
   The wind howled through the trees.
6. A tree limb <u>fell</u> against the house.
   A tree limb crashed against the house.
7. The little boy <u>cried</u> and <u>held</u> his mother.
   The little boy wailed and clutched his mother.
8. She <u>touched</u> his hair and <u>talked</u> to him.
   She stroked his hair and whispered to him.

Write a sentence about how the wind moves. Use two vivid words. Underline them.
Possible answer: The wind <u>stormed</u> across the <u>barren</u> desert.

144 Writing

RESOURCES

Writing Transparencies 16A, 16B
Writing Rubrics and Anchor Papers p. 24

Poem

A **poem** uses vivid words to describe a person, place, thing, event, or feeling. A poem has many or all of these characteristics.

- Words are arranged in *lines*. Each line may be a complete sentence or a group of words that makes sense.
- Words are used in fresh ways to create pictures, or images.
- Lines may be arranged in groups called *stanzas*.
- Some lines may *rhyme*. This means that the ending sounds of two words are the same.
- The lines have *rhythm*. Their sounds make a musical pattern.

Poem is arranged in two four-line stanzas.

Vivid words create a picture of the waves in motion.

All the lines have a similar rhythm.

Each pair of lines rhymes.

Waves

The waves flow in from far away.
They journey each and every day,
Come crashing, splashing toward the land,
To meet me here upon the sand.

The waves leap up; they lift up high.
They travel almost to the sky,
Climb higher than a man can reach,
And then collapse upon the beach.

Writing **145**

Poem
ANALYZE THE MODEL

Read aloud the model and the callouts to the left of it. Prepare students to write their own poems.

PROMPT
Write a poem about an unusual person, thing, or event. Use vivid words to create mental pictures.

Getting Started Students can do any of the following.

- Use an organizer (pp. TR28–TR32).
- Talk with a group about unusual people, things, or events.
- Brainstorm words brought to mind by the phrase *something unusual*.

Editing/Revising Checklist

✓ Have I used vivid words to create a picture?

✓ Have I arranged my poem in lines?

✓ Have I used singular and plural pronouns to replace nouns?

Self-Evaluation Distribute copies of p. TR26 for students to fill out.

Scoring Rubric Poem

Rubric 4 3 2 1	4	3	2	1
Focus/Ideas	Poem with tight focus on topic	Poem with fairly clear focus on topic	Poem unfocused, with topic unclear	Lacks understanding of poem form
Organization/ Paragraphs	Clearly organized into lines and stanzas	Organization of lines and stanzas fairly consistent	Organization into lines and stanzas confused	No use of lines and stanzas
Voice	Imaginative, original voice	Some evidence of imagination	Tries for imaginative voice	No original voice
Word Choice	Vivid words and images	Some vivid words	Little attempt to use vivid words	Incorrect or limited word choice
Sentences	Clear sentences or effective non-sentences in line form	Sentences or word groups in line form	No sentences or meaningful word groups in lines	No attempt at sentences or word groups in lines
Conventions	Excellent control and accuracy	Reasonable control with few errors	Errors that may hinder understanding	Frequent errors that interfere with meaning

For 5- and 6-point rubrics, see *Writing Rubrics and Anchor Papers* p. 24.

Subject and Object Pronouns

- Define and identify subject and object pronouns.
- Use subject and object pronouns correctly in writing.
- Become familiar with subject and object pronoun assessment on high-stakes tests.

TEACH

Read aloud the definitions, examples, and instruction in the box on p. 146. Point out that students usually do not have to identify a pronoun as a subject or object pronoun before using it because the correct form is familiar to them. However, in some sentences, such as those with a compound subject, they need to distinguish between a subject and object pronoun and choose the correct one.

Model In the first example, it is clear that *she* is the subject of the sentence, so the subject pronoun is correct. The second sentence has a compound subject: two subjects joined by *and*. I have heard people mistakenly say something like *Her and me stayed home.* But if I know that *her* and *me* are object pronouns and cannot be used in the subject of a sentence, I won't make that mistake.

LESSON 17

Subject and Object Pronouns

A pronoun used as the subject of a sentence is called a **subject pronoun**. A pronoun used after an action verb or as the object of a preposition is called an **object pronoun**.

- *I, you, he, she, it, we,* and *they* are subject pronouns.
- *Me, you, him, her, it, us,* and *them* are object pronouns.

Subject Pronouns <u>She</u> hiked in the desert.
<u>He</u> and <u>I</u> stayed home.

Object Pronouns The plants surprised <u>her</u>.
She told <u>him</u> and <u>me</u> about <u>them</u>.

A Write *SP* if the underlined pronoun is a subject pronoun. Write *OP* if it is an object pronoun.

1. Scientists work in Antarctica, and <u>they</u> stay there all winter. SP
2. The long, cold winters do not discourage <u>them</u>. OP
3. My group and <u>I</u> studied the penguins in Antarctica. SP
4. A trip to Antarctica is a dream for <u>us</u>. OP
5. <u>You</u> should plan a trip too. SP
6. <u>We</u> saw an active volcano in Hawaii. SP
7. My brothers and sisters walked near <u>it</u>. OP
8. Michael and <u>she</u> saw a lava flow. SP

146 Grammar

RESOURCES

Daily Fix-It Lesson 17
See p. TR6.
See also Daily Fix-It Transparency 17.
Grammar Transparency 17

B Choose the correct pronoun for each sentence. Write the sentence.

1. (<u>We</u>, Us) took a trip to the Grand Canyon.
2. The view of the canyon amazed my cousin and (<u>me</u>, I).
3. Ted and (<u>I</u>, me) photographed the canyon's beautiful colors.
4. Some of (they, <u>them</u>) were red and brown.
5. A guide showed us the canyon, and we talked with (<u>her</u>, she).
6. Dad and (<u>they</u>, them) hiked many trails in the canyon.
7. The river was below (they, <u>them</u>).
8. The depth of the canyon surprised the guide and (<u>him</u>, he).
9. Dad and (<u>he</u>, him) said the deepest point is a mile deep.
10. The hike in the canyon fascinated (we, <u>us</u>).

C Revise each sentence or pair of sentences. Replace the underlined words with subject or object pronouns.

11. The Mississippi River is the longest river in the United States. <u>The Mississippi River</u> is more than 2,000 miles long. **It**
12. Many ships transport cargo on the river. <u>The ships</u> carry millions of tons of freight. **They**
13. Heavy snows and rains fell on the Mississippi River. A flood occurred because of <u>the heavy snows and rains</u>. **them**
14. When Hernando De Soto explored America in 1541, the journey led <u>Hernando De Soto</u> to the Mississippi River. **him**

Grammar **147**

Guided Practice A

Work through the exercise with students. Then have them identify the noun that each pronoun stands for in items 1, 2, 4, 6, and 7.

TEACHING TiP

- Discuss sentences in which students may make pronoun errors, such as *She saw her and me.* Point out that *She saw she and I* may sound correct. But if students know when to use subject pronouns and when to use object pronouns, they will not make this error. Here, object pronouns, *her* and *me*, are needed after the action verb *saw.*

Independent Practice
B and C

Have students complete the exercises. For Differentiated Instruction and Extra Practice, see p. TR14.

Differentiated Instruction

Strategic Intervention

Point out that when pronouns are used with prepositions, the pronouns are object pronouns. Write object pronouns and the following sentences on the board. Ask students to complete each sentence with a different object pronoun. Check pronouns off the list as they are used.

Julie came with ___.

Dan gave a ticket to ___.

Tim sat behind ___.

Jon got snacks for ___.

Maria left without ___.

Advanced

Have students write three sentences about an activity they participated in with another person. Challenge them to use at least three subjects and objects that include one or more pronouns, such as *he and I* or *Tina and me.* Have them exchange papers with a partner. Partners should underline each compound subject and object and make sure pronouns are used correctly.

ELL

Write the following sentence patterns on the board.

___ *greeted* ___.

___ *scared* ___.

___ *helped* ___.

___ *amazed* ___.

___ *confused* ___.

Pair students with different abilities. Have them complete each sentence with a subject pronoun and an object pronoun, using as many different pronouns as possible. Let pairs take turns reading aloud their sentences.

Remind students that they may be asked to identify the correct pronoun in a phrase such as *Jane and I* or *Terry and her*. They can decide whether the subject pronoun or object pronoun is correct by saying the sentence with just the pronoun and not the rest of the phrase.

Jane and (I, me) came over.
  I came over. (correct)
  Me came over. (incorrect)
Jane and I came over.

I called Terry and (she, her).
  I called she. (incorrect)
  I called her. (correct)
I called Terry and her.

Monitor Progress

Check Grammar

| **If...** students have difficulty choosing between subject and object pronouns, | **then...** have them identify whether each underlined noun appears in a test item before or after the verb. |

Test Preparation

✐ Write the letter of the word that can replace the underlined word or group of words.

1. <u>Those deserts</u> are very hot.
  Ⓐ They   **C** Him
  B She   **D** Them

2. The desert plants interest <u>Jay</u>.
  A he   **Ⓒ** him
  B they   **D** us

3. The hot weather agrees with <u>desert animals</u>.
  A it   **Ⓒ** them
  B they   **D** him

4. Anna and <u>Kate</u> studied snakes.
  A they   **Ⓒ** she
  B her   **D** them

5. They saw <u>a king snake</u> under the rocks.
  A they   **C** she
  B he   **Ⓓ** it

6. They showed pictures to Rob and <u>Ted</u>.
  Ⓐ him   **C** he
  B they   **D** she

7. <u>Rob</u> saw a big toad.
  A Them **Ⓒ** He
  B Him   **D** They

8. A jackrabbit hopped by Ty and <u>Kay</u>.
  A she   **C** they
  Ⓑ her   **D** he

148 Grammar

Review

☑ Write *SP* if the underlined pronoun is a subject pronoun. Write *OP* if it is an object pronoun.

1. Ellie went to Japan, and <u>she</u> saw Mount Fuji. SP
2. It delighted James and <u>her</u>. OP
3. Ellie's family and <u>he</u> climbed the mountain. SP
4. She sent a postcard to <u>us</u>. OP
5. <u>You</u> should see Mount Hood in Oregon. SP
6. <u>I</u> saw Mount McKinley in Alaska last year. SP
7. The trip to Alaska was wonderful for Jamal and <u>me</u>. OP
8. Seeing the highest peak in North America was a thrill for <u>him</u>. OP

☑ Choose the correct pronoun for each sentence. Write the sentence.

9. (Them, <u>They</u>) climbed Mount Kilimanjaro.
10. Climbing the highest peak in Africa was not hard for (<u>them</u>, they).
11. Jill and (her, <u>she</u>) saw the Matterhorn.
12. This peak in the Alps looked like a pyramid to Jill and (she, <u>her</u>).
13. Raj and (<u>he</u>, him) said the highest peak in California is Mount McKinley.
14. They told (<u>us</u>, we) it is in the Sierra Nevada range.
15. Kelly and (me, <u>I</u>) live in the Rocky Mountains.
16. Pikes Peak is near (we, <u>us</u>).

Grammar **149**

Summarize

Ask students to explain subject and object pronouns and when to use each.

- A subject pronoun is used as the subject of a sentence.
- An object pronoun is used after an action verb or as the object of a preposition.
- *I, you, he, she, it, we,* and *they* are subject pronouns. *Me, you, him, her, it, us,* and *them* are object pronouns.

Grammar-Writing Connection

Explain that using subject and object pronouns makes writing less wordy by avoiding the repetition of nouns.

Wordy: Tanya said the Amazon River interested <u>Tanya</u>, and <u>Tanya</u> wrote a report on <u>the Amazon River</u>.

Less wordy: Tanya said the Amazon River interested <u>her</u>, and <u>she</u> wrote a report on <u>it</u>.

Style

TEACH

- Read aloud the information about style in the box.
- Ask students to tell in their own words what style is. *(the quality that makes one piece of writing different from others)*

Guided Writing

Read the paragraphs in Exercise 1 with the class. Ask students to point out specific features that helped them identify the style of each one.

Independent Writing

Ask volunteers to read aloud their responses to Exercise 2. Have students identify the style of each response.

Monitor Progress

Check Style

If... students need more help with style,	then... read aloud passages from a reading text with recognizable styles, such as descriptive and imaginative, and have students identify them.

 WRITER'S CRAFT

Style

Style is the quality that makes one piece of writing different from others. There are many features that give each piece of writing a unique style.

- word choice
- length of sentences
- kinds of sentences
- details, including facts, sensory details, and colorful comparisons

 Write the word that describes the style of each paragraph.

factual   imaginative

1. Once upon a time a family of sky-blue fish set out on a journey. Imagine their surprise when they came upon another fish family. These fish were the coral color of a sunset. Both families traveled on together in bright, shimmery waves. Someday the fish will invite you to visit their ocean. You will see a traveling rainbow! *imaginative*

2. A desert is a place that gets fewer than 10 inches of rain each year. Sand may cover about 10 to 20 percent of a desert. Some of the sand blows into tall dunes. Deserts are dry, but many kinds of plants and animals live there. Plants include cactuses and mesquite trees. *factual*

Write a paragraph about your neighborhood. Use a factual or an imaginative style.

150 Writing

RESOURCES

Writing Transparencies 17A, 17B
Writing Rubrics and Anchor Papers p. 25

Describing a Setting

Setting is the time and place of a story. *Time* is when the story happens, and *place* is where the story happens.

- The description of the setting creates a mood for readers.
- Vivid words help readers see, hear, and smell the place.
- Facts and other details describe the place.

Topic sentence answers where and when about setting.

Vivid verbs create a lively style.

Sensory details describe sights, sounds, and smells of setting.

Saturday Morning in Eastwood

The town of Eastwood sparkles on an early Saturday morning. The sun shines gently on the clean shop windows. The air feels cool and damp. The streets are quiet, and the air smells fresh without the weekday cars and trucks going by. A jogger dashes by, and two dog owners lunge after their pets on early-morning walks. Soon the smells of bacon and coffee float out of the Breadbasket Café. Families will stop by for a hearty breakfast. Then they will head off to soccer games and trips to the zoo. Another busy Saturday has begun!

Writing **151**

Describing a Setting

ANALYZE THE MODEL

Read aloud the model and the callouts to the left of it. Prepare students to write their own setting descriptions.

PROMPT

Describe a setting that is interesting or unusual. Use specific details and vivid words to create a unique style.

Getting Started Students can do any of the following.

- Use an organizer (pp. TR28–TR32).
- Close their eyes and visualize the place.
- Brainstorm places that are quiet, fun, beautiful, or strange.

Editing/Revising Checklist

✓ Does my description include sensory details?

✓ Does my description have a recognizable style?

✓ Have I used subject and object pronouns correctly?

Self-Evaluation Distribute copies of p. TR26 for students to fill out.

Scoring Rubric — Description of a Setting

Rubric 4 3 2 1	4	3	2	1
Focus/Ideas	Description with tight focus on specific setting	Description with fairly clear focus on setting	Description unfocused, with no clear setting	No understanding of description or setting
Organization/ Paragraphs	Details in logical spatial organization	Organization of details fairly consistent	Organization of details confused	No organization of details
Voice	Sees setting in unique way	Some evidence of unique viewpoint	Little evidence of unique viewpoint	No clear viewpoint
Word Choice	Vivid words that create engaging style	Some vivid words and sense of style	Little attempt to use vivid words	Incorrect or limited word choice
Sentences	Unique sentence construction	Some individuality in sentence construction	No individuality in sentence construction	Poorly constructed sentences
Conventions	Excellent control and accuracyScoring Rubric txt	Reasonable control with few errors	Errors that may hinder understanding	Frequent errors that interfere with meaning

For 5- and 6-point rubrics, see Writing Rubrics and Anchor Papers p. 25.

Possessive Pronouns

OBJECTIVES

- Define and identify possessive pronouns.
- Use possessive pronouns correctly in writing.
- Become familiar with possessive pronoun assessment on high-stakes tests.

TEACH

Read aloud the definitions, examples, and instruction in the box on p. 152. Remind students of what they know about possessive nouns, as in the phrase *Ramon's chair*. Explain that possessive pronouns perform the same function.

Think Aloud

Model It makes sense that there are possessive pronouns to take the place of possessive nouns. But I notice that, while possessive nouns have an apostrophe to show possession, possessive pronouns do not have apostrophes.

Possessive Pronouns

Some pronouns show who or what owns, or possesses, something. This kind of pronoun is a **possessive pronoun**. *My, mine, your, yours, her, hers, our, ours, his, their, theirs,* and *its* are possessive pronouns.

- <u>Your</u> rock collection is larger than <u>mine</u>.

A Write the possessive pronoun in each sentence.

1. There are many kinds of rocks in my neighborhood. my
2. Your walls and floors are made of rock. Your
3. The cement in our driveway comes from rocks. our
4. Mr. Ferguson used limestone walls in his house. his
5. Mrs. Ray used marble floors in hers. hers
6. Their color is pale gray. Their
7. That area is beautiful because its rocks are red. its
8. Did you see colorful rocks on your hike? your
9. I saw yellow and orange rocks on mine. mine
10. The best views of the mountains are ours. ours
11. Do you think the best view is yours? yours
12. The neighbors probably think theirs is the best! theirs

152 Grammar

RESOURCES

Daily Fix-It Lesson 18
   See p. TR6.
   See also Daily Fix-It Transparency 18.
Grammar Transparency 18

B Choose the possessive pronoun in ( ) that could replace the underlined words in each sentence. Write the sentence.

1. <u>These scientists'</u> work is finding and studying rocks. (Your, <u>Their</u>)
2. Brian's uncle found rocks in <u>Brian's and my</u> neighborhood. (your, <u>our</u>)
3. <u>The scientist's</u> most important find was a black rock. (<u>His</u>, Our)
4. <u>The rock's</u> surface was smooth and shiny. (His, <u>Its</u>)
5. Brian's uncle looked at <u>Brian's</u> rock collection. (<u>his</u>, her)
6. Another scientist looked at <u>the collection I own</u>. (yours, <u>mine</u>)
7. Show the scientist <u>the rocks you own</u>. (hers, <u>yours</u>)
8. The scientists will study <u>the rocks that Brian and I own</u>. (his, <u>ours</u>)

C Revise each sentence. Replace the underlined words with possessive pronouns. Write the sentences.

9. The white cliffs of Dover got that name because <u>the cliffs'</u> limestone is white. their
10. Julia and I saw the cliffs with <u>Julia's and my</u> parents. our
11. My dad went to England because <u>my dad's</u> company sent him there. his
12. When we visited the country, we enjoyed many of <u>the country's</u> sights. its
13. Julia's favorite was the Lake District, and <u>my favorite</u> was Stonehenge . mine
14. Julia took my picture at Stonehenge, and I took <u>Julia's picture</u> in the Lake District. hers

Grammar **153**

PRACTICE

Guided Practice **A**

Work through the exercise with students. Then have them identify what is possessed in each item, for example, *neighborhood* in *my neighborhood*.

TEACHING TIP

• Point out that some possessive pronouns, such as *my* and *your*, come before a noun. Others, such as *mine* and *yours*, are used alone.

Independent Practice **B** **and** **C**

Have students complete the exercises. For Differentiated Instruction and Extra Practice, see p. TR14.

Differentiated Instruction

Strategic Intervention

Have students find a picture that shows ownership, such as a woman with a car or a dog with a dish of food. Ask students to write a sentence that describes the picture and uses a possessive pronoun, such as *The dog likes its food.* You may wish to show the pictures and work with students to write the sentences.

Advanced

Have pairs of students discuss their favorite hobbies or after-school activities. Then have them each write two or three sentences comparing their preferences. Challenge students to use at least three possessive pronouns in their sentences.

ELL

Ask each student to choose an object, such as a pencil, stone, or rubber band; show it to the group; and then put it into a box. Mix the objects and have students take turns picking an object out of the box and making up a sentence about it that includes a possessive pronoun. Model the process: *This blue stone is hers. His pencil is red.* As you say the sentence, gesture toward the person to whom the object belongs.

Remind students that they may be asked to identify possessive pronouns. They should not confuse possessive pronouns with possessive nouns. Possessive nouns have apostrophes. Possessive pronouns do not have apostrophes.

Example: <u>Tim's</u> rocks were the most unusual. (possessive noun)

<u>His</u> rocks were the most unusual. (possessive pronoun)

Monitor Progress

Check Grammar

If... students have difficulty identifying possessive pronouns,	**then...** discuss how to eliminate incorrect choices and choose the correct pronoun for each test item.

Test Preparation

✓ Write the letter of the pronoun that correctly completes each sentence.

1. I will show you __A__ secret place for finding rocks.

   A my   **C** yours
   B your   **D** its

2. The stones are small, but __B__ value is high.

   A our   **C** her
   B their **D** its

3. These blue rocks are __C__ favorites.

   A its   **C** my
   B it's   **D** mine

4. My sister put one on __C__ necklace.

   A ours   **C** her
   B theirs **D** mine

5. The stone is large, and __D__ color is bright.

   A their **C** our
   B her   **D** its

6. I put one in my collection, and you put one in __B__.

   A our   **C** my
   B yours **D** your

7. Ty's green stones are larger than __D__.

   A our   **C** my
   B their **D** mine

8. I found this stone, and I think __C__ color is beautiful.

   A it's   **C** its
   B theirs **D** their

Review

☑ Write the possessive pronoun in each sentence.

1. Chad and Jenny went to a cliff near <u>their</u> house.
2. The cliff had many rocks against <u>its</u> sides.
3. Jenny had a rock hammer in <u>her</u> backpack.
4. Chad said, "<u>My</u> first rock is marble."
5. Chad put seven rocks in <u>his</u> bag.
6. Jenny put nine rocks in <u>hers</u>.
7. All the rocks were theirs.
8. Can you find rocks in <u>your</u> neighborhood?

☑ Choose the possessive pronoun in ( ) that could replace the underlined words in each sentence. Write the sentences.

9. Rocks help us learn how <u>your and my</u> earth has changed. (<u>our</u>, their)
10. We can see how animals looked from <u>the animals'</u> fossils. (its, <u>their</u>)
11. <u>Mr. Kenny's</u> swamp was home to dinosaurs. (<u>His</u>, Our)
12. A dinosaur was buried in <u>the swamp's</u> mud. (his, <u>its</u>)
13. The dinosaur's bones left <u>the bones'</u> shape in the mud. (its, <u>their</u>)
14. <u>Ms. Shaw's</u> team found many dinosaur fossils. (<u>Her</u>, Hers)
15. Scientists display <u>the scientists'</u> fossils in museums. (<u>their</u>, theirs)
16. I will show you <u>the fossils that I own</u>. (my, <u>mine</u>)

Grammar **155**

Summarize

Ask students to tell about possessive pronouns and give examples of them.

- A possessive pronoun shows who or what owns something.
- *My, mine, your, yours, her, hers, our, ours, his, their, theirs,* and *its* are possessive pronouns.

Grammar-Writing Connection

Explain that using possessive pronouns makes writing smoother by avoiding the repetition of a noun.

Repetitious: Sandra showed us <u>Sandra's</u> rocks in <u>Sandra's</u> room.

Smoother: Sandra showed us <u>her</u> rocks in <u>her</u> room.

Get Your Reader's Attention

- Identify characteristics of a memoir.
- Write a memoir, using techniques to get your reader's attention.
- Develop criteria for judging a piece of writing.

TEACH

- Read aloud the information in the box about getting your reader's attention.
- Ask students to tell in their own words how to get your reader's attention. *(write a catchy title, write a vivid or interesting opening sentence, create suspense)*

 Guided Writing

Read aloud the sentences in Exercise 1 with students. Ask them to identify the techniques used to get readers' attention. *(vivid opening sentence, suspense)*

 Independent Writing

Ask volunteers to read aloud their responses to Exercise 2. Have listeners identify words and phrases that get their attention.

Monitor Progress

Check Get Your Reader's Attention

If... students need more help with getting readers' attention,	**then...** locate reading passages that are especially attention-getting and have students identify the techniques used.

 WRITER'S CRAFT

Get Your Reader's Attention

When you write, **get your reader's attention** from the start. Here are some ways:

- Write a catchy title that puts questions in your reader's mind. To answer the questions, the reader must read your story.
- Write an opening sentence that creates a vivid image or states an interesting fact.
- Create suspense. Give clues about the important events. Make your reader curious about what will happen.

Tell how the following sentences get a reader's attention.
Possible answers on page TR36

1. The sky was as dark as ink, with no moon and no stars. We looked nervously at the sky and then at one another. Would we find what we had come for in this strange place?

Write answers for the following items:

2. Write an opening sentence for a story about an exciting boat trip on rough waters.
3. Write a title for a story about coming face to face with a bear in the woods.
4. You are writing a story about hearing strange sounds while you are camping in your backyard. Write two sentences that will create suspense for your reader.

156 Writing

RESOURCES

Writing Transparencies 18A, 18B
Writing Rubrics and Anchor Papers p. 26

Memoir

In a **memoir,** a person tells a story about an event in his or her life. The event is often one that changed the writer in some way.

Title makes readers ask, "How *did* the writer become a rock climber?"

First sentence creates a vivid image that makes readers curious.

Facts and images create suspense for readers.

Last two sentences tell how the experience has changed the writer.

How I Became a Rock Climber

I never pictured myself high above the ground, attached to a huge rock. But that's where I was one day last summer. I was visiting my cousins in Colorado, and my uncle drove my cousins and me to a big rock in the desert. It seemed huge! Uncle Dan explained the safety rules to us. He also gave us helmets. What would we need those for?

Uncle Dan put an iron spike into a crack in the rock. He attached a rope to the spike. He showed us how to hold the rope and climb the rock. I was scared at first, and it was hard work. But it was fun! Soon I had climbed higher than I had ever gone in my favorite oak tree. Uncle Dan showed us how to get down. Each week I practice on the rock-climbing equipment at the local gym. I can't wait until next summer's rock-climbing trip in Colorado!

Writing **157**

Memoir
ANALYZE THE MODEL

Read aloud the model and the callouts to the left of it. Prepare students to write their own memoirs.

PROMPT

Write a memoir about an important experience. Use what you've learned about how to get your reader's attention.

Getting Started Students can do any of the following.

- Use an organizer (pp. TR28–TR32).
- Recall memorable times in their lives that they may want to include.
- With a partner, discuss unusual or exciting experiences.

Editing/Revising Checklist

☑ Does my memoir tell how the experience changed me?

☑ Does my memoir get readers' attention?

☑ Have I used possessive pronouns correctly?

Self-Evaluation Distribute copies of p. TR26 for students to fill out.

Scoring Rubric Memoir

Rubric 4 3 2 1	4	3	2	1
Focus/Ideas	Memoir with tight focus on important experience	Memoir with fairly tight focus on experience	Memoir unfocused or experience not important	Shows lack of understanding of memoir
Organization/ Paragraphs	Details in time order	Most details in time order	Confused time order	No time order
Voice	Expresses why event was important	Some expression of experience's importance	Little expression of experience's importance	No clear voice
Word Choice	Vivid words that get reader's attention	Some vivid words that get reader's attention	Little attempt to get reader's attention	Incorrect or limited word choice
Sentences	Uses variety to get reader's attention	Some variety in sentences	Lacks variety in sentences	Poorly constructed sentences
Conventions	Excellent control and accuracy	Reasonable control with few errors	Errors that may hinder understanding	Frequent errors that interfere with meaning

For 5- and 6-point rubrics, see Writing Rubrics and Anchor Papers p. 26.

Contractions

OBJECTIVES

- Define and identify contractions.
- Use contractions correctly in writing.
- Become familiar with contraction assessment on high-stakes tests.

TEACH

Read aloud the definitions, examples, and instruction in the box on p. 158. Point out that although contractions are considered informal, they are acceptable in all kinds of speaking and in most kinds of writing. Contractions usually are not used in formal writing such as research reports.

Think Aloud **Model** As I look over the list of contractions that combine a pronoun and a verb, I notice that I know several contractions that are not listed. But I see that they follow one of the patterns that is listed. For example, the contraction of *they have* is *they've*. I know that I can make similar contractions for *I have—I've, we have—we've,* and *you have—you've.*

Contractions

A **contraction** is a word made by putting two words together. When words are joined in a contraction, an apostrophe is used to show where a letter or letters have been left out.

- Some contractions combine a pronoun and a verb: *I + will = I'll; they + would = they'd; she + is = she's; it + is = it's; he + has = he's; they + have = they've; you + are = you're.*

- Some contractions combine a verb and *not*: *has + not = hasn't; had + not = hadn't; was + not = wasn't; did + not = didn't; could + not = couldn't; will + not = won't.*

Contractions We've gone swimming every day, but we won't go tomorrow.

A Write the contraction in each sentence. Then write the words that make up the contraction.

1. Swimming was popular long ago, and it's still popular today. it's; it is
2. Swimmers began competing in the 1896 Olympics, and they've competed ever since. they've; they have
3. Women didn't compete in the Olympics until 1912. didn't; did not
4. Wasn't Mark Spitz a winner of seven gold medals in 1972? wasn't; was not
5. American swimmers couldn't beat Spitz's record in 2004. couldn't; could not

158 Grammar

RESOURCES

Daily Fix-It Lesson 19
    See p. TR7.
    See also Daily Fix-It Transparency 19.
Grammar Transparency 19

B Write the contraction for the underlined words.

1. My grandpa likes to swim, and <u>he is</u> a good swimmer. he's
2. He <u>did not</u> swim in a pool when he was young. didn't
3. <u>He would</u> swim in the pond on his parents' farm. He'd
4. He <u>could not</u> wait to dive in on a hot summer day. couldn't
5. He <u>had not</u> had swimming lessons. hadn't
6. He <u>was not</u> afraid of the frogs and ducks in the pond. wasn't
7. <u>They would</u> all swim together. They'd
8. He <u>will not</u> forget his swimming pond. won't
9. Now <u>he will</u> swim in an indoor pool. he'll
10. Today <u>I will</u> go swimming with Grandpa. I'll

C Expand each group of words to create an interesting sentence. Replace two words in each group of words with a contraction. **Possible answers:**

11. I am trying out I'm trying out for the swim team.
12. We are practicing We're practicing early every morning.
13. My friends are not discouraged My friends aren't discouraged by the hard work.
14. We will learn We'll learn the backstroke this week.
15. I did not know I didn't know that stroke.
16. I had not done I hadn't done the butterfly before.
17. It is good to learn It's good to learn new things.
18. The coach says we are The coach says we're all good swimmers.
19. The team has not The team hasn't been chosen yet.
20. I will be happy I'll be happy if I make the team.

Grammar **159**

PRACTICE

Guided Practice Ⓐ

Work through the exercise with students. Afterwards, have them use each contraction in a sentence of their own.

TEACHING TIP

- Have students spell contractions that follow each pattern but are not listed on the chart, such as *he'll*, *we'd*, and *we're*.

- Point out that possessive nouns also have apostrophes. Remind students that possessive pronouns do not have apostrophes; they should not confuse contractions with possessive pronouns, such as *your* and *you're*.

Independent Practice Ⓑ and Ⓒ

Have students complete the exercises. For Differentiated Instruction and Extra Practice, see p. TR14.

Differentiated Instruction

Strategic Intervention

Make a flash card for each pronoun and verb combination listed on p. 158. Have students take turns choosing a card and writing the contraction for the two words on the board. Repeat the activity with cards for the verb + *not* combinations.

Advanced

Students may make up bingo-like cards using a pattern that is five squares across and five squares down. Each square would contain a contraction. The caller's list includes the word pairs from which each contraction is made. The game may be played by large or small groups.

ELL

Encourage English language learners to be creative as they create sentences in Exercise C. Welcome even silly responses as long as they make sense in the context.

Remind students that they may be asked to use contractions correctly. They should not confuse contractions with words that sound the same but have different meanings and spellings.

Example: <u>They're</u> jumping off the dock. (contraction)

They might hurt <u>their</u> feet. (possessive pronoun)

Monitor Progress

Check Grammar

If... students have difficulty identifying contractions,	then... have them locate contractions in their reading materials and tell the two words that make up each contraction.

Test Preparation

Write the letter of the correct contraction for the underlined words.

1. People <u>do not</u> swim just in pools.
   - **A** doesn't
   - **B** don't
   - **C** isn't
   - **D** didn't

2. <u>They will</u> swim wherever there is water.
   - **A** They're
   - **B** They'll
   - **C** They'd
   - **D** Their

3. <u>He is</u> swimming in a lake.
   - **A** He'd
   - **B** She's
   - **C** He's
   - **D** His

4. <u>We are</u> in a river.
   - **A** We'd
   - **B** You're
   - **C** Were
   - **D** We're

5. I have swum in the ocean when <u>it is</u> warm.
   - **A** it's
   - **B** its
   - **C** I'm
   - **D** I'll

6. <u>Have not</u> people swum in the English Channel?
   - **A** Hadnt
   - **B** Hasn't
   - **C** Hadn't
   - **D** Haven't

7. You <u>were not</u> swimming in the pond.
   - **A** wasn't
   - **B** weren't
   - **C** won't
   - **D** we'll

8. Lakes <u>are not</u> as warm as pools.
   - **A** isn't
   - **B** don't
   - **C** arent
   - **D** aren't

Review

✔ Write the contraction in each sentence. Then write the words that make up the contraction.

1. She's doing the backstroke in the swim meet. She's; she is
2. Eddie hasn't done the backstroke before. hasn't; has not
3. He'll probably do the butterfly. He'll; he will
4. Maggie didn't practice the breaststroke. didn't; did not
5. She'd like to do the backstroke. She'd; she would
6. Wouldn't you like to practice the butterfly? Wouldn't; would not
7. Tyler won't be at practice tomorrow. won't; will not
8. He's going to the dentist. He's; he is
9. I think it's all right to miss practice sometimes. it's; it is
10. I'm sure Tyler will practice the next day. I'm; I am

✔ Write the contraction for the underlined words.

11. If you are a good swimmer, you can learn to dive. you're
12. She will dive from a springboard. She'll
13. He has learned to do a forward dive. He's
14. She is not ready to do a half-twist. isn't
15. His body was not straight when he hit the water. wasn't
16. They will practice before the meet. They'll
17. She is jumping at the end of the board. She's
18. She does not jump high enough. doesn't
19. They are applauding for her. They're
20. They could not believe how good she was. couldn't

Summarize

Ask students to tell about contractions and name some examples.

- A contraction is a word made by putting two words together and using an apostrophe to show where a letter or letters have been left out.
- Some contractions, such as *I'll,* combine a pronoun and a verb.
- Some contractions, such as *didn't,* combine a verb and *not.*

Grammar-Writing Connection

Explain that contractions are not generally used in formal writing such as research reports. However, contractions give informal writing a conversational tone and make dialogue sound realistic.

Too formal: "I cannot come to your house after school," Toby said.

Realistic: "I can't come to your house after school," Toby said.

Supporting Details

- Identify characteristics of a description of a goal.
- Describe a goal, using supporting details.
- Develop criteria for judging a piece of writing.

TEACH

- Read aloud the information in the box about supporting details.
- Ask students to tell in their own words what supporting details are. *(facts or examples that give more information about the main idea)*

Guided Writing

Read each item in Exercise 1 with the class. Then have volunteers tell the main idea of each paragraph and explain why one sentence in each is not a supporting detail.

Independent Writing

Ask volunteers to read aloud their responses to Exercise 2. After each response is read, ask the class to identify the main idea that it supports.

Monitor Progress

Check Supporting Details

If... students need more help with supporting details,	**then...** locate factual paragraphs in students' reading materials. Have them identify the main idea and one or more supporting details in each paragraph.

 WRITER'S CRAFT

Supporting Details

> **Supporting details** in your writing should give more information about the main idea. For example, if you want to describe the way something looks or feels, your supporting details should be vivid descriptions. If your purpose is to inform your reader, your supporting details should be facts.

 Write the sentence from each paragraph that is not a supporting detail.

1. Members of our community swim team work hard. Swimming is fun for the members. Team members must train five days each week. They must swim for one hour each day. Swimming is fun for the members.

2. I had always wanted to participate in the diving competition. I stood high atop the diving board, feeling strong and confident. Then I decided that I did not want to dive. I knew I could perform one of my best dives ever in front of dozens of people. Then I decided that I did not want to dive.

 Write one supporting detail for each main idea. Possible answers:

3. My first swimming lesson was an interesting experience. I found that swimming came as naturally to me as to a fish in the ocean.

4. Everyone should learn to swim at a young age. Pools, lakes, or oceans can be dangerous places for people who do not know how to swim.

5. Swimming is an excellent form of exercise. It strengthens your arm and leg muscles.

RESOURCES

Writing Transparencies 19A, 19B
Writing Rubrics and Anchor Papers p. 27

Describing a Goal

When **describing a goal,** a writer tells about something that he or she wanted to achieve and did achieve. The writer uses supporting details that tell how the goal was reached and why it was meaningful.

My 5K Race

First paragraph gives background information.

Each year our school has a field day. Students compete in running and jumping events. I didn't compete last year. There was only one event I wanted to enter: the 5-kilometer race. A 5K is not a quick sprint like the 50-yard dash. Running five kilometers takes endurance. I decided to enter next year's 5K race.

Details explain how the writer prepared to reach the goal.

My brother helped me train three days a week at the school track. At first I ran out of breath quickly. My side hurt. Soon I could run three kilometers without stopping. I was slow at first, but each week I felt stronger. Sometimes I felt as if I could run forever! When field day rolled around, I was ready.

Details describe how the goal was finally reached.

Halfway through, two other runners and I led the race. The stiff competition made me even stronger. I won the race!

Last three sentences tell why accomplishing the goal was meaningful.

I was thrilled, but not because I beat other runners. I had set a tough goal. I had achieved it through hard work.

Writing **163**

Describing a Goal

ANALYZE THE MODEL

Read aloud the model and the callouts to the left of it. Prepare students to write their own descriptions of a goal.

PROMPT

Describe a goal that you set and reached. Use supporting details to explain how you reached it.

Getting Started Students can do any of the following.

- Use an organizer (pp. TR28–TR32).
- Make a list of goals you feel you've accomplished.
- Discuss stories about people who accomplished goals.

Editing/Revising Checklist

☑ Does my description focus on how I achieved a goal?

☑ Does my description have details that support my main idea?

☑ Have I used contractions correctly?

Self-Evaluation Distribute copies of p. TR26 for students to fill out.

Scoring Rubric — Description of a Goal

Rubric 4 3 2 1	4	3	2	1
Focus/Ideas	Description with tight focus on meaningful goal	Description with fairly consistent focus on goal	Unfocused description or poorly described goal	No description of goal
Organization/ Paragraphs	Details in time order	Most details in time order	Confused time order	No time order
Voice	Sincere and honest; engages readers	Some uniqueness of viewpoint	Little evidence of unique experience	Lacks clear voice
Word Choice	Vivid words that create lively details	Some vivid words that create lively details	Little attempt to create lively details	Incorrect or limited word choice
Sentences	Style and variety in creating details	Some individual style and variety	Monotonous length and/or style	Poorly constructed sentences
Conventions	Excellent control and accuracy	Reasonable control with few errors	Errors that may hinder understanding	Frequent errors that interfere with meaning

For 5- and 6-point rubrics, see Writing Rubrics and Anchor Papers p. 27.

Prepositions

- Define and identify prepositions.
- Use prepositions correctly in writing.
- Become familiar with preposition assessment on high-stakes tests.

TEACH

Read aloud the definitions, examples, and instruction in the box on p. 164. Explain that prepositional phrases may tell *where* or *when* about the verb in a sentence, or they may give more details about the subject or another noun in a sentence.

Think Aloud

Model I'm familiar with all the words listed, but it might be hard to remember that each is a preposition. One way to recognize a preposition is that it always begins a prepositional phrase. So if you said *The eagle lived on,* *on* wouldn't be a preposition. The entire phrase *on a cliff* tells *where* about the verb *lived* and is a prepositional phrase. The word *on* is the preposition of the phrase.

LESSON 20

Prepositions

A **preposition** is the first word in a group of words called a prepositional phrase. A **prepositional phrase** ends with a noun or pronoun called the **object of the preposition**. A prepositional phrase tells more about other words in a sentence.

Preposition	The eagle lived <u>on</u> a cliff.
Prepositional Phrase	The eagle lived <u>on a cliff</u>.
Object of Preposition	The eagle lived on a <u>cliff</u>.

Here are some prepositions: *about, above, across, after, against, along, among, around, at, before, behind, below, beneath, beside, between, beyond, by, down, during, except, for, from, in, inside, into, near, of, off, on, onto, out, outside, over, past, since, through, throughout, to, toward, under, underneath, until, up, upon, with, within, without.*

A Write the preposition in each sentence.

1. My family drove <u>through</u> the Rocky Mountains.
2. A huge bird flew <u>across</u> the sky.
3. It settled <u>above</u> a rocky cliff.
4. It stopped <u>beside</u> a huge nest.
5. <u>Inside</u> the nest, baby eagles rested.
6. The word <u>for</u> a baby eagle is *eaglet.*
7. An eaglet is covered <u>with</u> fuzz.
8. Eaglets leave the nest <u>after</u> 12 weeks.

164 Grammar

RESOURCES

Daily Fix-It Lesson 20
   See p. TR7.
   See also Daily Fix-It Transparency 20.
Grammar Transparency 20

B Write the prepositional phrase in each sentence. Underline the preposition.

1. Are eagles the strongest birds in the world? <u>in</u> the world
2. They fly even during bad weather. <u>during</u> bad weather
3. Eagles stay far from people. <u>from</u> people
4. The golden eagle has been called the "king of birds." <u>of</u> birds
5. An eagle has strong claws on its feet. <u>on</u> its feet
6. It carries prey with its claws. <u>with</u> its claws
7. Eagles are among the heaviest birds. <u>among</u> the heaviest birds
8. They glide high above the trees. <u>above</u> the trees
9. An eagle catches a fish near the water's edge. <u>near</u> the water's edge
10. It uses its wings for paddles. <u>for</u> paddles
11. The eagle carries its prey to its nest. <u>to</u> its nest
12. It tears the fish into pieces. <u>into</u> pieces

C Choose a preposition from the box that makes sense in each sentence. Write the sentences.

inside	upon	without	across	of	to

13. A nest ___ eagles is called an aerie.
A nest of eagles is called an aerie.
14. Each year, the eagle returns ___ the same aerie.
Each year, the eagle returns to the same aerie.
15. Eagles lay eggs ___ their aeries.
Eagles lay eggs inside their aeries.
16. The mother eagle sits ___ the eggs.
The mother eagle sits upon the eggs.
17. The father eagle flies ___ the valley.
The father eagle flies across the valley.
18. He does not return ___ food.
He does not return without food.

Guided Practice A

Work through the exercise with students. Let them use the list of prepositions if they need to. Afterwards, have them identify the prepositional phrase and the object of the preposition in each sentence.

TEACHING TiP

• Point out that the object of a preposition is always a noun or pronoun. Explain that if a word that can be a preposition is not followed by an object, it is not being used as a preposition in that sentence.

Independent Practice B and C

Have students complete the exercises. For Differentiated Instruction and Extra Practice, see p. TR14.

Differentiated Instruction

Strategic Intervention

Write these short sentences on the board.

Tigers prowl.

Elephants play.

Monkeys climb.

Birds call.

Have students add a prepositional phrase to each sentence and then read their sentences aloud.

Advanced

Challenge students to learn more about a particular bird or other animal in the library or on the Internet. Have them write four or five sentences about their findings, using at least three prepositional phrases. Ask them to exchange papers with a partner and underline the prepositional phrases and circle the prepositions.

ELL

To build on the grammar concept of the lesson, display a picture that shows several buildings, people, animals, or other objects. Ask students questions about the picture that can be answered by a sentence with a prepositional phrase. For example, *Where is the dog playing? (The dog is playing in the yard.)* Make sure students use each preposition correctly.

TEST-TAKING TIP

Some words can be prepositions or not, depending on their use in a sentence. Remember that a preposition is part of a phrase and is followed by a noun or a pronoun. It cannot stand alone.

Not a preposition: The eagle flew <u>down</u>.

Preposition: The eagle flew <u>down</u> the mountain.

Monitor Progress

Check Grammar	
If... students have difficulty identifying prepositions,	**then...** work with them to eliminate incorrect answers in the test items.

Test Preparation

Write the letter of the word in each sentence that is a preposition.

1. An eagle flies over the lake.

   A An   **C** the
   B over   **D** lake

2. It dives into the water.

   A It   **C** into
   B dives   **D** water

3. A bald eagle sits upon a branch.

   A bald   **C** a
   B branch   **D** upon

4. White feathers grow on its head.

   A head   **C** on
   B its   **D** grow

5. In the wilderness there are many eagles.

   A In   **C** there
   B the   **D** are

6. A nest near the water holds two eggs.

   A nest   **C** the
   B near   **D** holds

7. A baby eagle with white fuzz hatches.

   A with   **C** fuzz
   B white   **D** hatches

8. A big eagle brings food to the nest.

   A big   **C** to
   B food   **D** nest

Review

✓ Write the preposition in each sentence.

1. Golden eagles live throughout North America. throughout

2. They have golden brown feathers on their necks. on

3. The harpy eagle lives within the rain forest. within

4. It is known for its yellow feet. for

5. The serpent eagle of Asia eats snakes. of

6. The rain forest is home to the Philippine eagle. to

7. Steppe eagles fly over Egypt each year. over

8. A harsh call is made by the African fish eagle. by

9. About 40 years ago, bald eagles were endangered. About

10. Their numbers have increased since that time. since

✓ Write the prepositional phrase in each sentence. Underline the preposition.

11. My cousin from Arizona is a birdwatcher. <u>from</u> Arizona

12. He finds many birds outside his house. <u>outside</u> his house

13. He views them through strong lenses. <u>through</u> strong lenses

14. He saw a huge golden eagle in the desert. <u>in</u> the desert

15. A woodpecker with a red head perched nearby. <u>with</u> a red head

16. A little roadrunner jogged past him. <u>past</u> him

17. An owl sat upon a cactus. <u>upon</u> a cactus

18. Sparrows and wrens fly around him. <u>around</u> him

19. A quail hurries along the ground. <u>along</u> the ground

20. My cousin looks at birds until dark. <u>until</u> dark

Summarize

Ask students to describe prepositions, prepositional phrases, and objects of prepositions.

- A preposition is the first word in a group of words called a *prepositional phrase.*
- A prepositional phrase tells more about other words in a sentence.
- The object of a preposition is a noun or pronoun at the end of a prepositional phrase.

Grammar-Writing Connection

Explain that prepositional phrases add important details to writing by telling exactly where something occurs or how two things are related.

Vague: An eagle flew.

Specific: An eagle flew <u>from the tall trees</u>.

Transitions to Show Order

OBJECTIVES

- Identify characteristics of a plot summary.
- Write a plot summary, using transitions to show order.
- Develop criteria for judging a piece of writing.

TEACH

- Read aloud the information in the box about transitions to show order.
- Ask students to tell in their own words what transitions are. *(words and phrases such as* then *that show the order in which things happen)*

Guided Writing

Read each item in Exercises 1 and 2 with students. Have volunteers explain their choices.

Independent Writing

Ask volunteers to read aloud their responses to Exercise 3. Have listeners identify the transitions the writer used.

Monitor Progress

Check Transitions to Show Order

If... students need more help with transitions to show order,	then... have them read recipes from a cookbook and explain how transition words help show order.

WRITER'S CRAFT

Transitions to Show Order

> Events in a story happen in a certain order. Transition words and phrases such as *first, then, later,* and *after a while* show the order of the events.

 Write the word or phrase that shows order.

1. Jacob saw a bird's nest. Later, he looked at the nest through his binoculars. **Later**

2. After a while, Jacob saw a big hawk swoop into the tree. **After a while**

 Add a phrase from the box or your own word or phrase to each sentence.

during the day	on Saturday
at night	on Sunday

Possible answers:

3. Molly went birdwatching in the woods. She went birdwatching at the pond. **On Saturday, Molly went birdwatching in the woods. On Sunday, she went birdwatching at the pond.**

4. The owl slept on the tree stump. The owl hunted for food. **During the day, the owl slept on the tree stump. At night, the owl hunted for food.**

 Write two or three sentences about something that happened in your backyard, a park, or another natural place. Use transitions to show the order of events. **Possible answer: Last Saturday I watched a squirrel in our backyard. At first it snuffled around in the grass. After a while, it found a nut.**

168 Writing

RESOURCES

Writing Transparencies 20A, 20B
Writing Rubrics and Anchor Papers p. 28

Writing for Tests

> **Prompt** Describe the <u>plot</u>, or <u>important events,</u> of a <u>story</u>. Tell what happens in the story to a <u>friend who has not read it.</u>

Plot summary begins with first story event. Other events are described in time order.

Words and phrases show when each event happens.

Summary tells main events of the plot but not all the details.

Goldilocks and the Three Bears

A little girl, Goldilocks, goes inside a house in the woods. In the kitchen, she sits in each chair. One is too big and one is too little, but the third one is the right size. Next Goldilocks tests the porridge on the table. One bowl is too hot and one is too cold, but the third is just right. By now Goldilocks is tired, so she goes upstairs to the bedroom. One bed is too hard and one is too soft. The third one is just right, and Goldilocks falls asleep. Meanwhile, the mother, father, and baby bear who live in the house return home. They see that someone has used their chairs and eaten their food. They go upstairs and find Goldilocks. Goldilocks awakens to see the bears looking at her. Frightened, she runs away and never wanders into the woods again.

Writing **169**

Writing for Tests

ANALYZE THE MODEL

Read aloud the model and the callouts to the left of it. Prepare students to write about plot summaries.

> ### PROMPT
> Describe the plot, or important events, of a story. Tell the story's events to a friend who hasn't read it.

Getting Started Students should do the following.

- Read the prompt and develop a plan for what they want to say.
- Support their ideas with facts, examples, and details.
- Check their writing for errors.

Editing/Revising Checklist

☑ Does my plot summary describe only important events?

☑ Have I used transitions to show the order of events?

☑ Have I used prepositional phrases to tell more?

Self-Evaluation Distribute copies of p. TR26 for students to fill out.

Scoring Rubric — Plot Summary

Rubric 4 3 2 1	4	3	2	1
Focus/Ideas	Summary that focuses on main events of plot	Summary that focuses mostly on main events of plot	Summary that focuses on details as well as main events of plot	Summary with little or no focus on story plot
Organization/ Paragraphs	Clear, consistent use of time order	Fairly consistent use of time order	Time order not clear	No organization of details
Voice	Clearly knows story events	Shows fair knowledge of story	Writer vague about story plot	Not familiar with story
Word Choice	Excellent use of transitions to show order	Uses some transitions to show order	Little use of transitions to show order	No use of transitions to show order
Sentences	Varied, well-constructed sentences	Sentences well constructed; some variety	Little variety; some sentences poorly constructed	Lacks variety; fragments and run-ons
Conventions	Excellent control and accuracy	Reasonable control with few errors	Errors that may hinder understanding	Frequent errors that interfere with meaning

For 5- and 6-point rubrics, see Writing Rubrics and Anchor Papers p. 28.

Adjectives and Articles

- Define and identify adjectives and articles.
- Use adjectives and articles correctly in writing.
- Become familiar with adjective and article assessment on high-stakes tests.

TEACH

Read aloud the definitions, instructions, and examples in the box on p. 170. Point out that adjectives may tell *how many* or *which one* as well as describe specific characteristics such as color or size about a noun.

Model I know that adjectives can vividly describe a person, place, or thing. For example, *blue, huge,* and *stormy* are all adjectives. But I see that words such as *many* and *several* can be adjectives as well. Also, some words we use all the time before nouns—*a, and,* and *the*—are a kind of adjective.

LESSON 21

Adjectives and Articles

An **adjective** is a word that can describe a person, place, or thing. Adjectives tell more about nouns. *A, an,* and *the* are special adjectives called **articles**.

Adjectives <u>Many</u> people wore <u>bright</u> clothes to the <u>annual</u> parade.

Articles <u>The</u> child wore <u>an</u> orange sweater and <u>a</u> blue jacket.

- The articles *a* and *an* are used only with singular nouns. *A* is used before a word that begins with a consonant sound: *a box, a red coat. An* is used before a word that begins with a vowel sound: *an egg, an empty box, an old coat.*
- Use *the* before singular or plural nouns: *the earring, the earrings.*

A Write the adjective that describes each underlined noun.

1. A kimono is made of vivid <u>cloth</u>. vivid
2. The Japanese wear kimonos for special <u>occasions</u>. special
3. They wear wide <u>belts</u> with their kimonos. wide
4. We will wear fancy <u>kimonos</u> to the party. fancy

Write the article in ( ) that correctly completes each sentence.

5. In Hawaii, a muumuu is (<u>a</u>, an) long dress.
6. I bought (a, <u>an</u>) attractive muumuu in Honolulu.
7. My dad bought (an, <u>the</u>) brightest shirt he could find.

170 Grammar

RESOURCES

Daily Fix-It Lesson 21
  See p. TR7.
  See also Daily Fix-It Transparency 21.
Grammar Transparency 21

B Write the adjectives, including the articles, in each sentence. The number in ( ) tells you how many are in the sentence.

1. Noriko took a long trip to faraway Japan. (3) a, long, faraway
2. She stayed with elderly Aunt Chiyoko. (1) elderly
3. She loved the bright, noisy city of Tokyo. (3) the, bright, noisy
4. Aunt Chiyoko had a small apartment. (2) a, small
5. The family ate dinner at a low table. (3) The, a, low
6. They ate some unusual fish with delicious sauce. (3) some, unusual, delicious
7. Noriko and Aunt Chiyoko visited an elegant garden. (2) an, elegant
8. The small, fancy trees in the garden were called *bonsai*. (4) The, small, fancy, the
9. One was an evergreen bonsai. (2) an, evergreen
10. Noriko had an excellent time on the trip. (3) an, excellent, the

C Add an adjective for each blank. Write the new sentences. Possible answers:

11. The ___ garden had ___ flowers.
The beautiful garden had colorful flowers.
12. A ___ tree was covered with ___ blossoms.
A pear tree was covered with white blossoms.
13. The ___ weather signaled an ___ spring.
The warm weather signaled an early spring.
14. ___ people walked among the ___ beds of flowers.
Many people walked among the brilliant beds of flowers.
15. Two ___ rabbits hopped around a ___ bush.
Two little rabbits hopped around a nearby bush.

Grammar **171**

PRACTICE

Guided Practice Ⓐ

Work through the exercise with students. Point out that the adjectives in items 1–4 describe specific characteristics of the nouns they modify. For items 5–7, have students explain the reasons for their choices.

TEACHING TIP

• Point out that well-chosen adjectives can help readers by specifying exactly the person, place, or thing that is being described. They can also help readers see, hear, feel, taste, or smell what is being described.

Independent Practice Ⓑ **and** Ⓒ

Have students complete the exercises. For Differentiated Instruction and Extra Practice, see p. TR15.

Differentiated Instruction

Strategic Intervention

Point out that the article *an* is used not only before nouns that begin with a vowel sound, but before a modifier beginning with a vowel sound that comes before the noun, such as *an ugly duck*. Have students write *a, an,* and *the* on three self-stick notes. Write words and phrases such as *awful day, ocean,* and *red ant* on chart paper. Have students come to the chart and put the correct article in front of a word or phrase.

Advanced

Have each student write five vivid adjectives on paper. Then have students write three or four sentences about a parade without using any adjectives except articles. Have students exchange sentences with a partner and insert each of the adjectives they listed into the partner's sentences. Point out that sentences may be silly. Have volunteers read aloud interesting sentences.

ELL

Write cloze sentences in which articles and adjectives are left out. Have students complete the sentences using appropriate articles and vivid adjectives.

TEST-TAKING TIP

You may be asked to identify adjectives in a sentence. Some adjectives tell how something looks, sounds, feels, tastes, or smells, such as *small, loud, rough, sweet,* or *fresh.* Adjectives can also tell how many or how much, such as *many, some,* or *two.*

Monitor Progress

Check Grammar

| If... students have difficulty identifying adjectives, | then... ask them to point out adjectives in a reading passage and identify the noun that each adjective tells about. |

Test Preparation

Write the letter of the word that is an adjective.

1. The team is playing a big game.
   - A team
   - B playing
   - **C big**
   - D game

2. The players are wearing orange shirts.
   - A players
   - B are
   - C shirts
   - **D orange**

3. Most of them have sturdy shoes.
   - A Most
   - **B sturdy**
   - C shoes
   - D them

4. The other players have green shirts.
   - **A other**
   - B players
   - C have
   - D shirts

5. Each one wears long socks.
   - A one
   - B wears
   - **C long**
   - D socks

6. Some girls are dancing after school.
   - A after
   - B school
   - C girls
   - **D Some**

7. The dancers wear soft shoes.
   - **A soft**
   - B shoes
   - C dancers
   - D wear

8. They attend class in the new gym.
   - **A new**
   - B gym
   - C attend
   - D class

Review

✓ **Write the adjective that describes each underlined noun.**

1. Many <u>holidays</u> are celebrated in Japan. Many
2. Popular <u>celebrations</u> include the New Year's Day Festival. Popular
3. People wear fancy <u>kimonos</u>. fancy
4. Many tie red <u>belts</u> around their kimonos. red
5. Wide <u>sashes</u> are called *obis*. Wide
6. Cities and towns have colorful <u>parades</u>. colorful
7. Families have splendid <u>feasts</u>. splendid
8. People give nice <u>gifts</u> to their friends and family. nice
9. Some <u>people</u> celebrate for several days. Some
10. Special <u>festivities</u> such as these are fun for everyone. Special

✓ **Choose the article in ( ) that correctly completes each sentence. Write the sentence.**

11. Midori is writing (a, <u>an</u>) unusual kind of poem.
12. (An, <u>The</u>) poem is from Japan and is called a *haiku*.
13. It is (<u>a</u>, an) very short poem.
14. It describes (a, <u>an</u>) interesting part of nature.
15. Japan has (<u>a</u>, an) fascinating kind of theater too.
16. (A, <u>The</u>) actors often portray characters from history.
17. (A, <u>The</u>) makeup on these players is unusual.
18. (A, <u>The</u>) players are all men.

Grammar **173**

Summarize

Ask students to tell about adjectives and articles and give examples of each.

- An adjective is a word that describes a person, place, or thing.
- The articles *a, an,* and *the* are special adjectives.
- *A* and *an* are used before singular nouns. *A* is used before words that begin with a consonant sound. *An* is used before words that begin with a vowel sound. *The* is used before singular or plural nouns.

Grammar-Writing Connection

Explain that choosing vivid, precise adjectives can make writing more lively and interesting.

General: Maria wore a dress.
Specific: Maria wore a <u>silky, yellow</u> dress.

Strong Adjectives

- Identify characteristics of an editorial.
- Write an editorial using strong adjectives.
- Develop criteria for judging a piece of writing.

TEACH

- Read aloud the information about strong adjectives in the box.
- Ask students to tell in their own words what strong adjectives are. *(words that describe nouns in a specific way, so readers can see, hear, feel, taste, and touch what the writer is describing)*

Guided Writing

Read each item in Exercise 1 with the class. Have volunteers name the strong adjectives and tell which nouns they describe.

Independent Writing

Ask volunteers to read aloud their responses to Exercise 2. Have listeners identify the strong adjectives the writer added.

Monitor Progress

Check Strong Adjectives

If... students need more help with strong adjectives,	**then...** have them locate some in a descriptive passage or poem and identify the senses to which they appeal.

 WRITER'S CRAFT

Strong Adjectives

> **Strong adjectives** describe nouns in a specific, lively way. Strong adjectives help readers see, hear, feel, taste, and touch what the writer is describing.

 Find four strong adjectives in each set of sentences. Write the adjectives.

1. The dancers wore baggy pants with brilliant shirts and soft velvet vests. baggy, brilliant, soft, velvet
2. The music made a jolly clattering as the energetic performers bounced across the glossy wooden floor of the ballroom. jolly, energetic, glossy, wooden
3. The enthusiastic singer let out a shrill note that could be heard by the noisy dancers all the way across the enormous ballroom. enthusiastic, shrill, noisy, enormous

 Add a strong adjective to describe each underlined noun. Write the sentences. Underline the adjectives. Possible answers:

4. The crowd cheered as the players ran onto the field.
   The eager crowd cheered as the nervous players ran onto the wet field.
5. Several police officers stopped the bystanders outside the gates. Several burly police officers stopped the angry bystanders outside the wooden gates.
6. The children rushed into the hall as their father came in the door. The excited children rushed into the narrow hall as their tired father came in the door.

RESOURCES

Writing Transparencies 21A, 21B
Writing Rubrics and Anchor Papers p. 29

Editorial

An **editorial** appears in a newspaper or magazine. An editorial states the writer's opinion about a topic. It supports the opinion with facts and examples.

First sentence states the writer's opinion.

Writer uses strong adjectives to make the details lively and persuasive.

Second paragraph contains facts and examples that support the writer's opinion.

All Students Should Wear School Uniforms

I think students in public schools should wear uniforms. I visited two schools last week. At one school, all the students wore neat blue pants and clean white shirts. At the other school, the students wore a jumble of styles, from torn jeans to expensive leather jackets. The students with uniforms were polite. Students at the school without uniforms seemed disorganized and rude.

First of all, uniforms make students' lives easier. With uniforms, kids don't have to think about what to wear each day, and they don't need to worry about being in style. Second, uniforms make students feel they are part of a group. This makes them work hard together. Their neat appearance makes them behave more politely.

Students can express their personalities with their clothes on weekends. But during the school day, uniforms are the way to go!

Writing **175**

Editorial

ANALYZE THE MODEL

Read aloud the model and the callouts to the left of it. Prepare students to write their own editorials.

PROMPT

Write an editorial expressing your opinion on an issue related to clothing styles. Use strong adjectives.

Getting Started Students can do any of the following.

- Use an organizer (pp. TR28–TR32).
- Discuss current clothing styles and related issues with a group.
- Write a journal entry about a clothing issue.

Editing/Revising Checklist

☑ Does my editorial clearly state my opinion on the issue?

☑ Have I used strong adjectives to make my details persuasive?

☑ Are adjectives and articles used correctly?

Self-Evaluation Distribute copies of p. TR26 for students to fill out.

Scoring Rubric Editorial

Rubric 4 3 2 1	4	3	2	1
Focus/Ideas	Editorial with strong focus on issue and opinion	Editorial with fair focus on issue and opinion	Editorial unfocused on issue and/or opinion	Editorial with issue and opinion not described
Organization/Paragraphs	Order that emphasizes key details	Attempts to emphasize key details	Confused order	No order
Voice	Knowledgeable and sincere	Some evidence of authority and sincerity	Little evidence of sincere voice	No clear voice
Word Choice	Uses strong adjectives that help persuade	Uses some strong adjectives	Little attempt to use strong adjectives	Incorrect or limited word choice
Sentences	Style and variety in lengths and kinds	Attempts to use individual style and variety	Monotonous lengths and/or style	Poorly constructed sentences
Conventions	Excellent control and accuracy	Reasonable control with few errors	Errors that may hinder understanding	Frequent errors that interfere with meaning

For 5- and 6-point rubrics, see Writing Rubrics and Anchor Papers p. 29.

Adjectives That Compare

OBJECTIVES

- Define and identify adjectives that compare.
- Use comparative and superlative adjectives correctly in writing.
- Become familiar with comparative and superlative adjective assessment on high-stakes tests.

TEACH

Read aloud the definitions, instruction, and examples in the box on p. 176. Point out that many people mistakenly use the superlative adjective form when they are comparing only two people, places, or things. For example, *Of my two brothers, Jay is tallest.* The correct form is comparative: *Of my two brothers, Jay is taller.*

Think Aloud

Model In reading the examples, I see that using the *-er* form or the *-est* form of the adjective is sufficient to make comparisons. I don't need to add the word *more* or *most* although I have heard people mistakenly say, for example, *This is the most hottest day of the summer.*

Adjectives That Compare

Adjectives are often used to make comparisons. To compare two people, places, or things, you usually add *-er* to an adjective. To compare three or more people, places, or things, you usually add *-est* to an adjective.

Puerto Rico has <u>warmer</u> weather than Florida.
Northern Africa has the <u>warmest</u> weather of all.

Sometimes you must change the spelling of an adjective when you write the *-er* or *-est* form.

Drop final *e*	rare	rarer	rarest
Change *y* to *i*	spicy	spicier	spiciest
Double final consonant	hot	hotter	hottest

A Write the adjective that compares in each sentence.

1. My family had a longer stay in China than in Kenya. longer
2. I think China has the strangest animals in the world. strangest
3. The giant panda is the heaviest panda of all. heaviest
4. Pandas have the oddest diets of any animal. oddest
5. To them, bamboo plants are tastier than fruits. tastier
6. Of the two countries, my family had a nicer time in Kenya. nicer
7. We saw the brightest cloth in the world at the market. brightest
8. We had the hottest day I can remember. hottest
9. The night was cooler than the day. cooler
10. The air is thinner in the mountains than along the coast. thinner

176 Grammar

RESOURCES

Daily Fix-It Lesson 22
See p. TR8.
See also Daily Fix-It Transparency 22.
Grammar Transparency 22

B Choose the adjective in ( ) that correctly completes each sentence. Write the sentences.

1. Which is the (greater, <u>greatest</u>) sport of all?
2. Soccer attracts the (bigger, <u>biggest</u>) crowds in the world.
3. Baseball has (<u>larger</u>, largest) crowds here than in Mexico.
4. Are baseball players (<u>stronger</u>, strongest) than golfers?
5. Cricket is the (stranger, <u>strangest</u>) game I have ever seen.
6. It is usually a (<u>longer</u>, longest) game than baseball.
7. Are baseball rules (<u>clearer</u>, clearest) than cricket rules?
8. Football has the (louder, <u>loudest</u>) fans of any sport.
9. Basketball is the (easier, <u>easiest</u>) sport of all.
10. Is basketball the (cooler, <u>coolest</u>) sport in the world?

C Complete each sentence by adding the *-er* or *-est* form of an adjective in the box. Use each adjective only once. Write the new sentences.

pretty	cheap	busy	nice	rich

Possible answers:

11. That city has the ____ market in the world.
    That city has the busiest market in the world.
12. The pottery is ____ than the pottery at home.
    The pottery is nicer than the pottery at home.
13. Some shoppers are ____ than others.
    Some shoppers are richer than others.
14. The daisies are the ____ flowers I have ever seen.
    The daisies are the prettiest flowers I have ever seen.
15. The vegetables are ____ than those in the grocery store.
    The vegetables are cheaper than those in the grocery store.

Grammar **177**

Guided Practice Ⓐ

Work through the exercise with students. Have them tell whether each adjective compares two things or more than two things. Ask them to point out clues that helped them figure out how many things are being compared.

TEACHING TIP

- Point out that although the *-er* ending may indicate an adjective that compares, many other words, such as the nouns *teacher* and *stranger*, also have that ending.

Independent Practice
Ⓑ and Ⓒ

Have students complete the exercises. For Differentiated Instruction and Extra Practice, see p. TR15.

Differentiated Instruction

Strategic Intervention

Have each student look outside and write an adjective that describes the scene, such as *sunny, snowy,* or *green.* Have students exchange adjectives with a partner. Partners write one sentence using the *-er* form of the adjective and one using the *-est* form. Then partners can exchange sentences and check to see that the forms were used and spelled correctly.

Advanced

Display a chart from the Internet or an encyclopedia that compares facts, such as the heights of mountains in the United States or the populations of world cities. Have students write four sentences based on facts in the chart. Two sentences should use the comparative form of an adjective, and two should use the superlative form of an adjective.

ELL

Remind English learners that to compare two or more things, you tell how they are alike and different. On slips of paper, write adjectives in both the comparative and superlative forms, such as *smaller, smallest, deeper,* and *deepest,* one adjective on each slip. Put the slips in a box and have students take turns drawing one. Students make up a sentence using the adjective. Model the process: *The red book is smaller than the blue book.* Write the sentences on the board and read them aloud with students.

You may be asked to choose the correct comparative or superlative adjective form in a sentence. Remember that the -est ending is used only to compare three or more items.

Incorrect: Of the two tests, this was <u>hardest</u>.

Correct: Of the two tests, this was <u>harder</u>.

Monitor Progress

Check Grammar

If... students have difficulty choosing the correct adjectives that compare,	then... discuss the clues in each test item that indicate the correct answer.

Test Preparation

✓ Write the letter of the word that correctly completes each sentence.

1. Juan's new house is __B__ than his old house.
   - **A** biger
   - **B** bigger
   - **C** biggest
   - **D** more bigger

2. His yard is the __C__ one he has ever seen.
   - **A** larger
   - **B** largeer
   - **C** largest
   - **D** largeest

3. His school is the __B__ school in the city.
   - **A** old
   - **B** oldest
   - **C** older
   - **D** most older

4. He lives in a __A__ neighborhood than before.
   - **A** quieter
   - **B** quiet
   - **C** more quietest
   - **D** quietest

5. Anna's new house is __D__ than her old house.
   - **A** fancy
   - **B** fanciest
   - **C** fancyest
   - **D** fancier

6. Her bedroom is the __B__ room in the house.
   - **A** tinyer
   - **B** tiniest
   - **C** tinyest
   - **D** tiny

Review

☑ Write the adjective that compares in each sentence.

1. Grandpa is the greatest storyteller in the world. greatest
2. He is also the thinnest family member from Puerto Rico. thinnest
3. He says Puerto Rico is the loveliest country of all. loveliest
4. It has the finest people in the world. finest
5. His tales of Puerto Rico are funnier than Uncle Luis's. funnier
6. His jokes are even sillier than mine. sillier
7. Sometimes Grandpa acts even stranger than I do. stranger
8. He is the cleverest member of our family. cleverest
9. I can't think of a family jollier than ours. jollier
10. We have the happiest times of all with Grandpa. happiest

☑ Choose the adjective in ( ) that correctly completes each sentence. Write the sentences.

11. Who can make the (<u>tastier</u>, tastiest) pizza, Ed or you?
12. I will use the (spicier, <u>spiciest</u>) sauce in the kitchen.
13. Then I will add the (hotter, <u>hottest</u>) sausage I can find.
14. These mushrooms are (<u>fresher</u>, freshest) than those.
15. This cheese is (mild, <u>milder</u>) than the other kind.
16. Those tomatoes are (<u>sweeter</u>, sweetest) than usual.
17. The peppers are the (green, <u>greenest</u>) ones I have ever seen.
18. The oven is (<u>warmer</u>, warmest) than before.
19. I am a (<u>finer</u>, finest) cook than Ed.
20. My pizza is the (rich, <u>richest</u>) pizza ever!

Grammar **179**

Summarize

Ask students to describe adjectives that compare and explain when to use each form.

- Adjectives can compare two or more people, places, or things.
- To compare two things, you usually add -er to an adjective. To compare more than two things, you usually add -est to an adjective.
- Sometimes you must change the spelling of an adjective before adding the -er or -est ending.

Grammar-Writing Connection

Explain that using the comparative and superlative forms of adjectives is useful for comparing and contrasting two or more things.

Comparative: Alaska is a <u>colder</u> place than Minnesota.

Superlative: The South Pole is the <u>coldest</u> place in the world.

Persuasive Words

OBJECTIVES

- Identify characteristics of an opinion.
- Write an opinion, using persuasive words.
- Develop criteria for judging a piece of writing.

TEACH

- Read aloud the information about persuasive words in the box.
- Ask students to tell in their own words what persuasive words are. *(words that state a judgment made by the writer to get readers to agree with the writer's opinion)*

 Guided Writing

Read each item in Exercise 1 with the class. Ask students to summarize the opinion stated in each item and point out the persuasive words and phrases.

 Independent Writing

Ask volunteers to read aloud their responses to Exercise 2. Have listeners identify persuasive words and phrases and discuss whether they are effective.

Monitor Progress

Check Persuasive Words

If... students need more help with persuasive words,	then... locate editorials or letters to the editor in student news magazines and have students identify persuasive words in them.

 WRITER'S CRAFT

Persuasive Words

> **Persuasive words** are words that state a judgment made by the writer. Some persuasive words are *should, must, best, worst, most,* and adjectives ending in *-est*. They are used to get readers to agree with the writer's opinion.
>
> You <u>should</u> try a Chinese meal <u>because</u> it includes the <u>healthiest</u> and <u>tastiest</u> foods in the world. It has the <u>most interesting</u> variety of foods.

 Find three persuasive words or phrases in each set of sentences. Write the persuasive words and phrases.

1. You <u>should</u> visit Africa. The <u>friendliest</u> people live there, and they have the <u>most</u> unusual stories to tell.

2. That part of the park is the <u>worst</u> place to camp of all. It has the <u>ugliest</u> scenery and the <u>coldest</u> water.

3. Everyone <u>must</u> get together to clean up our downtown. We have the <u>nicest</u> neighborhoods and <u>best</u> schools in the county, so why is our downtown area so dirty?

 Write details to support the following opinion. Use at least three persuasive words or phrases in your details.

You should root for my favorite team. **Possible answer: You should root for the Cougars baseball team. It has the most talented players in the county. The field it plays on is the most beautiful one I've ever seen. Its fans are the most loyal ones around.**

180 Writing

RESOURCES

Writing Transparencies 22A, 22B
Writing Rubrics and Anchor Papers p. 30

Writing Your Opinion

In **writing your opinion,** you state a strong viewpoint about a topic. Your purpose is to persuade your readers to agree with you. Support your opinion with facts, examples, and descriptions.

Writer asks questions to attract readers' attention.

Sentence states writer's opinion.

Facts and descriptions support writer's opinion.

Writer uses persuasive words.

The Best Place to Live

Would you like to live in a place that is warm all year? Would you like a place where flowers brighten all four seasons? Would you like a place where the nicest people in the world live? Then you would love Florida! I think Florida is the best place to live.

Florida has the most beautiful scenery in the world. Relax and observe the wading birds and mangrove trees in the Everglades. Lie on a white sandy beach and feel the gentle breeze blow through the palm trees. Do you like amusement parks and sea parks? You will find the most fun parks in Florida. Florida has big, busy cities such as Miami and quiet wilderness areas as well. Here's the best thing about Florida: my family lives here! Florida is the greatest place to live in the world.

Writing **181**

Writing Your Opinion

ANALYZE THE MODEL

Read aloud the model and the callouts to the left of it. Prepare students to write their own opinions.

PROMPT

Write an opinion about where the best place to live is. Use persuasive words to convince your readers.

Getting Started Students can do any of the following.
- Use an organizer (pp. TR28–TR32).
- With partners, brainstorm different specific and general places to live.
- Make a list of benefits of living in the place of their choice.

Editing/Revising Checklist
☑ Have I clearly stated my opinion?
☑ Have I used persuasive words to support my opinion?
☑ Are adjectives that compare used correctly?

Self-Evaluation Distribute copies of p. TR26 for students to fill out.

Scoring Rubric — Writing Your Opinion

Rubric 4 3 2 1	4	3	2	1
Focus/Ideas	Strong focus on opinion and good support for it	Fair focus on opinion and some support	Unfocused opinion and/or inadequate support	Opinion and support not described
Organization/ Paragraphs	Order that emphasizes key details	Attempts to emphasize key details	Confused order	No order
Voice	Unusually persuasive	Fairly persuasive	Not persuasive	No attempt to be persuasive
Word Choice	Strong persuasive words	Some persuasive words	Little attempt to use persuasive words	Incorrect or limited word choice
Sentences	Variety in kind; uses compounds	Some variety and use of compounds	No variety in kinds	Poorly constructed sentences
Conventions	Excellent control and accuracy	Reasonable control with few errors	Errors that may hinder understanding	Frequent errors that interfere with meaning

For 5- and 6-point rubrics, see Writing Rubrics and Anchor Papers p. 30.

Adverbs

- Define and identify adverbs.
- Use adverbs correctly in writing.
- Become familiar with adverb assessment on high-stakes tests.

TEACH

Read aloud the definitions, instruction, and examples in the box on p. 182. Point out that adverbs always tell more about the verb in a sentence.

Model When I read the examples, I quickly recognize the word *happily* as an adverb because I know that words ending in *-ly* are often adverbs that tell how something happens. The words *yesterday* and *inside* are not as easy to identify, but I notice that they both tell more about a verb in the sentence. *Yesterday* tells when the family moved, and *inside* tells where they carried boxes.

LESSON 23

Adverbs

An **adverb** is a word that can tell when, where, or how something happens.

<u>Yesterday</u>, the family moved into a new home. (when)
They carried boxes <u>inside</u>. (where)
They <u>happily</u> unpacked the boxes. (how)

- Adverbs can come before or after the verbs they describe.
- Adverbs that tell how something happens often end in *-ly*.

A Write the adverb in each sentence.

1. Recently Jangmi said good-bye to her house in Korea. Recently
2. Then she left the house. Then
3. She wandered around. around
4. Jangmi quietly looked at her big bedroom. quietly
5. She now was happy about her new home. now
6. The house has a playroom downstairs. downstairs
7. There is a beautiful garden outside. outside
8. The builders arranged the bricks beautifully on the new house. beautifully
9. The painters carefully painted each room. carefully
10. The workers cleaned the house thoroughly. thoroughly
11. Jangmi will unpack her boxes later. later
12. Finally, the house will belong to its new owners. Finally

182 Grammar

RESOURCES

Daily Fix-It Lesson 23
   See p. TR8.
   See also Daily Fix-It Transparency 23.
Grammar Transparency 23

B Write the adverb in each sentence. Then write whether the adverb tells *when, where,* or *how.*

1. The Wilsons often discuss their need for a new home.
   often; when
2. Today Maria suggested a familiar city neighborhood.
   Today; when
3. Maria's dad had a store there.
   there; where
4. Dad supported Maria's suggestion heartily.
   heartily; how
5. Tom always had wanted an oceanside home.
   always; when
6. Then Maria's mom mentioned a pretty little town.
   Then; when
7. Both the city and the beach were nearby.
   nearby; where
8. Surprisingly, everyone liked Mom's idea.
   Surprisingly; how
9. The family quickly made their plans.
   quickly; how
10. Soon they will find a new home in the town.
    Soon; when

C Make each sentence more specific by adding an adverb from the box. Write the new sentences. Use each adverb only once.

often	fondly	soon	eagerly	first	later

Possible answers:

11. Will's family looks forward to their trip to Korea.
    Will's family eagerly looks forward to their trip to Korea.
12. They will go to the capital city of Seoul.
    First they will go to the capital city of Seoul.
13. They will go to a village near the sea.
    Later they will go to a village near the sea.
14. Will's parents have described their native country.
    Will's parents often have described their native country.
15. They remember their early years in Korea.
    They fondly remember their early years in Korea.
16. The whole family will have memories of Korea.
    Soon the whole family will have memories of Korea.

Grammar **183**

PRACTICE

Guided Practice Ⓐ

Work through the exercise with students. Afterwards, you might have them tell whether each adverb tells *when, where,* or *how* about the verb.

TEACHING TIP

- Explain that one way to recognize adverbs is to try placing them in a different position in a sentence. For example, *The painters worked carefully* could be revised as *The painters carefully worked.* However, the adjective *careful* in *The painters were careful* cannot be put in a different position.

Independent Practice Ⓑ and Ⓒ

Have students complete the exercises. For Differentiated Instruction and Extra Practice, see p. TR15.

Differentiated Instruction

Strategic Intervention

On the board, make a chart with the headings *When, Where,* and *How.* Help students brainstorm adverbs, such as *tomorrow, later, outdoors, down, gladly,* and *strangely,* and write them under the correct heading. Then have students choose one adverb from each column and write a sentence using it.

Advanced

Have students write a sentence about a formal or informal musical activity in which they have participated. Tell them to write a simple sentence with no adverbs. For example, *I sang to my brother.* Then have them rewrite the sentence, adding at least three adverbs. If possible, they should use one adverb that tells *when,* one that tells *where,* and one that tells *how.* For example, *Yesterday I quietly sang to my brother outside.*

ELL

Provide a cooperative language experience in which students play Add an Adverb. Each player adds a word to the sentence that Player 1 creates.

Player 1: The apple turned red.

Player 2 (adds adverb that tells *when*): Yesterday the apple turned red.

Player 3 (adds adverb that tells *how*): Yesterday the apple suddenly turned red.

TEST-TAKING TIP

You may be asked to choose the correct adverb form in a sentence. Remember that the -ly ending is often added to an adjective to make an adverb.

Incorrect: The bell rang very <u>sudden</u>.

Correct: The bell rang very <u>suddenly</u>.

Monitor Progress

Check Grammar

| **If...** students have difficulty identifying adverbs, | **then...** help them find adverbs in their reading materials; identify whether they tell *how, when,* or *where;* and name the verbs they describe. |

Test Preparation

✓ Write the letter of the word that is an adverb.

1. Today the class is studying Korea.
- **A** is
- **C** class
- **B** studying
- **D** Today ⓓ

2. Lee hardly remembers his years in Korea.
- **A** remembers
- **C** hardly ⓒ
- **B** his
- **D** years

3. The country has grown rapidly.
- **A** rapidly ⓐ
- **C** has
- **B** grown
- **D** country

4. People are everywhere on the streets.
- **A** are
- **C** People
- **B** everywhere ⓑ
- **D** on

5. Korea usually has had close ties to Japan.
- **A** has
- **C** close
- **B** usually ⓑ
- **D** ties

6. The people generally speak Korean.
- **A** people
- **C** speak
- **B** generally ⓑ
- **D** Korean

7. Families have always respected older people.
- **A** people
- **C** always ⓒ
- **B** older
- **D** have

8. Sometimes people wear traditional clothes.
- **A** wear
- **C** clothes
- **B** traditional
- **D** Sometimes ⓓ

9. People in Korea eat rice often.
- **A** often ⓐ
- **C** in
- **B** People
- **D** rice

10. Pictures clearly show Korea's charm.
- **A** show
- **C** clearly ⓒ
- **B** Pictures
- **D** show

Review

☑ Write the adverb in each sentence.

1. Yesterday I studied holidays in other countries.
   Yesterday
2. Koreans celebrate the fall harvest annually.
   annually
3. The holiday is interestingly called the Moon Festival.
   interestingly
4. In China, people happily celebrate the Chinese New Year.
   happily
5. They have colorful parades outside.
   outside
6. The French joyfully celebrate independence on Bastille Day.
   joyfully
7. It always occurs on July 14.
   always
8. May Day is celebrated differently in different places.
   differently
9. People often celebrate springtime on May Day.
   often
10. Many countries honor their workers then.
    then

☑ Write the adverb in each sentence. Then write whether the adverb tells *when*, *where*, or *how*.

11. Homes everywhere have different characteristics.
    everywhere; where
12. Japanese homes usually have straw mats on floors.
    usually; when
13. Korean floors have heat pipes underneath.
    underneath; where
14. Some Africans firmly pack mud for walls.
    firmly; how
15. In parts of Mongolia, people may set up tents anyplace.
    anyplace; where
16. American builders work differently in each area.
    differently; how
17. New Orleans designers often decorate homes with wrought iron. often; when
18. Builders frequently make East Coast homes from brick.
    frequently; when

Grammar **185**

Summarize

Ask students to define adverbs and give examples of their use.

- An adverb tells *how, when,* or *where* about a verb.
- An adverb can come before or after the verb it describes.
- Adverbs that tell *how* often end in *-ly.*

Grammar-Writing Connection

Explain that adverbs make descriptions of actions more specific and vivid.

General: Jangmi packed her clothes.

Specific: Jangmi <u>sadly</u> packed her clothes.

Use Reasons to Persuade

- Identify characteristics of an ad.
- Write an ad, using reasons to persuade.
- Develop criteria for judging a piece of writing.

TEACH

- Read aloud the information in the box about using reasons to persuade.
- Ask students to tell in their own words what using reasons to persuade means. *(giving readers logical, specific reasons why they should act)*

 ## Guided Writing

Read the ad and questions in Exercise 1 with students. Ask them to identify details in the ad that help them answer the questions.

 ## Independent Writing

Ask volunteers to read aloud their responses to Exercise 2. Discuss with students how the writers try to persuade their readers.

Monitor Progress

Check Use Reasons to Persuade

If... students need more help with using reasons to persuade,	**then...** show ads for various products and have students identify the reasons used in the ads to persuade readers to buy the products.

 WRITER'S CRAFT

Use Reasons to Persuade

When your goal is to convince readers to buy a product or use a service, **use reasons to persuade** them. A reason is a specific answer to the question "Why?" When you want readers to take an action, give them logical, specific reasons why they should act. Use vivid descriptive words and persuasive words in your reasons.

You should visit Hawaii. It has the <u>most beautiful beaches</u>. It has the <u>warmest, sunniest weather all year</u>.

 Read the ad. Then write answers to the questions.

> Visit San Antonio, Texas. You can stroll along the River Walk and enjoy a meal outdoors. Go to the Alamo and see where history was made. Attend the colorful Fiesta San Antonio in April or go to the annual rodeo in February.

1. What does the writer want to persuade readers to do?
go to San Antonio
2. What reasons does the writer use to persuade readers?
Readers can stroll and eat on the River Walk, visit the Alamo, and go to a festival and a rodeo.

Write two reasons to persuade readers to take each action.
Possible answers:
3. Come to the school fair. All your friends will be there. You can win prizes playing entertaining games.
4. Join the soccer team.
You will get good exercise. You will learn how to be part of a team.

186 Writing

RESOURCES

Writing Transparencies 23A, 23B
Writing Rubrics and Anchor Papers p. 31

Ad

Ads are written to convince readers to buy a product or use a service. Ads use persuasive words, reasons, and vivid descriptions to encourage readers to act.

Come to Washington, D.C.

Writer begins to list reasons why people should visit Washington.

Writer uses vivid descriptions to appeal to readers' senses.

Writer includes persuasive words to convince readers.

Are you looking for the perfect family vacation? Then visit Washington, D.C.! Washington has many exciting museums, such as the National Air and Space Museum. The Jefferson Memorial and other beautiful monuments sit elegantly on the green banks of the Potomac River. In spring white blossoms bloom on the cherry trees along the river. Of course, the best reason to visit Washington is to see where American history was made. You can visit the Capitol and see our government at work. You can also visit the White House and see where Abraham Lincoln lived. You could spend two weeks in Washington, D.C., and still not see all the educational and inspiring sights. Make your plans today to come to our nation's capital.

Writing 187

Ad

ANALYZE THE MODEL

Read aloud the model and the callouts to the left of it. Prepare students to write their own ads.

PROMPT

Write an ad that might be in a travel brochure for a specific place. Give specific reasons for going there.

Getting Started Students can do any of the following.

- Use an organizer (pp. TR28–TR32).
- Brainstorm a list of interesting travel destinations.
- Look through illustrated travel brochures and magazines.

Editing/Revising Checklist

☑ Does my ad clearly focus on a specific place?

☑ Does my ad give readers reasons for going to the place?

☑ Are adverbs used correctly?

Self-Evaluation Distribute copies of p. TR26 for students to fill out.

Scoring Rubric Ad

Rubric 4 3 2 1	4	3	2	1
Focus/Ideas	Ad with strong focus on place	Ad with fair focus on place	Ad unfocused on place	Place not described in ad
Organization/ Paragraphs	Reasons given in logical order	Reasons given in fair order	Confused order	No order
Voice	Unusually vivid and persuasive	Fairly vivid and persuasive	Not vivid or persuasive	No attempt to be persuasive
Word Choice	Strong sensory and persuasive words	Some sensory and persuasive words	Few or no sensory or persuasive words	Incorrect or limited word choice
Sentences	Uses variety of sentences	Some variety of sentences	No variety	Poorly constructed sentences
Conventions	Excellent control and accuracy	Reasonable control with few errors	Errors that may hinder understanding	Frequent errors that interfere with meaning

For 5- and 6-point rubrics, see Writing Rubrics and Anchor Papers p. 31.

Adverbs That Compare

OBJECTIVES

- Define and identify adverbs that compare.
- Use comparative and superlative adverbs correctly in writing.
- Become familiar with comparative and superlative adverb assessment on high-stakes tests.

TEACH

Read aloud the definitions, instruction, and examples in the box on p. 188. Point out that adverbs can be used to compare, just as adjectives can. Both adverbs and adjectives use one form to compare two things and another form to compare three or more things.

Model In the first set of examples, I can see that the word *high* tells how the cakes rise, so *high* is an adverb. In the second sentence, two things are compared, so the *-er* form of *high* is used. In the third sentence, the action of the cake is compared to those of all cakes, so the *-est* form of *high* is correct. In the second set of examples, I notice that *more* is used before the adverb *slowly* to compare two actions. *Most* is used to compare many actions.

Adverbs That Compare

You can use **adverbs** to compare actions. The *-er* form of an adverb compares two actions. The *-est* form of an adverb compares three or more actions.

> That baker's cakes rise <u>high</u>.
> That baker's cakes rise <u>higher</u> than Mr. Lee's cakes.
> That baker's cakes rise <u>highest</u> of any cakes.

Most adverbs that end in *-ly* use *more* and *most* to make comparisons.

> Tom ate breakfast <u>slowly</u>.
> Tom ate breakfast <u>more slowly</u> than Alison.
> Tom ate breakfast <u>most slowly</u> of all the children.

A Write the adverb that compares in each sentence.

1. Mrs. Sanchez works harder than the bakery's owner. harder
2. Mr. Lane rolls out pastry dough more rapidly than Ms. Delroy. more rapidly
3. Mrs. Sanchez makes delicious treats fastest of all the bakers. fastest
4. The sweet rolls disappear most quickly of all. most quickly
5. One oven cooks faster than the other oven. faster
6. Everyone worked more carefully than usual. more carefully
7. Mrs. Sanchez was finished sooner than the others. sooner
8. Her scones baked most rapidly of all. most rapidly
9. Mrs. Fisher's bagels took longer than Ms. Delroy's turnovers. longer
10. Mr. Ling's muffins cooked slowest of all. slowest

188 Grammar

RESOURCES

Daily Fix-It Lesson 24
See p. TR8.
See also Daily Fix-It Transparency 24.
Grammar Transparency 24

B Choose the correct word in ( ) to complete each sentence. Write the sentences.

1. Of all her family members, Sharon cooked (more often, <u>most often</u>).

2. She chose a career (<u>earlier</u>, earliest) than her friend Dave did.

3. She decided (<u>sooner</u>, soonest) than Dave to be a chef.

4. Of all the students in her cooking class, Sharon studied (harder, <u>hardest</u>).

5. She prepared food (<u>more quickly</u>, most quickly) than her best friend.

6. She kneaded bread (more rapidly, <u>most rapidly</u>) of all the bakers in class.

7. Sharon cooked in her restaurant (<u>more confidently</u>, most confidently) than her assistant.

8. She baked (more creatively, <u>most creatively</u>) of any chef in the city.

9. She chose vegetables (<u>more carefully</u>, most carefully) than her chief rival.

C Complete each sentence. Use the -er or -est form of an adverb in the box. Use each adverb only once.

fast	calmly	often

10. Pablo makes tacos ____ than Manuel.
    Pablo makes tacos faster than Manuel.
11. Tom cooks spaghetti ____ than Paul does.
    Theresa cooks spaghetti more often than Paula does.
12. Of all his friends, Taylor works ____ in the kitchen.
    Of all his friends, Taylor works most calmly in the kitchen.

Grammar **189**

PRACTICE

Guided Practice **A**

Work through the exercise with students. Afterwards, you might have them identify clues that help them figure out how many actions are being compared.

TEACHING TIP

- Point out that people may mistakenly use -er or -est to make the comparative forms of one-syllable words such as *quick* or *slow*. Explain that words such as *quick* and *slow* must have an -ly ending to be used as adverbs. Therefore, *more* or *most* must be added for the comparative forms.

Independent Practice **B** and **C**

Have students complete the exercises. For Differentiated Instruction and Extra Practice, see p. TR15.

Differentiated Instruction

Strategic Intervention

Say each sentence below. Ask students to make up a related sentence using the same adverb in the comparative form and then in the superlative form. Model the process: *The trombone player played loudly. (The trumpet player played more loudly than the trombone player. The drummer played loudest of all.)*

The librarian spoke kindly.

The robin sang sweetly.

The first-graders worked busily.

The story ended strangely.

Advanced

Have students find two or three sentences in their reading materials that use adverbs that compare. Ask them to write the adverbs and then write sentences of their own using the same forms.

ELL

Help students think of words that name kinds of transportation. *(car, truck, plane, ship, rocket, bus, bike)* Write the words on the board. Then have students think of sentences that compare two or more of the items. Model the process: *A rocket goes higher than a plane. Bikes travel most slowly.* Write the sentences on the board and read them together. Have volunteers underline the adverbs that compare.

You may be asked to choose the correct adverb that compares in a sentence. Remember that you should not use *more* with the *-er* form of an adverb or *most* with the *-est* form of an adverb.

Incorrect: The rolls bake <u>more faster</u> than the bread.

Correct: The rolls bake <u>faster</u> than the bread.

Monitor Progress

Check Grammar

If... students have difficulty with adverbs that compare,	then... discuss the reason for eliminating each incorrect answer in the test items.

Test Preparation

Write the letter of the word that correctly completes each sentence.

1. Stacy tries new foods __B__ than Tim.
  A often
  B more often
  C most often
  D oftenest

2. Tim eats sandwiches __D__ than salads.
  A eagerly
  B most eagerly
  C eagerer
  D more eagerly

3. Stacy eats vegetables __C__ than meats.
  A frequently
  B frequenter
  C more frequently
  D most frequently

4. Of all her neighbors, Stacy grows vegetables __D__.
  A easy
  B more easily
  C more easy
  D most easily

5. She plants tomatoes __A__ than carrots.
  A earlier
  B earliest
  C early
  D most earliest

6. She waits for them to ripen __C__ than I do.
  A patiently
  B most patiently
  C more patiently
  D patienter

Review

Write the adverb that compares in each sentence.

1. Of all her sisters, Charla awakens earliest.
   earliest
2. She waits for breakfast more eagerly than Michelle.
   more eagerly
3. The bagels toast longer than usual.
   longer
4. Michelle waits more patiently than Charla does.
   more patiently
5. Tamara pours cereal more carefully this morning than yesterday.
   more carefully
6. Charla eats breakfast fastest of anyone in the family.
   fastest
7. Tamara eats breakfast more calmly than her sister.
   more calmly
8. Of the three girls, Michelle goes to school most enthusiastically.
   most enthusiastically

Choose the correct word in ( ) to complete each sentence. Write the sentences.

9. Of all the people in the neighborhood, Mr. Green cooks (more skillfully, <u>most skillfully</u>).

10. He makes pie crust (<u>more rapidly</u>, most rapidly) than the French chef does.

11. Of all his friends, he makes tacos (faster, <u>fastest</u>).

12. He puts a pizza together (<u>more quickly</u>, most quickly) than Dana does.

13. He tries new recipes (most fearlessly, <u>more fearlessly</u>) than Edward does.

14. Mr. Green prepares a feast (<u>most calmly</u>, more calmly) of all the cooks I know.

Grammar **191**

REVIEW

Summarize

Ask students to explain adverbs that compare and how to form them.

- The *-er* form of an adverb compares two actions. The *-est* form of an adverb compares three or more actions.
- Use *more* and *most* to make comparisons with most adverbs that end in *-ly*.

Grammar-Writing Connection

Explain that we can compare the actions of two or more people, animals, or things with the superlative forms of adverbs.

Comparative: The dog howled <u>louder</u> than the wolf.

Superlative: The hyena howled loudest of all the animals.

Put Reasons in Order

TEACH

- Read aloud the information in the box about putting reasons in order.
- Ask students to tell in their own words what putting reasons in order means. *(putting reasons in the best order to persuade readers, such as ending with the most important reason and signaling it with a phrase)*

 Guided Writing

Read each item in Exercise 1 with students. Ask them to point out clues that helped them determine the best sentence order for each paragraph.

 Independent Writing

Ask volunteers to read aloud their responses to Exercise 2. Have listeners discuss whether the writer's reasons are in the best order.

Monitor Progress

Check Put Reasons in Order

If... students need more help with putting reasons in order,	**then...** find one or more pieces of persuasive writing with well-ordered reasons. Have students point out phrases that signal the most important reason.

 WRITER'S CRAFT

Put Reasons in Order

When you use reasons to persuade readers or to explain your opinion, **put the reasons in order**. You might begin with your least important reason and end with your most important reason. You can signal your most important reason with a phrase such as *best of all* or *most important*.

 Read the first sentence of each paragraph and the reasons that support it. Then write the letters of the sentences to show the best order for a good paragraph.

1. You should eat green vegetables as often as possible.
   B, C, A
   A Most importantly, green vegetables have many vitamins that will make you healthy.
   B First of all, green vegetables look bright and colorful on the dinner table.
   C In addition, there are many delicious recipes for green vegetables.

2. Try baking your own breads and rolls at home.
   A, C, B
   A Baking bread fills your home with wonderful aromas.
   B Best of all, baked goods are delicious treats for your family and friends.
   C Better yet, baking is fun and creative.

 Why is it important to eat a good breakfast? Write three or four sentences to answer this question. Put your reasons in order. Signal your most important reason with a phrase.

192 Writing   Possible answer on page TR37

RESOURCES

Writing Transparencies 24A, 24B
Writing Rubrics and Anchor Papers p. 32

Answer a Question

When you are writing to **answer a question**, give reasons to explain your answer. Put your reasons in order, from least important to most important.

First sentence states writer's opinion.

Remaining sentences give reasons for writer's opinion. They are arranged in order from least important to most important.

Reasons include vivid sensory details to get readers' attention.

What is your favorite food?

My favorite food is spaghetti. I like spaghetti because it is Italian like my grandma. In fact, my grandma makes the best spaghetti in the world. Spaghetti is great for a quick lunch or a nice family dinner. It's the perfect meal when I'm hungry. You can easily prepare other foods to serve with spaghetti, such as a crisp green salad and hot garlic bread. Spaghetti has many nourishing things in it. Pasta has protein plus carbohydrates for energy. The tomato sauce has meat in it, which also contains protein. The tomatoes are full of Vitamin C. Most importantly, I like spaghetti because it tastes delicious!

Writing **193**

Answer a Question
ANALYZE THE MODEL

Read aloud the model and the callouts to the left of it. Prepare students to write their own answers to a question.

PROMPT

Write an answer to this question: What is your favorite kind of food? Put your reasons in a good order.

Getting Started Students can do any of the following.

- Use an organizer (pp. TR28–TR32).
- Look through magazines for ideas.
- With the class, brainstorm foods from different cultures.

Editing/Revising Checklist

☑ Have I clearly answered the question?
☑ Are my reasons in the best possible order?
☑ Have I used adverbs that compare correctly?

Self-Evaluation Distribute copies of p. TR26 for students to fill out.

Scoring Rubric — Answer a Question

Rubric 4 3 2 1	4	3	2	1
Focus/Ideas	Answer strongly focused on specific food	Answer well focused on specific food	Answer sometimes not focused on topic	Specific food not described in answer
Organization/ Paragraphs	Persuasive reasons in order	Persuasive reasons in some order	Confused order	No order
Voice	Individual and persuasive	Fairly individual and persuasive	Not individual or persuasive	No attempt to be persuasive
Word Choice	Vivid sensory and persuasive words	Some sensory and persuasive words	Few or no sensory or persuasive words	Incorrect or limited word choice
Sentences	Variety in lengths and kinds	Some variety in lengths and kinds	No variety in lengths or kinds	Poorly constructed sentences
Conventions	Excellent control and accuracy	Reasonable control with few errors	Errors that may hinder understanding	Frequent errors that interfere with meaning

For 5- and 6-point rubrics, see Writing Rubrics and Anchor Papers p. 32.

Conjunctions

- Define and identify conjunctions.
- Use conjunctions correctly in writing.
- Become familiar with conjunction assessment on high-stakes tests.

TEACH

Read aloud the definitions, instruction, and examples in the box on p. 194. Point out that conjunctions may join words, as in compound subjects or verbs; groups of words, as in compound predicates; or sentences, as in a compound sentence.

Model When I read the first three examples, I see that the three conjunctions, *and, but,* and *or,* have different meanings. In the first sentence, *and* is used to add information. In the second sentence, *but* is used to show a difference. In the third sentence, *or* is used to show a choice. When the conjunctions are used to combine two sentences, a comma is placed after the word that comes before the conjunction.

Conjunctions

A **conjunction** is a word that connects words or groups of words.

- To add information, use the conjunction *and*. To show a difference, use the conjunction *but*. To show a choice, use the conjunction *or*.

   James played ball <u>and</u> listened to music.
   He had never played stickball, <u>but</u> he enjoyed it.
   He could stay inside <u>or</u> play outside.

- You can use a conjunction to combine two sentences into a compound sentence. Add a comma before the conjunction in a compound sentence.

   James had played baseball. He had never played stickball.
   James had played baseball, but he had never played stickball.

A Write the conjunction in each sentence.

1. New York is a huge city, but it has many smaller neighborhoods. **but**
2. Many artists and writers live in Greenwich Village. **and**
3. Central Park has gardens, playgrounds, and a zoo. **and**
4. You can see a play or a musical near Times Square. **or**
5. Harlem is in New York City, and it is an interesting neighborhood. **and**

194 Grammar

RESOURCES

Daily Fix-It Lesson 25
   See p. TR9.
   See also Daily Fix-It Transparency 25.
Grammar Transparency 25

B Choose the correct word in ( ) to complete each sentence. Write the sentences.

1. You can view art at museums (but, <u>and</u>) galleries.
2. You can go for the day (but, <u>or</u>) for an hour.
3. The museum has some very old art, (or, <u>but</u>) it has new pieces too.
4. You can take a tour (<u>or</u>, but) wander around alone.
5. You can't see everything in one day, (and, <u>but</u>) you can always come back.
6. One gallery has sculptures, (<u>and</u>, or) another has collages.
7. You can just view the art, (and, <u>or</u>) you can buy it.
8. Often you can meet an artist (but, <u>or</u>) hear the artist speak.
9. That gallery is small, (<u>but</u>, or) it has some wonderful paintings.
10. Art galleries are fun, (or, <u>and</u>) they are educational as well.

C Combine each pair of sentences using *and, but,* or *or.* Write the new sentences. Remember that compound sentences need commas. **Possible answers:**

11. The painting shows Boston. The collage shows New York.
The painting shows Boston, and the collage shows New York.
12. The styles are different. Both pieces of art show the liveliness of cities. The styles are different, but both pieces of art show the liveliness of cities.
13. The picture was painted in 2001. It shows a scene from the 1800s. The picture was painted in 2001, but it shows a scene from the 1800s.
14. See the collage in person. View it on the Internet.
See the collage in person, or view it on the Internet.
15. Some artists painted Boston. Many more painted New York.
Some artists painted Boston, but many more painted New York.

Grammar **195**

Guided Practice **A**

Work through the exercise with students. Then ask them to name the words, groups of words, or sentences that each conjunction connects.

TEACHING TiP

- Explain that using conjunctions in writing helps avoid too many short, choppy sentences. However, students should not overuse conjunctions by stringing many clauses or phrases together with *and* or *but.*

Independent Practice **B** and **C**

Have students complete the exercises. For Differentiated Instruction and Extra Practice, see p. TR15.

Differentiated Instruction

Strategic Intervention

Ask each student to write a sentence about going to the zoo. Have students include the conjunction *and, but,* or *or* in their sentence. Ask them to exchange papers with partners who then underline the conjunction in the sentence.

Advanced

Ask students to find sentences in their reading materials in which the conjunctions *and, but,* and *or* are used to join words, groups of words, or sentences. Have students mark the sentences with self-stick notes. Let pairs of students take turns reading each sentence aloud and describing what the conjunction does. *(Ty or Will ate the pie. Or joins two subjects and shows a choice.)*

ELL

Ask each student to suggest a simple sentence about pets. *(I like big dogs. I like tiny kittens.)* Write the sentences on the board or on chart paper. Have students choose two of the sentences and combine parts or whole sentences using the conjunctions *and, but,* and *or.* *(I like big dogs and tiny kittens.)* Point out that the two sentences must be related in some way. Write the new sentences and read them together.

You may be asked to choose the conjunction that makes sense in a sentence. Remember that *and* adds information, *but* shows a difference, and *or* shows a choice.

Incorrect: You may go out, <u>and</u> you may stay at home.

Correct: You may go out, <u>or</u> you may stay at home.

Monitor Progress

Check Grammar

If... students have difficulty using conjunctions,	then... show them how to test each word in the sentence to eliminate incorrect answers.

Test Preparation

✓ Write the letter of the word that best completes each sentence.

1. Dan likes sightseeing, _C_ Jo likes it too.

   A unless   **C** and

   B only   **D** or

2. Dan likes museums, _B_ he likes parks better.

   A or   **C** and

   B but   **D** since

3. Jo likes the science museum, _A_ Dan prefers the art museum.

   A but   **C** since

   B or   **D** with

4. Jo likes tall buildings _B_ big stores.

   A but   **C** since

   B and   **D** while

5. Dan would prefer a zoo _D_ a playground.

   A but   **C** yet

   B nor   **D** or

6. The city has all of these _A_ more.

   A and   **C** since

   B or   **D** nor

7. Sightseeing is fun, _B_ it is tiring.

   A and   **C** since

   B but   **D** with

8. At the end of the day, you can stop _C_ rest.

   A but   **C** and

   B yet   **D** because

196 Grammar

Review

✔ Write the conjunction in each sentence.

1. We went to the Empire State Building and rode to the top. **and**

2. It has 102 stories and is 1,250 feet high. **and**

3. It was once the world's tallest building, but it is not anymore. **but**

4. You can see the city from the 86th or the 102nd floor. **or**

5. The Empire State Building is a famous sight, but it is also a busy office building. **but**

6. There are pictures at the library or on the Internet. **or**

7. You should go to New York City and see this building. **and**

8. You cannot see a building this tall in Texas or in Florida. **or**

✔ Write the correct word in ( ) to complete each sentence.

9. The parks in my town are nice, (or, <u>but</u>) they are not like Central Park.

10. Central Park is in New York City, (but, <u>and</u>) it is 2½ miles long.

11. You can visit the park's zoo (but, <u>or</u>) bird house.

12. Outside the park is noisy traffic, (and, <u>but</u>) inside is peace and quiet.

13. You can take a picnic (<u>or</u>, but) get a snack in the park.

14. People walk, skate, (but, <u>and</u>) jog in the park.

Grammar **197**

Summarize

Ask students to describe conjunctions.

- A conjunction is a word that connects words or groups of words.

- The conjunction *and* adds information; *but* shows a difference; and *or* shows a choice.

- A conjunction can combine two sentences to make a compound sentence. A comma is placed before the conjunction.

Grammar-Writing Connection

Explain that by using conjunctions, writers can combine words and phrases to avoid wordiness and repetition.

Wordy: The day was hot. The day was sunny.

Not wordy: The day was hot <u>and</u> sunny.

Know Your Audience

- Identify characteristics of a story review.
- Write a story review that shows you know your audience.
- Develop criteria for judging a piece of writing.

TEACH

- Read aloud the information in the box about knowing your audience.
- Ask students to tell in their own words what knowing your audience means. *(thinking about your readers' age, interests, and opinions to choose the most persuasive details to use)*

Guided Writing

Read each paragraph in the exercise with students. Ask them to point out details that help them identify the audience for each paragraph.

Independent Writing

Ask students to suppose that they are writing a review of a movie about a talking cat for a 4-year-old child. Have them write a sentence or two that would be suitable for the review.

Monitor Progress

Check Know Your Audience

If... students need more help with knowing their audience,	**then...** read with them a news story for adults and one for students their age. Have them point out details that show the writer's awareness of the audience.

WRITER'S CRAFT

Know Your Audience

When your goal is to persuade readers to agree with your viewpoint, you need to **know your audience.** To know your audience, think about the age, interests, and opinions of your readers. Keep these in mind as you choose your details.

Tell for which audience each paragraph was written.

third graders	nature lovers	high-school students

1. *Winter Dreams* by F. Scott Fitzgerald tells the story of a young man who wants to marry a young woman from a wealthy family. The story takes place in the 1920s, but anyone who worries about going to college, getting a job, and someday getting married will enjoy it.
   high-school students
2. Whales face many dangers, such as icebergs and polluted waters. Everyone wants to protect whales and other sea animals. *A Symphony of Whales* is an inspiring story about a girl who comes up with a unique way to help a group of whales stuck in an icy sea.
   nature lovers
3. *Suki's Kimono* is a great story about a young girl who wears what she wants no matter what her classmates think. If you've ever worn something that others didn't think was cool, or even if you've wanted to, you'll love this story.
   third graders

198 Writing

RESOURCES

Writing Transparencies 25A, 25B
Writing Rubrics and Anchor Papers p. 33

Story Review

In a **story review,** you explain to readers why they should read a particular story or not. You describe what you like and dislike about the story.

First two sentences state writer's opinions of story.

Writer supports opinion with reasons. Transitions show order of reasons.

Writer ends with most important reason and tells readers what they should do.

A True-to-Life Story

Me and Uncle Romie is a story that will make you both happy and sad. You will enjoy reading about the main character, James. First of all, the story has a colorful setting. James goes to New York City for the first time. It is fun to read about the city's sights and James's responses to them. Second, the story's characters seem real. James is happy sometimes. Other times he is unsure of himself, sad, or homesick. Everyone can identify with these feelings. Finally, James has interesting relationships with his aunt and uncle. At the story's beginning, he does not know these family members. By the end, he knows both them and himself much better. This story will remind readers of their own unique family members. For an enjoyable reading experience, read *Me and Uncle Romie.*

Writing   **199**

Story Review
ANALYZE THE MODEL

Read aloud the model and the callouts to the left of it. Prepare students to write their own story reviews.

PROMPT

Write a review of a story you like for readers who might also like it. Explain why they might like it.

Getting Started Students can do any of the following.

- Use an organizer (pp. TR28–TR32).
- Look at stories in the reading textbook.
- Discuss stories they have enjoyed.

Editing/Revising Checklist

- ☑ Does my review give my opinion of the story?
- ☑ Do I show that I know who my audience is?
- ☑ Have I used conjunctions correctly?

Self-Evaluation Distribute copies of p. TR26 for students to fill out.

Scoring Rubric   Story Review

Rubric 4 3 2 1	4	3	2	1
Focus/Ideas	Review with strong focus on story and audience	Review with good focus on story and audience	Story recommendation and awareness of audience incomplete or unclear in review	Story not reviewed
Organization/ Paragraphs	Supporting reasons in logical order	Reasons in fairly logical order	Confused order	No order
Voice	Original and persuasive	Fairly original and persuasive	Not original or persuasive	No attempt to be persuasive
Word Choice	Vivid sensory and persuasive words	Some sensory and persuasive words	Few or no sensory or persuasive words	Incorrect or limited word choice
Sentences	Good mix of simple and compound sentences	Some variety of simple and compound sentences	No compound sentences	Poorly constructed sentences
Conventions	Excellent control and accuracy	Reasonable control with few errors	Errors that may prevent understanding	Frequent errors that interfere with meaning

For 5- and 6-point rubrics, see *Writing Rubrics and Anchor Papers* p. 33.

Capital Letters

OBJECTIVES

- Define and identify capital letters.
- Use capital letters correctly in writing.
- Become familiar with capital letter assessment on high-stakes tests.

TEACH

Read aloud the instruction and examples in the box on p. 200. Point out that in holidays with more than one word, each important word is capitalized.

Think Aloud **Model** In the first incorrect example, the day of the week, the month, and the holiday should all be capitalized. In the second incorrect example, *grandpa* should not be capitalized because the word *my* is used before it. If it were used by itself— *I went to the park with Grandpa*—it would be capitalized. In the same way, in the sentence *I saw our uncle, uncle* is not capitalized, but in the sentence *I saw Uncle Ted, Uncle* is capitalized.

LESSON 26

Capital Letters

Use **capital letters** for proper nouns. Proper nouns include days of the week, months of the year, and holidays. Titles for people and abbreviations of the titles should be capitalized when they are used with a person's name. Do not capitalize titles when they are used by themselves.

Incorrect	The fourth thursday in november is thanksgiving.
Correct	The fourth Thursday in November is Thanksgiving.
Incorrect	My Grandpa visits on hanukkah and labor day.
Correct	My grandpa visits on Hanukkah and Labor Day.

A Write correctly the words in each sentence that should have capital letters. If a sentence has no capitalization mistakes, write *C*.

1. Today dr. chang said Americans have many symbols of freedom.
   Dr. Chang
2. My mom and dad display our flag each july.
   July
3. That is when our country celebrates independence day.
   Independence Day
4. Some people display flags from january to december.
   January; December
5. One monday in june I spotted a bald eagle.
   Monday; June
6. Bald eagles stand for freedom in the United States.
   C

200 Grammar

RESOURCES

Daily Fix-It Lesson 26
    See p. TR9.
    See also Daily Fix-It Transparency 26.
Grammar Transparency 26

B Write the sentences. Use capital letters correctly.

1. The art students are taking a trip with ms. collins in february.
2. They will see a statue of mr. lincoln on presidents' day.
3. On tuesday they will visit a statue of president Washington.
4. They will also see wooden carvings in mr. toma's studio.
5. They will see bronze statues on wednesday.
6. On thursday, february 25, the students plan to study paintings of cowboys.
7. Stacy's uncle will show us his marble statues on friday.
8. He made aunt Ellen a statue for valentine's day.
9. On saturday, everyone will return to New York.
10. Next year the art trip will take place over memorial day.

C Answer each question with a complete sentence. Use capital letters correctly. **Possible answers:**

11. Which holiday did you celebrate most recently?
    I recently celebrated Veterans Day.
12. In what month does this holiday occur?
    Veterans Day occurs in November.
13. What is a holiday for which you receive gifts?
    I receive gifts for Christmas.
14. On which day of the week do you get up latest?
    I get up latest on Saturday.
15. In which month did you go on a trip away from home?
    I went on a trip in August.
16. Who is your favorite coach?
    My favorite coach is Coach Reilly.

Grammar **201**

Guided Practice Ⓐ

Work through the exercise with students. Have them explain their choices in capitalizing or not capitalizing specific words.

TEACHING TiP

- Remind students that capitalization is used for proper nouns, which name particular persons, places, or things. Each day of the week is a particular day; each month of the year is a particular month. *Grandpa* and *Uncle Ted* name particular people.

Independent Practice Ⓑ and Ⓒ

Have students complete the exercises. For Differentiated Instruction and Extra Practice, see p. TR16.

Differentiated Instruction

Strategic Intervention	**Advanced**	**ⒺⓁⓁ**
Write each of these phrases on a slip of paper: *month of your birthday; favorite holiday; favorite aunt or uncle; teacher you have had; the next big holiday; favorite day of the week.* Put the slips in a box. Have students draw a slip and write on the board a sentence using a proper noun that fits their category. Check capitalization.	Have students write a paragraph about a holiday they enjoy celebrating. Ask them to use at least five proper nouns in the paragraph. Have them exchange papers with partners and check each other's writing for correct capitalization.	Ask volunteers to write on the board in lists the days of the week and the months of the year in English. Point to the names at random and have students make up sentences with them. Write the sentences on the board, read them together, and highlight the capital letters. You may wish to have volunteers add the names of the days and the months in their home languages.

Remind students that they may be asked to identify which words should be capitalized in a sentence. They need to remember that days of the week, months of the year, and holidays should be capitalized. Titles for people and abbreviations of the titles should be capitalized when they are used with a person's name, but not when they are used by themselves.

Incorrect: My Aunt came on Thursday for thanksgiving with uncle Rob.

Correct: My aunt came on Thursday for Thanksgiving with Uncle Rob.

Monitor Progress

Check Grammar

If... students have difficulty using capital letters,	**then...** find a reading passage with several capitalized words and have students explain the reason each word was capitalized.

Test Preparation

☑ Write the letter of the word or words that should be capitalized. If no words should be capitalized, choose *none*.

1. My family saw the Statue of Liberty in july.
   - **A** none
   - **B** saw
   - **Ⓒ** july
   - **D** family

2. We took a ferry to the statue on independence day.
   - **A** ferry
   - **B** statue
   - **C** none
   - **Ⓓ** independence day

3. The statue was made in the 19th century by mr. bartholdi.
   - **Ⓐ** mr. bartholdi
   - **B** century
   - **C** mr.
   - **D** none

4. He modeled the face on his mother's.
   - **A** mother's
   - **B** modeled
   - **C** face
   - **Ⓓ** none

5. The statue's pedestal was made by mr. Hunt.
   - **A** pedestal
   - **B** statue's
   - **C** none
   - **Ⓓ** mr.

6. This artwork was dedicated by our 22nd president.
   - **A** dedicated
   - **B** artwork
   - **Ⓒ** president
   - **D** none

Review

✓ Rewrite correctly the words in each sentence that should have capital letters. If a sentence has no capitalization mistakes, write *C*.

1. Last summer my family visited some American monuments.
   C

2. In july we went to the Gateway Arch in St. Louis.
   July

3. It was designed by mr. eero Saarinen.
   Mr. Eero

4. In august we visited Mount Rushmore in South Dakota.
   August

5. A ceremony is held there each summer night from monday through sunday.
   Monday; Sunday

6. On a saturday in september we saw a monument in New York.
   Saturday; September

7. It was the tomb of general Grant.
   General

8. My grandma said the memorial honors mrs. grant also.
   Mrs. Grant

✓ Write the sentences. Use capital letters correctly.

9. In april, we saw a memorial for president franklin delano roosevelt, our 32nd president.

10. I went with aunt janet to the memorial.

11. On tuesday we saw sculptures of the president.

12. On wednesday we learned more about mrs. Roosevelt.

13. My aunt and uncle saw the memorial on veterans day.

14. Roosevelt was born on january 30, 1882.

15. The memorial was dedicated may 2, 1997.

16. In june, uncle ed will take me to the Jefferson Memorial.

Grammar **203**

Summarize

Ask students to identify words that should be capitalized.

- Days of the week, months of the year, and holidays should be capitalized.

- Titles for people and abbreviations of titles should be capitalized when they are used with a person's name but not when they are used alone.

Grammar-Writing Connection

Explain that using proper nouns can make writing more specific.

General: We visited the statue on the holiday.

Specific: We visited the Statue of Liberty on the Fourth of July.

Paraphrasing

- Identify characteristics of taking notes.
- Take notes, using paraphrasing.
- Develop criteria for judging a piece of writing.

TEACH

- Read aloud the information about paraphrasing in the box.
- Ask students to tell in their own words what paraphrasing is. *(putting the main ideas of a book or article into your own words)*

Guided Writing

Read each item in the exercise with students. Have them discuss which paraphrase is better. Ask them which paraphrase included unimportant information and omitted important information.

Independent Writing

Ask students to find facts about another American symbol, such as the Washington Monument, on the Internet or in the library. Have them paraphrase the information and share it with the class.

Monitor Progress

Check Paraphrasing

If... students need more help with paraphrasing,	**then...** read aloud a short news article and have them paraphrase its main ideas.

 WRITER'S CRAFT

Paraphrasing

When you take notes on facts in a book or article, you **paraphrase** the article. Use these tips.

- Paraphrase only the main ideas, not unimportant details. Make sure you paraphrase the facts correctly.
- Use your own words, not those of the author.
- Copy especially interesting sentences in quotation marks.

 Read the paragraph and each paraphrase of the paragraph. Write the best description from the box for each paraphrase.

Includes main ideas   Omits important information

The Liberty Bell is a symbol of American freedom. It was made in England and sent to Philadelphia. It cracked on its first ring and was repaired. On July 8, 1776, the bell was rung in honor of adopting the Declaration of Independence. Today the bell can be seen in Liberty Bell Pavilion in Philadelphia.

1. The Liberty Bell was made in England. It got cracked, but Americans fixed it. Omits important information
2. The Liberty Bell stands for freedom to Americans because it was rung in 1776 when the Declaration of Independence was adopted. The Liberty Bell is still displayed in Philadelphia. Includes main ideas

204 Writing

RESOURCES

Writing Transparencies 26A, 26B
Writing Rubrics and Anchor Papers p. 34

Taking Notes

When you **take notes,** write the most important facts in an article. Try to put ideas into your own words. Put any phrases that you pick up word for word in quotation marks.

Notes are written in list form.

Writer uses abbreviations and does not always use complete sentences.

Notes on "The Story of the Statue of Liberty"

Americans forgot about the S of L.

No money to finish the base

N.Y. newspaper asked public for money, and statue was finished.

Celebration—speeches, songs, speech by Pres. Cleveland—in 1886 when statue was in place. Bartholdi uncovered statue's face.

People coming on ships to live in America first see S of L.

Fireworks above S of L part of July 4th celebration each year

Writer uses quotation marks to show phrase is a direct quote from the original text.

"a truly unforgettable sight"

Writing **205**

Taking Notes
ANALYZE THE MODEL

Read aloud the model and the callouts to the left of it. Prepare students to write their own notes.

PROMPT

Take notes on an article about an American symbol. Be sure to paraphrase only the main ideas.

Getting Started Students can do any of the following.

- Use an organizer (pp. TR28–TR32).
- Read part of the article with others. Discuss the main ideas.
- Practice paraphrasing individual sentences in shortened note form.

Editing/Revising Checklist

☑ Do my notes include the article's main ideas?

☑ Do my notes paraphrase, not copy, the article's words?

☑ Have I used capital letters correctly?

Self-Evaluation Distribute copies of p. TR26 for students to fill out.

Scoring Rubric Taking Notes

Rubric 4 3 2 1	4	3	2	1
Focus/Ideas	All important ideas included in notes	Most important ideas included in notes	Many unimportant ideas included in notes	Article's ideas not paraphrased in notes
Organization/ Paragraphs	Paraphrases in order similar to original	Paraphrases in fairly logical order	Confused order	No order
Voice	Clear and knowledgeable	Fairly clear and knowledgeable	Not clear or knowledgeable	No sense of voice
Word Choice	Precise words used for clarity	Mostly precise words used	Few or no precise words	Incorrect or limited word choice
Sentences	Shortened forms and fragments used consistently	Shortened forms used fairly consistently	No shortened forms used	No understanding of correct forms for notes
Conventions	Excellent control and accuracy	Reasonable control with few errors	Errors that may hinder understanding	Frequent errors that interfere with meaning

For 5- and 6-point rubrics, see Writing Rubrics and Anchor Papers p. 34.

Abbreviations

TEACH

Read aloud the definitions, instruction, and examples in the box on p. 206. Explain that the abbreviations *Mr.*, *Mrs.*, *Ms.*, and *Dr.* and a few others can be used in sentences. However, most other abbreviations are only used in addresses and in notes.

Model As I look over the examples of abbreviations, I realize that they are useful when I need to shorten long words that I use frequently. I know that different abbreviations are appropriate in different kinds of writing. We can use *Mr.*, *Ms.*, *Mrs.*, and *Dr.* in all kinds of writing. However, abbreviations for months and days are generally not used in formal writing. Also, short names, such as *May, June,* and *July,* do not need to be abbreviated because they are not very long.

LESSON 27

Abbreviations

An **abbreviation** is a shortened form of a word. Many abbreviations begin with a capital letter and end with a period.

- Some titles used for names of people are abbreviations. For example, *Dr.* is the abbreviation for *Doctor*. The title *Miss* is not abbreviated.

  Mr. Mark Elton Lewis   Ms. Susan Wang
  Mrs. Mendes

- An **initial** is the first letter of a name. It is written with a capital letter and is followed by a period.

  Mr. Mark E. Lewis   S. B. Wang   C. M. Mendes

- The names of days and months can be abbreviated. *May, June,* and *July* are not abbreviated.

Days of the Week
Sun. Mon. Tues. Wed. Thurs. Fri. Sat.
Months of the Year
Jan. Feb. Mar. Apr. Aug. Sept. Oct. Nov. Dec.

A Write each abbreviation. Be sure to capitalize letters and use periods correctly. If a phrase is correct, write *C*.

1. ms. Janine Lee
   Ms. Janine Lee
2. jan 24
   Jan. 24
3. Dr N D Bond
   Dr. N. D. Bond
4. thurs, aug 2
   Thurs., Aug. 2
5. B. C. Pepper
   C
6. Mon., Dec. 13
   C
7. mrs M A Dixon
   Mrs. M. A. Dixon
8. tues, oct 8
   Tues., Oct. 8

206 Grammar

B Some abbreviations can be used in sentences. Write the sentences. Write the abbreviations and initials correctly.

1. Mr. G. t. Bryant has several birds.
2. He takes them to an animal doctor, dr. E. Rodriguez.
3. His son P. J. helps care for the family's birds.
4. The Bryants bought a bright yellow canary from ms. Gray's pet store.
5. They named it Archie, after their friend Archibald p. McNabb.
6. One day mrs. Bryant noticed that Archie had stopped singing.
7. Neither dr. Rodriguez nor her assistant ms. r. m. Lee knew what was wrong.
8. They talked with Gen. F. X. Loomis, an army bird specialist.
9. "Maybe he needs friends," gen. Loomis said.
10. The next day mr. Bryant bought two more canaries from ms. Gray.

C The following items are notes for a report. Rewrite each note. Use abbreviations and initials correctly for titles, names, days, and months whenever possible.

11. Mister Roger Tory Peterson, bird lover, born Friday, August 28, 1908
    Mr. R. T. Peterson, bird lover, born Fri., Aug. 28, 1908
12. Roger Tory Peterson, member of National Audubon Society, named for John James Audubon R. T. Peterson, member of National Audubon Society, named for J. J. Audubon
13. Mister Peterson wrote *A Field Guide to the Birds,* 1934
    Mr. Peterson wrote *A Field Guide to the Birds,* 1934
14. Roger Tory Peterson died Sunday, July 28, 1996
    R. T. Peterson died Sun., July 28, 1996

PRACTICE

Guided Practice **A**
Work through the exercise with students. Have them explain what is correct or incorrect about each item and how they knew.

TEACHING TiP

• Discuss appropriate places to use abbreviations of days of the week and months of the year—letters and notes. Point out that abbreviations of titles, such as *Mr.* and *Dr.,* are acceptable in all kinds of writing.

Independent Practice **B** and **C**
Have students complete the exercises. For Differentiated Instruction and Extra Practice, see p. TR16.

Differentiated Instruction

Strategic Intervention
Make flash cards with a day of the week or month of the year written on each card. Have students work in pairs. One partner mixes the cards and show each one to the partner. The partner writes the abbreviation for each word. Partners then switch roles. When both have finished writing, they check each other's work.

Advanced
Ask students to write a brief story about a pet. Tell them to use names that include titles and initials for each character in the story, for example, *Dr. D.D. Perry.* Have students exchange stories with a partner, read the stories, and circle each name with a title or initial.

ELL
Have students work with more proficient English speakers to write several sentences about activities they have enjoyed, using a day of the week and/or a month of the year in each sentence. *(On Monday I played soccer. In July I visited my cousins.)* Have students exchange papers with another pair of students and circle each day or month and write its abbreviation.

Remind students that they may be asked to identify the correct abbreviation for a word. They must remember that abbreviations for words that begin with a capital letter, such as days of the week and months of the year, also begin with a capital letter. Most abbreviations end with a period.

Words: Mister Coleman's birthday party—Saturday, January 15

Abbreviations: Mr. Coleman's birthday party—Sat., Jan. 15

Monitor Progress

Check Grammar

If... students have difficulty identifying correct abbreviations,	**then...** discuss why certain items in the test are incorrect.

Test Preparation

Write the letter of the correct abbreviation for each word or group of words.

1. December
   - **A** dec
   - **B** Dec
   - **C** Decem
   - Ⓓ Dec.

2. Wednesday
   - **A** Wed
   - Ⓑ Wed.
   - **C** wed
   - **D** wednes.

3. Doctor Ray
   - **A** dr Ray
   - **B** Dr Ray
   - Ⓒ Dr. Ray
   - **D** dr. Ray

4. February
   - **A** Feb
   - **B** feb
   - **C** feb.
   - Ⓓ Feb.

5. Monday, March 2
   - **A** Mon, March 2
   - Ⓑ Mon., Mar. 2
   - **C** Mon., mar. 2
   - **D** mon., march 2

6. Mister King
   - Ⓐ Mr. King
   - **B** mr King
   - **C** Mr King
   - **D** mr. King

Review

☑ Write each name or date. Be sure to capitalize letters and use periods correctly. If a phrase is correct, write *C*.

1. Mrs Tanya Bright
Mrs. Tanya Bright

2. Dr. Barbara A. Finch
C

3. Sun, aug 12
Sun., Aug. 12

4. Mr and Mrs. J. T Adams
Mr. and Mrs. J. T. Adams

5. R. j. Moss
R. J. Moss

6. Thurs, sept. 1
Thurs., Sept. 1

7. Ms. Joan L. Rose
C

8. Tues., nov 13
Tues., Nov. 13

9. Mr Carlton b Hayes
Mr. Carlton B. Hayes

10. mon, oct. 30
Mon., Oct. 30

11. miss h Elena Ruiz
Miss H. Elena Ruiz

12. Sat., Apr. 28
C

☑ Some abbreviations can be used in sentences. Write the sentences. Write the abbreviations and initials correctly.

13. Our teacher, mr. t. n. Frost, likes pet birds.

14. Dr. Marian k. Hardy told our class about parrots.

15. My neighbor, j. g. Jones, owns a rainbow-colored parrot from South America.

16. Mrs. Sanchez said parakeets are related to parrots.

17. "Where do parakeets come from?" asked ms. Torres.

18. dr. Hardy said they live in many warm places around the world.

19. My friend k. v. said they used to live in Florida.

20. That white cockatoo with a yellow crest belongs to mr. and mrs. Frost.

21. "A cockatoo is a kind of parrot," said mrs. Sanchez.

22. Mrs. Sanchez, ms. Torres, dr. Hardy, and mr. Frost are experts on parrots.

Grammar **209**

Summarize

Ask students to tell about abbreviations and explain how to use them.

• An abbreviation is a shortened form of a word. It usually begins with a capital letter and ends with a period.

• An initial is the first letter of a name. It is written with a capital letter and followed by a period.

• Names of days and months, except *May, June,* and *July,* can be abbreviated.

Grammar-Writing Connection

Explain that using abbreviations when taking notes or writing outlines saves time and space for writers.

Unabbreviated: Some birds fly south in October or November.

Abbreviated: Some birds fly south in Oct. or Nov.

Including Important Details

OBJECTIVES

- Identify characteristics of outlining.
- Write an outline, including important details.
- Develop criteria for judging a piece of writing.

- Read aloud the information in the box about including important details.
- Ask students to tell in their own words what including important details means. *(putting in facts and examples appropriate for the topic, audience, and purpose)*

Guided Writing

Read the outline and paragraph in Exercise 1 aloud with students. Discuss with them how considering audience, purpose, and topic helps them distinguish between important and unimportant details.

Independent Writing

Ask volunteers to read aloud their responses to Exercise 2. Have students discuss whether each response includes only important details.

Monitor Progress

Check Including Important Details

If... students need more help with including important details,	**then...** read aloud several factual paragraphs and have students choose the details they would include in a report.

 WRITER'S CRAFT

Including Important Details

When you write a research report, use the facts in your outline. Keep your topic, audience, and purpose in mind. Then **include the important details** about your topic.

The information below is part of an outline on the hua mei bird. The paragraph that follows it adds unimportant details to the information in the outline. Copy the sentences that have unimportant details.

- **B.** Appearance
  - **1.** 4–5 in. long
  - **2.** Grayish-yellow with black speckles
  - **3.** White marks above eyes
- **C.** Special Features
  - **1.** Fighting birds
  - **2.** Can be taught to sing
  - **3.** Name means "painted eyebrows"

The hua mei bird is 4 or 5 inches long. ~~Canaries are much more colorful than this bird.~~ It has unusual white marks above its eyes. These marks led to the bird's name, which is Chinese for "painted eyebrows." The hua mei is a fighting bird. ~~I prefer peaceful birds.~~ People have taught the hua mei bird to sing. ~~Its melody is probably beautiful.~~

Write sentences about parrots based on the following details: 3 inches to 3 ft. long; brightly colored; thick, hooked bill. **Possible answer: Parrots can be from three inches to three feet long. They are brightly colored and have thick, hooked bills.**

RESOURCES

Writing Transparencies 27A, 27B
Writing Rubrics and Anchor Papers p. 35

Outlining

An **outline** organizes information about a topic. Before writing a research report, use your notes to make an outline.

- For most outlines, use words and phrases, not complete sentences. You may use abbreviations.
- Use Roman numerals for the main topics.
- Use capital letters for subtopics.
- Use numbers for details about the subtopics.

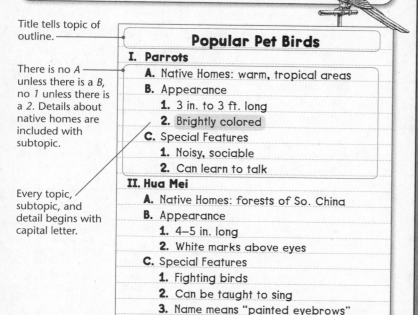

Title tells topic of outline.

There is no *A* unless there is a *B*, no *1* unless there is a *2*. Details about native homes are included with subtopic.

Every topic, subtopic, and detail begins with capital letter.

Popular Pet Birds

I. Parrots
- **A.** Native Homes: warm, tropical areas
- **B.** Appearance
  - **1.** 3 in. to 3 ft. long
  - **2.** Brightly colored
- **C.** Special Features
  - **1.** Noisy, sociable
  - **2.** Can learn to talk

II. Hua Mei
- **A.** Native Homes: forests of So. China
- **B.** Appearance
  - **1.** 4–5 in. long
  - **2.** White marks above eyes
- **C.** Special Features
  - **1.** Fighting birds
  - **2.** Can be taught to sing
  - **3.** Name means "painted eyebrows"

Writing **211**

Outlining
ANALYZE THE MODEL

Read aloud the model and the callouts to the left of it. Prepare students to write their own outlines.

PROMPT

Write an outline on a kind of pet bird. Use facts you find in the library or on the Internet.

Getting Started Students can do any of the following.

- Use an organizer (pp. TR28–TR32).
- With a group, brainstorm different kinds of pet birds.
- Look through books and on the Internet for possible choices of pet birds.

Editing/Revising Checklist

☑ Is my outline arranged by main topics, subtopics, and details?

☑ Does my outline have the important details about my subject?

☑ Have I used abbreviations whenever possible?

Self-Evaluation Distribute copies of p. TR26 for students to fill out.

Scoring Rubric Outlining

Rubric 4 3 2 1	4	3	2	1
Focus/Ideas	All important ideas included in outline	Most important ideas included in outline	Unimportant ideas included in outline	Facts not reflected in outline
Organization/ Paragraphs	Logical organization of heads and subheads	Organization mainly logical	Confused order	No order
Voice	Clear and logical	Fairly clear and logical	Not clear or logical	No voice
Word Choice	Precise words used for clarity	Mostly precise words used	Few or no precise words	Incorrect or limited word choice
Sentences	Phrases and fragments used consistently	Phrases and fragments used fairly consistently	No shortened forms used	No understanding of what to write in outline
Conventions	Excellent control and accuracy	Reasonable control with few errors	Errors that may hinder understanding	Frequent errors that interfere with meaning

For 5- and 6-point rubrics, see Writing Rubrics and Anchor Papers p. 35.

Combining Sentences

OBJECTIVES

- Define combining sentences.
- Use sentence combining correctly in writing.
- Become familiar with sentence combining assessment on high-stakes tests.

TEACH

Read aloud the instruction and examples in the box on p. 212. Explain that combining sentences eliminates too many short, choppy sentences and adds more interesting sentence rhythms to writing.

Think Aloud **Model** As I read the examples, I see that combining sentences can accomplish two goals. By combining two complete sentences, I can avoid having too many short sentences. Several short, choppy sentences in a row makes writing sound monotonous. By combining sentence parts, such as two subjects or two predicates, I can avoid unnecessary repetition. The key to combining sentences is making sure the ideas in the sentences are related. They must be about the same topic.

Combining Sentences

When you **combine sentences**, you join two sentences that are about the same topic. You make them into one sentence.

- You can join two simple sentences to form a compound sentence. Add a comma and a conjunction such as *and, but,* or *or.*

    We saw a mural. Its bright colors amazed us.
    We saw a mural, and its bright colors amazed us.

- You can combine two sentences that have the same subject.

    The mural was in a cave. The mural seemed very old.
    The mural was in a cave and seemed very old.

- You can combine two sentences that have the same predicate.

    Michael liked the mural. I liked the mural.
    Michael and I liked the mural.

A Combine each pair of short sentences into a compound sentence. Use a comma and the conjunction in ( ).

1. People in France explored caves. They found murals. (and)
   People in France explored caves, and they found murals.
2. Were the murals painted by modern people? Were they painted by cave people long ago? (or) Were the murals painted by modern people, or were they painted by cave people long ago?
3. The murals showed animals from long ago. The art style dates back thousands of years. (and) The murals showed animals from long ago, and the art style dates back thousands of years.
4. People can view the cave murals. They must be careful. (but) People can view the cave murals, but they must be careful.

212 Grammar

RESOURCES

Daily Fix-It Lesson 28
   See p. TR10.
   See also Daily Fix-It Transparency 28.
Grammar Transparency 28

B Combine each pair of sentences with a conjunction that works. Use the underlined words only once in your new sentence. Do not use commas in your sentences.

1. <u>Our teacher</u> saw an empty wall downtown. <u>Our teacher</u> got permission to paint a mural on it. Our teacher saw an empty wall downtown and got permission to paint a mural on it.
2. <u>We</u> drew pictures on the wall. <u>We</u> painted them with bright colors.
We drew pictures on the wall and painted them with bright colors.
3. Our teacher <u>worked every day for weeks</u>. The students <u>worked every day for weeks</u>.
Our teacher and the students worked every day for weeks.
4. Dancers <u>are pictured on the mural</u>. Musicians <u>are pictured on the mural</u>.
Dancers and musicians are pictured on the mural.
5. Our parents <u>came to see the mural</u>. Friends <u>came to see the mural</u>.
Our parents and friends came to see the mural.
6. <u>Making a mural is</u> fun. <u>Making a mural is</u> difficult.
Making a mural is fun but difficult.
7. <u>We could</u> make a mural next year. <u>We could</u> choose another kind of art.
We could make a mural next year or choose another kind of art.

C Combine the items in each pair. Combine subjects or predicates, or write compound sentences. Use a conjunction that works. Remember to use commas in compound sentences. **Possible answers:**

8. Robert draws well. Some other students draw even better.
Robert draws well, but some other students draw even better.
9. Robert might become a cartoonist. He might illustrate children's books.
Robert might become a cartoonist or illustrate children's books.
10. Sadie likes pastels. She doesn't like watercolors.
Sadie likes pastels, but she doesn't like watercolors.
11. Yolanda wants to be a sculptor. Michael wants to be a photographer.
Yolanda wants to be a sculptor, and Michael wants to be a photographer.
12. The students work hard. They have fun as well.
The students work hard but have fun as well.

Grammar **213**

Guided Practice Ⓐ

Work through the exercise with students. Ask volunteers to write their combined sentences on the board and have students check the punctuation and capitalization.

TEACHING TiP

- Explain that using a mixture of short sentences and longer sentences gives a piece of writing a pleasing variety and rhythm. Combining some sentences can help accomplish this.

Independent Practice Ⓑ and Ⓒ

Have students complete the exercises. For Differentiated Instruction and Extra Practice, see p. TR16.

Differentiated Instruction

Strategic Intervention

Ask students to write on paper several sentences describing an artwork they have made. Have them exchange papers with a partner. Partners should decide whether any sentences can be combined and then do so. Have them read aloud their combined sentences.

Advanced

Have students find an article that interests them in a publication such as a student news magazine. Ask them to find at least two sets of sentences in the article that could be combined. Have them write the combined sentences and share them with a partner.

ELL

Display a picture or artwork for students. Have them suggest simple sentences that describe the art. Write their sentences on the board. Then have students choose sentences that can be combined and tell you how to combine them. Write these on the board and compare them to the original sentences.

TEST-TAKING TIP

Point out that students may be asked to identify the correct way to combine two sentences. Tell them to remember that when two simple sentences are made into a compound sentence, a comma is added before the conjunction. Commas are not added when two subjects or two predicates are combined.

Incorrect: Jay drew and Mary painted. Jay painted the mural, and made a sculpture.

Correct: Jay drew, and Mary painted. Jay painted the mural and made a sculpture.

Monitor Progress

Check Grammar

| If... students have difficulty combining sentences, | then... show them student sentences that can be combined. Have students combine them. |

Test Preparation

✒ Write the letter of the words that complete the sentence correctly.

1. Jon likes __C__ prefers music.
   - **A** art, But Toby
   - **B** art or Toby
   - **C** art, but Toby
   - **D** art and Toby

2. You can go to the __D__ the concert.
   - **A** museum, or
   - **B** museum but
   - **C** museum, and
   - **D** museum or

3. I saw a __D__ saw a collage.
   - **A** mural and Andy
   - **B** mural or Andy
   - **C** mural, or Andy
   - **D** mural, and Andy

4. This picture is __C__ is larger.
   - **A** huge but that one
   - **B** huge and that one
   - **C** huge, but that one
   - **D** huge, or that one

5. I will look at __C__ paintings.
   - **A** sculptures but
   - **B** sculptures, and
   - **C** sculptures and
   - **D** sculptures, or

6. You can get into __B__ must wait in line.
   - **A** this show but you
   - **B** this show, but you
   - **C** this show, and you
   - **D** this show and you

Review

Combine each pair of short sentences into a compound sentence. Use a comma and the conjunction in ( ).

1. Paintings are popular. There are many other kinds of art. (but)
   Paintings are popular, but there are many other kinds of art.
2. Collages combine different items. Murals include many small pictures. (and)
   Collages combine different items, and murals include many small pictures.
3. Some sculptors use marble. Others use metals. (and)
   Some sculptors use marble, and others use metals.
4. Potters shape clay with their hands. They use a potter's wheel. (or)
   Potters shape clay with their hands, or they use a potter's wheel.
5. Will you make a vase? Would you rather shape a pot? (or)
   Will you make a vase, or would you rather shape a pot?
6. Enjoy the paintings at the museum. Don't forget the other art. (but)
   Enjoy the paintings at the museum, but don't forget the other art.

Combine each pair of sentences with a conjunction that works. Use the underlined words only once in your new sentence.

7. I like to go to the museum. I look at my favorite pictures.
   I like to go to the museum and look at my favorite pictures.
8. My favorite painting is set in the desert. My favorite painting shows an old barn.
   My favorite painting is set in the desert and shows an old barn.
9. Henri Matisse painted still lifes. Claude Monet painted still lifes.
   Henri Matisse and Claude Monet painted still lifes.
10. Vincent Van Gogh painted sunflowers. Vincent Van Gogh also drew a starry sky.
    Vincent Van Gogh painted sunflowers and also drew a starry sky.
11. Van Gogh's work is beautiful. Van Gogh's work is strange.
    Van Gogh's work is beautiful but strange.
12. I could become a painter. I could become a sculptor.
    I could become a painter or a sculptor.

Grammar **215**

REVIEW

Summarize

Ask students to describe ways of combining sentences.

- Two simple sentences can be combined to form a compound sentence by adding a comma and a conjunction such as *and, but,* or *or.*
- Two sentences with the same subject or two sentences with the same predicate can be combined without a comma.

Grammar-Writing Connection

Explain that combining sentences can help writers avoid wordiness caused by repeating subjects and predicates.

Wordy: The artists painted a bright background. The artists drew people at a celebration.

Less wordy: The artists painted a bright background and drew people at a celebration.

Topic Sentences

OBJECTIVES

- Identify characteristics of an informational paragraph.
- Write an informational paragraph with a topic sentence.
- Develop criteria for judging a piece of writing.

TEACH

- Read aloud the information about topic sentences in the box.
- Ask students to tell in their own words what a topic sentence is. *(a sentence, often the first in a paragraph, that tells the main idea of the paragraph)*

Guided Writing

Read each item in Exercise 1 with the class. Have students explain how they matched topic sentences to groups of details.

Independent Writing

Ask volunteers to read aloud their responses to Exercise 2. Ask listeners whether each topic sentence accurately and concisely states the paragraph's main idea.

Monitor Progress

Check Topic Sentences

If... students need more help with topic sentences,	then... find factual paragraphs with topic sentences for students to read and discuss.

 WRITER'S CRAFT

Topic Sentences

 A **topic sentence** tells the main idea of a paragraph. The topic sentence is often the first sentence of a paragraph that gives information.

Read the three topic sentences. Write the sentence that would be the best topic sentence for each group of details.

Topic Sentences
Many artists have painted murals.
Murals are not hard to make.
You can see murals in many different places.

1. Put a big piece of white paper on a bulletin board. Decide on a topic such as school sports. Have each person paint one scene for the mural.
Murals are not hard to make.
2. Some murals are painted on skyscrapers near city highways. Others are painted in neighborhood parks or inside public buildings.
You can see murals in many different places.
3. People who lived in caves long ago painted murals. An Italian artist, Michelangelo, painted a famous mural on a ceiling in the 1500s. Many Americans painted murals in the 1960s.
Many artists have painted murals.

 Write a topic sentence for the following details.

Some murals show important people. Others show beautiful places. Still others show events from history.
Possible answer: Murals have many different subjects.

216 Writing

RESOURCES

Writing Transparencies 28A, 28B
Writing Rubrics and Anchor Papers p. 36

Informational Paragraph

An **informational paragraph** gives facts on a topic. It usually begins with a topic sentence that tells the main idea of the paragraph. The other sentences in the paragraph give details that support the main idea. A concluding sentence sums up the paragraph.

Topic sentence gets readers' interest and tells paragraph's main idea.

Other sentences give facts about main idea.

Conclusion sums up paragraph's main idea.

Large Art

What is big and bright and enjoyed by many people? A mural is an art form that has all these traits. A mural is a painting on a large surface such as a wall, either inside or outside. The pictures on a mural tell a story. A mural may show events in history, such as the history of Native Americans. It may show famous people, such as jazz musicians. The bright colors and vivid styles of murals attract everyone's attention. Many famous artists have painted murals. People like you and me can paint murals too. Murals are artworks for everyone.

Writing **217**

Informational Paragraph

ANALYZE THE MODEL

Read aloud the model and the callouts to the left of it. Prepare students to write their own informational paragraphs.

PROMPT

Write an informational paragraph about an art form such as a mural or collage. Include a topic sentence.

Getting Started Students can do any of the following.

- Use an organizer (pp. TR28–TR32).
- Write down facts they already know about the art form.
- Find information in the library or on the Internet.

Editing/Revising Checklist

☑ Does my paragraph include a topic sentence?

☑ Do my paragraph's details support the main idea?

☑ Have I combined related sentences whenever possible?

Self-Evaluation Distribute copies of p. TR26 for students to fill out.

Scoring Rubric — Informational Paragraph

Rubric 4 3 2 1	4	3	2	1
Focus/Ideas	Main idea supported by many facts in paragraph	Main idea supported by some facts in paragraph	Main idea unclear or few supporting facts in paragraph	Not a paragraph; lacks clarity and development
Organization/ Paragraphs	Strong topic sentence; order of details logical	Good topic sentence and logical order	Confused order	No order
Voice	Clear and knowledgeable	Involved with subject	Weak voice	No voice
Word Choice	Precise, vivid words	Mostly precise, vivid words	Some vague or incorrect words	Limited word choice
Sentences	Well crafted; combining evident	Some sentence combining evident	No sentence combining evident	Fragments or run-on sentences
Conventions	Excellent control and accuracy	Reasonable control with few errors	Errors that may hinder understanding	Frequent errors that may interfere with meaning

For 5- and 6-point rubrics, see Writing Rubrics and Anchor Papers p. 36.

Commas

- Define and identify commas.
- Use commas correctly in writing.
- Become familiar with comma assessment on high-stakes tests.

TEACH

Read aloud the instruction and examples in the box on p. 218. Point out that commas are used only for specific purposes and not simply when a writer feels like indicating a pause in a sentence.

Think Aloud

Model I know that I use a comma before a conjunction that joins two sentences, so the first example looks familiar. In the second example, I notice that commas keep readers from becoming confused about the items in a series. I also notice that a comma is placed before the conjunction *and.* The remaining examples are uses of commas that are important when writing a letter, an address, or a date.

LESSON 29

Commas

Use a **comma** and a conjunction to join two sentences.

I went outside, and I saw some ants.

Use **commas** to separate words in a series.

The ants were small, brown, and very active.

Use a **comma** after the greeting and the closing of a friendly letter.

Dear Ellie,   Your friend,

Use a **comma** between the name of a city and a state in an address.

Casper, WY 82602   Cleveland, Ohio

Use a **comma** to separate the month and day from the year.

April 28, 2007

A Write *C* if commas are used correctly in the sentence. Write *NC* if commas are not used correctly.

1. Ants are social insects, and they live in groups called colonies. C
2. Ants may live in rotten logs leaves or thorns. NC
3. I finished my report on ants on October 3, 2007. C
4. An ant's sting is painful but it isn't poisonous. NC
5. That scientist lives in Miami, Florida. C

218 Grammar

RESOURCES

Daily Fix-It Lesson 29
See p. TR10.
See also Daily Fix-It Transparency 29.
Grammar Transparency 29

B Write each line of the letter. Add commas where they are needed.

1. Dear Caroline,

2. Frankie and I went to the park, and we took a picnic lunch.

3. On our picnic we had sandwiches, pickles, and fruit.

4. It was summer, and the day was very hot.

5. Coming toward us was a line of big ants, little ants, and medium ants.

6. Frankie said there are many ants in Tulsa, Oklahoma.

7. We moved our food, and Frankie left stale bread on the table.

8. Soon red ants, brown ants, and black ants were eating the bread.

9. The date of our victory over the ants was August 15, 2006.

10. Your friend,
Eliza

C Answer each question with a complete sentence. Make your writing clear by using commas correctly.
Possible answers are on page TR37.

11. What are three of your favorite hobbies?

12. What was the month, date, and year when you turned 6?

13. What is the name of the city and state or city and country where you were born?

14. What two subjects do you enjoy most at school? Write a compound sentence for your answer.

15. Do you like ants? Write a compound sentence for your answer.

Grammar **219**

Guided Practice A

Work through the exercise with students. For sentences with correct comma usage, have students explain why the commas are used. For sentences with incorrect comma usage, have students tell how commas should be used.

TEACHING TiP

- Emphasize that writers should not use commas in sentences based on a feeling that a comma belongs in a certain place. Instead they should rely on rules for where commas are used, memorizing the rules if necessary.

Independent Practice B and C

Have students complete the exercises. For Differentiated Instruction and Extra Practice, see p. TR16.

Differentiated Instruction

Strategic Intervention

Display a map of the United States. Have students take turns going to the map, choosing the names of a city and the state in which the city is located, and writing the names on the board, using commas correctly. Encourage students to find cities in different parts of the country. Continue until each student has had a turn.

Advanced

Have students write a short letter to a friend about an experience they have had with insects. Tell students to use correct letter form including correct placement of commas in the greeting, closing, and date. Check their writing.

ELL

Write items on the board that call for commas. Examples will be items in a series; names of a city and state; and the greeting, closing, and date of a letter. Call on volunteers from this group to insert commas where they belong.

Tell students they may be asked to identify the correct locations for commas in a sentence. Remind them that a comma is placed before the conjunction in a compound sentence and after the day of the month in a date. A comma is placed after each word in a series, including the last word before the conjunction.

Incorrect: Juan ran and, I walked.
The race was on June 10 2008.
We passed a park, a store
and a school.

Correct: Juan ran, and I walked.
The race was on June 10, 2008.
We passed a park, a store,
and a school.

Monitor Progress

Check Grammar

If... students have difficulty using commas,

then... point out passages with commas in their reading materials and have them tell why the commas are used.

Test Preparation

✔ Write the letter of the words that complete the sentence correctly.

1. Dear __C__
   - **A** Cousin Peter
   - **B** Cousin, Peter,
   - **C** Cousin Peter,
   - **D** Cousin, Peter

2. We went on a hike on __D__ .
   - **A** April 23 2007
   - **B** April, 23, 2007
   - **C** April 23. 2007
   - **D** April 23, 2007

3. Our hike took place near __A__ .
   - **A** Albany, New York
   - **B** Albany New York
   - **C** Albany, New, York
   - **D** Albany New, York

4. We hiked in the __B__ many insects.
   - **A** woods and we saw
   - **B** woods, and we saw
   - **C** woods, And we saw
   - **D** woods or we saw

5. We saw __D__ .
   - **A** beetles crickets and ants
   - **B** beetles crickets, and, ants
   - **C** beetles, crickets and, ants
   - **D** beetles, crickets, and ants

6. Your __A__
   - **A** favorite cousin, Tad
   - **B** favorite, cousin, Tad
   - **C** favorite cousin, Tad,
   - **D** favorite, cousin, Tad

Review

✓ Write *C* if commas are used correctly in the sentence. Write *NC* if commas are missing or are not used correctly.

1. My dad studies insects and he loves his work. NC
2. He has studied insects in Hawaii Brazil, and Costa Rica. NC
3. He saw enormous butterflies near San Jose, Costa Rica. C
4. Dad went to Africa on July 4 2003. NC
5. There he saw huge moths ants and mosquitoes. NC
6. One day we went to the park, and Dad showed me some grasshoppers. C
7. There are a million different insects and Dad wants to study them all. NC

✓ Write each sentence. Add commas where they are needed.

8. Some insects are helpful, and some are harmful.
9. Bees make honey, and silkworms create silk.
10. Ladybugs are harmless, but they eat many harmful insects.
11. Fleas, flies, and mosquitoes can carry diseases.
12. Moths eat cloth, and termites eat wood.
13. Locusts, weevils, and some beetles eat crops.
14. Did you hear this prediction from a scientist in Paris, France?
15. She said the world will be overrun by insects by January 1, 3000.
16. If insects come, I would prefer to be in Juneau, Alaska.

Grammar **221**

Summarize

Ask students to explain when commas are used.

- A comma is used before a conjunction when combining two sentences.
- A comma is used after the greeting and closing of a friendly letter.
- A comma is used between the names of a city and state in an address and between the day and year in a date.

Grammar-Writing Connection

Explain that using commas correctly makes writing clearer and more easily understood by readers.

Unclear: The ants found sugar cookies and cake in the kitchen.

Clear: The ants found sugar, cookies, and cake in the kitchen.

Elaborating

OBJECTIVES

- Identify characteristics of writing about a picture.
- Write about a picture, using elaboration.
- Develop criteria for judging a piece of writing.

TEACH

- Read aloud the information about elaborating in the box.
- Ask students to tell in their own words what elaborating is. *(using specific words to tell details that support the main idea)*

Guided Writing

Read each item in Exercise 1 with the class. Have students discuss the mental images created by the added details.

Independent Writing

Ask volunteers to read aloud their responses to Exercise 2. Discuss with students whether the details do a good job of showing what the writer is describing.

Monitor Progress

Check Elaborating

If... students need more help with elaborating,	**then...** point out and discuss with students some reading passages with interesting elaboration.

 WRITER'S CRAFT

Elaborating

When you **elaborate**, you write details to support your main idea. Use specific words to show what you are describing. Replace words and phrases such as *things* and *a lot of* with specific words.

No Those ants carried a lot of things.
Yes Those ants carried hundreds of cake crumbs.

 Choose words from the box to replace the underlined word or words in each sentence. Write the new sentence.

> like a weightlifter picking up a huge barbell
> books and magazine articles
> sugar crystals many times their weight
> a huge bread crumb
> ten times its size

1. Once I saw an ant carrying <u>something</u>.
   Once I saw an ant carrying a huge bread crumb.
2. The bread crumb was <u>very big</u>.
   The bread crumb was ten times its size.
3. Ants can lift <u>heavy things</u>.
   Ants can lift sugar crystals many times their weight.
4. This is <u>neat</u>.
   This is like a weightlifter picking up a huge barbell.
5. I want to read <u>a lot of stuff</u> about ants.
   I want to read books and magazine articles about ants.

 Elaborate on the following topic sentence by writing two details. Use specific words.
Possible answer is on page TR37.

   Ants come in many different colors and sizes.

222 Writing

RESOURCES

Writing Transparencies 29A, 29B
Writing Rubrics and Anchor Papers p. 37

Writing About a Picture

When you **write about a picture**, you describe the picture's details. You may explain why you think the picture is especially interesting, beautiful, or creative.

Topic sentence gets readers' interest and describes picture.

Next sentences use vivid descriptive words to elaborate on picture's traits.

Conclusion sums up why the picture is interesting.

A Big World

Huge creatures with antennae and six legs march through a dark forest covered with rocks and gravel. But wait! The huge creatures are really tiny ants. The forest is really blades of grass. The rocks and gravel are tiny grains of sand and dirt. This is a picture in *Two Bad Ants*, and it shows how big the world must look to ants. The picture shows a line of black ants marching along a white path. The ants are drawn in correct proportion to the grass. Yet people never see the ground and the grass from the ants' point of view. This picture gives people a whole new view of the world.

Writing **223**

Writing About a Picture

ANALYZE THE MODEL

Read aloud the model and the callouts to the left of it. Prepare students to write their own picture descriptions.

PROMPT

Describe a picture from a book that you think is interesting or creative. Elaborate on your topic sentence.

Getting Started Students can do any of the following.

- Use an organizer (pp. TR28–TR32).
- Find a picture and list details in it.
- Close their eyes and recall pictures that made a big impression.

Editing/Revising Checklist

☑ Is my topic sentence supported by my details?

☑ Have I elaborated by using specific words in the details?

☑ Have I used commas correctly?

Self-Evaluation Distribute copies of p. TR26 for students to fill out.

Scoring Rubric
Writing About a Picture

Rubric 4 3 2 1	4	3	2	1
Focus/Ideas	Main idea supported by various forms of elaboration	Main idea supported by some variety of elaboration	Main idea supported by few facts or details	Lacks clarity and development
Organization/ Paragraphs	Strong topic sentence; order of details logical	Good topic sentence and logical order	Confused order	No order
Voice	Original and observant	Fairly original and observant	Weak voice	No sense of voice
Word Choice	Precise, vivid words	Mostly precise, vivid words	Some vague or incorrect words	Limited word choice
Sentences	Well crafted; various lengths and kinds	Fair craft and variety	Little craft or variety	Fragments or run-on sentences
Conventions	Excellent control and accuracy	Reasonable control with few errors	Errors that may hinder understanding	Frequent errors that interfere with meaning

For 5- and 6-point rubrics, see Writing Rubrics and Anchor Papers p. 37.

Quotations

OBJECTIVES

- Define and identify quotations.
- Use quotations correctly in writing.
- Become familiar with quotation assessment on high-stakes tests.

TEACH

Read aloud the definition, instruction, and examples in the box on p. 224. Point out that the punctuation marks that indicate quotations are called quotation marks. Explain that quotations are used for dialogue, or the exact words characters say to one another. Dialogue can enliven all kinds of writing.

Think Aloud **Model** I'm familiar with quotation marks because they're used to show the exact words of speakers in stories about fictional characters or real people. As I read these examples, I can tell it's important to punctuate quotations correctly. Otherwise, readers will get confused about who's talking and whether the writer is repeating the speaker's exact words or simply paraphrasing.

LESSON 30

Quotations

Quotation marks (" ") show the exact words of a speaker.

- Use a comma to separate the speaker's exact words from the rest of the sentence.
- Capitalize the first word inside the quotation marks.
- Put the punctuation mark that ends the quotation inside the quotation marks.

  "I want to be a glassblower," said Elena.

  "Is that a hard job?" I asked.

  She replied, "You need good lungs!"

Quotation marks also indicate titles of short works, such as songs, poems, and stories.

  Elena sang "Burro Serenade."

Ⓐ Write *C* if a sentence is correct. If it is not correct, make the corrections that are needed.

1. "There are many ways to make glass into objects," Al said.
2. "You can blow the hot glass with a blowpipe," Kit said.
3. Taylor mentioned, "you can press the glass into a mold."
4. Kevin added, "You can pour hot glass into a mold." c
5. "You can make so many useful things with glass!" Sara exclaimed. c
6. I asked, "Are some lamps made of glass?"

224 Grammar

RESOURCES

Daily Fix-It Lesson 30
  See p. TR10.
  See also Daily Fix-It Transparency 30.
Grammar Transparency 30

B Write the sentences. Add capital letters, quotation marks, commas, and other punctuation marks as needed.

1. "I read an article about the desert," Rosanna said.
2. The title of the article was "Not Always Hot and Dry."
3. "At night deserts can get very cold," Russell explained.
4. Olivia asked, "aren't deserts different in different places?"
5. "Yes, some deserts are in cold climates," replied Ms. Lacy.
6. Manuel said, "I lived near the desert in Arizona."
7. "It was really hot in summer," he exclaimed.
8. Manuel wrote a poem called "Song of the Desert."
9. "What was it like in spring?" Anna asked.
10. "In spring it rained, and wildflowers grew," Manuel replied.

C Answer each question with a complete sentence. Make each answer a quotation followed by the words *I said*. Use quotation marks and other punctuation correctly.

Example Do you like to travel?
"Yes, I like to travel," I said.

Possible answers:
11. Do you like the desert, mountains, beach, or another natural place best? "I like the mountains best," I said.
12. What is your favorite part of this place? "The snow on the trees always looks beautiful," I said.
13. What would you do in this place if you took a trip there? "I would climb to the top of the highest mountain," I said.
14. What animals would you see in this place? "I would see foxes and mountain lions," I said.
15. What would you take on your trip? "I would take a camera," I said.

Grammar **225**

Guided Practice Ⓐ

Work through the exercise with students. Discuss with them how specific errors in punctuating quotations could confuse readers.

TEACHING TIP

- Emphasize that most end punctuation goes inside quotation marks. Point out the final example in the box on p. 224, noting that although the period is part of the sentence and not part of the song title, it still goes inside the quotation marks.

Independent Practice
B and **C**

Have students complete the exercises. For Differentiated Instruction and Extra Practice, see p. TR16.

Differentiated Instruction

Strategic Intervention

Help students locate a passage of dialogue in a story they have read. Read the dialogue aloud with them. Then have each student write one additional line of dialogue that would fit in the conversation. Let students take turns writing their quotations on the board. Check their punctuation.

Advanced

Have students use reference books to find two quotations by people they admire. Have them copy the quotations, using quotation marks correctly, and attributing the words to the speaker. For example, "Ask not what your country can do for you," said President Kennedy. Have students share their quotations in small groups.

ELL

Ask students what they think about their favorite outdoor places, such as a park or forest. Write what some of the students say as quotations on the board. *(Jenna said, "The park is cool and green." "The forest has trails," said Jorge.)* Then have students talk about outdoor places with a more proficient English speaker, later writing two quotations that tell things their partner said during the discussion.

Explain that students may be asked to identify which words should go inside quotation marks. In addition to showing the exact words of people, quotation marks indicate many kinds of titles, such as song, poem, and story titles. Titles of longer works such as books are indicated with italics in print or underlined in handwriting.

Examples: Jane read a story called "A Big Lizard." I read a poem called "Desert Nights."

Monitor Progress

Check Grammar

If... students have difficulty identifying quotations,	**then...** have them find examples of dialogue and titles in quotation marks in their reading materials and discuss them.

Test Preparation

✔ Write the letter of the choice that correctly completes the sentence.

1. "I can play the __B__
   - **A** flute, Ross said.
   - **B** flute," Ross said.
   - **C** flute, Ross said."
   - **D** flute" Ross said.

2. Tara asked, "What kind of music __D__
   - **A** do you play.
   - **B** do you play?
   - **C** do you play"?
   - **D** do you play?"

3. __A__ like lively songs."
   - **A** Ross said, "I
   - **B** Ross said, I
   - **C** "Ross said, I
   - **D** Ross said "I

4. "She has a wonderful __B__
   - **A** teacher, Tara exclaimed!"
   - **B** teacher!" Tara exclaimed.
   - **C** teacher! Tara exclaimed.
   - **D** teacher." Tara exclaimed.

5. __C__ songs do you like?"
   - **A** Ross asked. "What
   - **B** Ross asked, What
   - **C** Ross asked, "What
   - **D** Ross asked "What

6. __C__ is Ross's favorite.
   - **A** "Tomorrow
   - **B** "Tomorrow"
   - **C** "Tomorrow"
   - **D** Tomorrow"

226 Grammar

Review

✔ Write *C* if a sentence is correct. If it is not correct, make the corrections that are needed.

1. "The class read a story called "The Island Journey."
2. "Can we go on a trip?" Pablo asked.
3. "How about an imaginary trip?" Ms. Adams replied.
4. Chris asked, "How do we do that?" C
5. Ms. Adams said, "think about a place you want to go."
6. "I'm thinking about a beautiful island," Danny said.
7. "The water is bright blue," Sophia said.
8. "Green parrots are talking in the trees," Clifford said.
9. Ms. Adams exclaimed, "You're taking your trip already!" C

✔ Write the sentences. Add capital letters, quotation marks, commas, and other punctuation marks as needed.

10. "I went on a trip," Ross said.
11. Sam asked, "where did you go?"
12. "I went to the bottom of the ocean," Ross replied.
13. "I saw purple fish and orange seahorses," he said.
14. Amber said, "I went to the top of a mountain."
15. Tyler asked, "what was your favorite part of the trip?"
16. "I could see the world for miles around," Amber replied.
17. Tyler said, "I went to the desert at night."
18. "I saw animals' eyes gleaming in the dark," he whispered.

Grammar **227**

Summarize

Ask students to tell about quotations and how they are used.

- Quotation marks show a speaker's exact words.
- A comma separates the exact words from the rest of the sentence. A capital letter begins the quotation. The punctuation mark that ends the quotation goes inside the quotation marks.
- Quotation marks indicate the titles of short works such as songs, poems, and stories.

Grammar-Writing Connection

Explain that using quotations to show exactly what people said makes stories and articles more vivid and interesting.

Interesting: The little girl said she wanted to be a glassblower.

More interesting: The little girl said, "I want to be a glassblower!"

Strong Conclusions

 WRITER'S CRAFT

Strong Conclusions

> A **strong conclusion** sums up the main idea of a paragraph in a vivid way.

 Read each paragraph and its possible conclusions. Write the letter of the most effective conclusion for the paragraph.

1. A mountaintop looks beautiful from far away, but it is a harsh place for people who visit. The higher you go, the worse the weather gets. At the top of a high mountain, snow swirls in a stiff wind. Temperatures are below freezing. __C__

   A Mountains are very beautiful.

   B So everyone should climb mountains.

   C Unless you are an experienced mountain climber, the best way to enjoy a tall mountain is from the ground.

2. The rain forest is a noisy and colorful part of the natural world. Monkeys screech, frogs croak, and insects chirp. The plants create a lush green world that contrasts with the brilliant reds and yellows of flowers and birds. __A__

   A A rain forest has more sights and sounds than the most exciting adventure movie.

   B Some of the animals that you see in rain forests include monkeys and frogs.

   C You should avoid the rain forest altogether if you have certain kinds of allergies.

Writing Good Paragraphs

A **good paragraph** has a topic sentence that tells the paragraph's main idea. It has supporting details that tell more about the main idea and are organized in a logical way. A good paragraph ends with a strong conclusion.

Topic sentence gets readers' interest and states paragraph's main idea.

Next six sentences provide supporting details. They are arranged in two groups: plants and animals.

Conclusion vividly sums up paragraph's main idea.

Life in the Desert

The desert seems like a hot, empty place, but it is really full of life. Deserts are very dry as well as hot, but plants that need little water grow there. These include cactuses, grasses, and even some trees. When it does rain, wildflowers and green plants bloom. Many animals like the dry, hot desert climate. Snakes and lizards live under rocks during the day. Larger animals such as foxes and jackrabbits may also spend time in the desert. When you think of a desert, you may think of a dead brown landscape. However, you will find that nature has amazing variety there.

Writing **229**

Writing Good Paragraphs

ANALYZE THE MODEL

Read aloud the model and the callouts to the left of it. Prepare students to write their own good paragraphs.

PROMPT

Write a paragraph about a setting in a story. Include a topic sentence, elaboration, and a strong conclusion.

Getting Started Students can do any of the following.

- Use an organizer (pp. TR28–TR32).
- Page through the selections to recall interesting settings.
- With a partner, discuss interesting real and fictional settings.

Editing/Revising Checklist

☑ Does my paragraph clearly focus on a specific setting?

☑ Does my conclusion sum up my main ideas?

☑ Have I used quotation marks correctly?

Self-Evaluation Distribute copies of p. TR26 for students to fill out.

Scoring Rubric
Writing Good Paragraphs

Rubric 4 3 2 1	4	3	2	1
Focus/Ideas	Paragraph with strong focus on story setting	Paragraph with fairly strong focus on story setting	Paragraph with weak focus on story setting	Paragraph with little or no focus
Organization/ Paragraphs	Includes strong topic sentence and conclusion	Includes good topic sentence and conclusion	Has poor topic sentence and conclusion	No topic sentence or conclusion
Voice	Individual and knowledgeable	Fairly individual and knowledgeable	Weak voice	No voice
Word Choice	Precise, vivid words	Mostly precise, vivid words	Some vague or incorrect words	Limited word choice
Sentences	Well crafted; different kinds and lengths	Fair craft and variety	Little craft or variety	Fragments or run-on sentences
Conventions	Excellent control and accuracy	Reasonable control with few errors	Errors that may prevent understanding	Frequent errors that interfere with meaning

For 5- and 6-point rubrics, see *Writing Rubrics and Anchor Papers* p. 38.

Taking Tests

Follow these tips when writing for a test:

Before Writing

- Read the prompt carefully. What does it ask you to do?
- Write down key words that name your audience *(warn people who eat junk food)*, state the purpose of the composition *(give directions)*, and tell you how to organize your points *(provide step-by-step instructions)*.
- Use a graphic organizer to plan your composition.
- Determine the tone of your writing (friendly, formal).

During Writing

- Reread the prompt as you write to make sure you are on topic.
- Keep in mind your graphic organizer and stay focused.
- Write a good beginning. You might engage readers with a thought-provoking question or an interesting fact.
- Develop and elaborate ideas. Support your main idea, your observations, or your opinion.
- Write a strong ending. Try to write a "clincher" sentence to provide a clear ending. You might add a final comment of your own or challenge your reader with a command.

After Writing

- Check your grammar and mechanics (punctuation, spelling).
- Reread the prompt and review your work. There's still time to add words or correct errors.

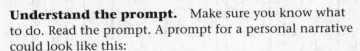

TEST TiP

Writing a Personal Narrative

Writing a strong opener can be difficult. Here are some suggestions:

- Set a mood—surprise, humor, suspense: *I thought I heard a faint moan, or it could have been the wind.*

- Ask your readers a question: *Have you ever wished you were invisible?*

- Set the scene: *It was 100 degrees, and dust was blowing around the playground.*

- Jump right into the action: *I was sprawled on the sidewalk with groceries scattered all over.*

Writing a Personal Narrative

A **test** may ask you to write a personal narrative. Your narrative needs to have a beginning, middle, and end. Use time-order words such as *then* and *after*. Follow the tips below.

Understand the prompt.   Make sure you know what to do. Read the prompt. A prompt for a personal narrative could look like this:

Write a personal narrative about an experience that made you feel proud of yourself. Be sure to choose just one experience or event for your narrative.

Key phrases are *personal narrative*, *proud of yourself*, and *one experience or event*.

Find a good topic.   Choose an important event that you remember well. Think about the details you want to include.

Organize your ideas.   Make a story organizer like this:

Event   I earned money to buy a new bike.

When?   Last summer

Why?   I outgrew my bike.

1. I needed a new bike and saw one I wanted.
2. I handed out flyers about jobs I could do.
3. I did jobs and earned money.
4. I bought the bike.

Write a good beginning. An exciting topic sentence will make your audience want to read more.

Develop and elaborate ideas. Use information from your story organizer. Include words that show time.

Write a strong ending. The end of your personal narrative can be exciting.

Check your work. Reread and make any changes.

See how the personal narrative below answers the prompt and has a clear beginning, middle, and end.

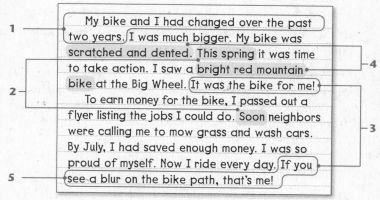

1. The opening sentence grabs the reader's attention.
2. Time-order words show the sequence of events.
3. Exclamatory sentences add interest.
4. Vivid details help readers picture the scene.
5. The strong ending shows the writer's personality.

TEST TIP

Writing a How-to Report

The focus of your report is *doing something*. You will use commands to tell readers how to perform the steps. Before you write the steps, visualize them in your mind. Then use words to create pictures of these steps for readers. Begin each step with a strong, precise verb: *fasten, outline, paint*. Avoid verbs such as *get* and *put* that don't go anywhere.

Writing a How-to Report

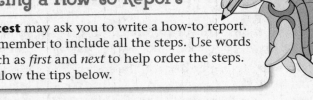

A **test** may ask you to write a how-to report. Remember to include all the steps. Use words such as *first* and *next* to help order the steps. Follow the tips below.

Understand the prompt.   Read the prompt carefully. A prompt for a how-to report could look like this:

Write a report that gives steps on how to make or do something. Make your report interesting and easy to understand. Explain all the steps and materials needed.

Key words and phrases are *steps, how to make or do something,* and *materials.*

Find a good topic.   Choose an activity you can do well.

Organize your ideas.   Create a how-to chart. Write the name of the task, the materials needed, an introduction, a list of steps, and an ending. A list of steps might look like the one below:

Steps	Get pine cone, string, peanut butter, margarine, and birdseed.
	Tie the string to the pine cone.
	Mix peanut butter and margarine and spread on pine cone.
	Roll pine cone in birdseed.

Write a good beginning. Write a strong opening sentence that tells readers what you are about to explain.

Develop and elaborate ideas. Refer to your chart to help you organize ideas. Use precise nouns and order words.

Write a strong ending. Use the ending to summarize.

Check your work. Read and check your report.

See how the how-to report below answers the prompt.

1 —
Do you like to watch birds in your yard? Then make this easy bird feeder. You will need a pine cone, a long string, peanut butter, margarine, and birdseed.

2 —
First, tie the string to the top of the pine cone. Then make a mixture of half peanut butter and half margarine. Spread it all over the pine cone. Next put some birdseed on a plate. Roll the pine cone around so birdseed sticks all over it.

Finally, hang the pine cone on a tree in your yard. Now see how many birds live in your neighborhood!

— 3

— 4

— 5

1. The opening question grabs the reader's attention.

2. The writer uses words that show the order of steps.

3. Precise nouns make the explanation clear.

4. The steps are in an order that makes sense.

5. The ending sums up the explanation.

TEST TiP

Writing a Compare/Contrast Essay

Organization is particularly important in a compare and contrast essay. Readers will get confused if you switch back and forth between similarities and differences without signaling which one you are telling about. One good way to organize a compare and contrast essay is to first describe all the similarities and then describe all the differences.

Writing a Compare/Contrast Essay

A **test** may ask you to write a compare/contrast essay. Use words that show likenesses (*and, also, both*) and differences (*although, while, but*). Follow the tips below.

Understand the prompt. Read the prompt carefully. A prompt for a compare/contrast essay could look like this:

Write an essay comparing and contrasting two things in nature, such as two seasons or two natural places. Show how they are alike and different.

A key phrase is *comparing and contrasting*.

Find a good topic. Choose two natural features that have many things in common as well as several differences.

Organize your ideas. Make a compare/contrast organizer. You can start with either likenesses or differences.

Main Idea Spring and fall, my favorite seasons, are different and alike.			
Different		**Same**	
Spring	**Fall**	**Spring**	**Fall**
Growth begins	Growth ends	In-between	In-between
New plants	Dying plants	Bright colors	Bright colors
		Not hot or cold	Not hot or cold

236 Taking Tests

Write a good beginning.   Draw your reader in.

Develop and elaborate ideas.   Build on your organizer.

Write a strong ending.   Sum up your ideas.

Check your work.   Change what you want.

See how the essay below follows the prompt.

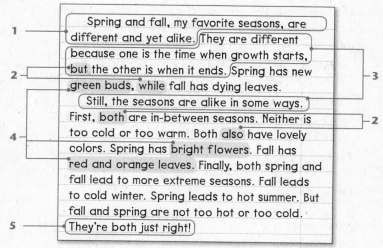

1   Spring and fall, my favorite seasons, are different and yet alike. They are different because one is the time when growth starts, but the other is when it ends. Spring has new green buds, while fall has dying leaves.
  Still, the seasons are alike in some ways. First, both are in-between seasons. Neither is too cold or too warm. Both also have lovely colors. Spring has bright flowers. Fall has red and orange leaves. Finally, both spring and fall lead to more extreme seasons. Fall leads to cold winter. Spring leads to hot summer. But fall and spring are not too hot or too cold. They're both just right!

1. The first sentence introduces the main idea.

2. Words for likenesses and differences make ideas clear.

3. The comparison and contrast points are clear.

4. Vivid word choice helps readers picture the seasons.

5. The conclusion sums up why the seasons are the writer's favorites.

TEST TiP

Writing a Story

Decide what the general tone of your story will be. Will it be funny, serious, sad, or something else? Keep your tone in mind as you select the details for your story. Know where you are going—how your story will end and how you will get to that ending.

Writing a Story

A **test** may ask you to write a story. You will need to think of a character and something that happens to him or her. Follow the tips below.

Understand the prompt.   Make sure you know what to do. Read the prompt carefully. A prompt for a story could look like this:

> Write a story about a character and one event that happens. The event could be interesting, funny, or scary. Be sure your story has a beginning, middle, and ending.

Key words and phrases are *story*, *character*, *one event*, *beginning*, *middle*, and *ending*.

Find a good topic.   Choose an interesting character and one specific thing that he or she does.

Organize your ideas.   Make a story organizer.

Character   Tim, who loves holidays

Setting   Tim's house

Event   Tim learns about a new holiday.

1. Tim's friend Lee comes to visit, wearing dragon costume.
2. Tim asks about the costume.
3. Lee tells Tim about Chinese New Year.
4. Tim plans to celebrate Chinese New Year too.

Write a good beginning. An interesting opening sentence will make your reader eager to read on.

Develop and elaborate ideas. Use information from your story organizer.

Write a strong ending. Show how your character changes.

Check your work. Reread your work carefully. Make needed changes.

See how the story below follows the prompt.

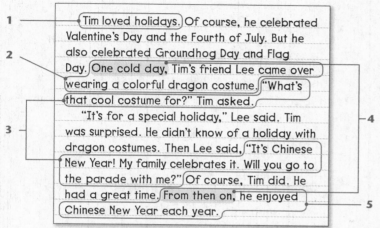

1. Tim loved holidays. Of course, he celebrated Valentine's Day and the Fourth of July. But he also celebrated Groundhog Day and Flag Day. One cold day, Tim's friend Lee came over wearing a colorful dragon costume. "What's that cool costume for?" Tim asked.

"It's for a special holiday," Lee said. Tim was surprised. He didn't know of a holiday with dragon costumes. Then Lee said, "It's Chinese New Year! My family celebrates it. Will you go to the parade with me?" Of course, Tim did. He had a great time. From then on, he enjoyed Chinese New Year each year.

1. The opening sentence tells about the main character.
2. The story event is introduced in the first paragraph.
3. Quotations add interest.
4. Time-order words show the sequence of events.
5. The ending tells how the event changes the main character.

TEST TiP

Writing a Persuasive Letter

Know your audience. Keep your audience in mind as you write your letter. You know the kinds of reasons that will likely convince him or her. For example, going on a trip because your best friend is going is not a fact that will impress your mom or dad. The fact that the trip is educational might be more effective.

Writing a Persuasive Letter

A **test** may ask you to write a persuasive letter. When you choose your topic, think of reasons that will convince your reader. Use words such as *should* and *most important*. Follow the tips below.

Understand the prompt. Make sure you know what to do. Read the prompt carefully. A prompt for a persuasive letter could look like this:

> Think of a place that you would like to visit. Write a letter to your parents persuading them to vacation there.

Key phrases are *letter*, *parents*, *persuading*, and *vacation*.

Find a good topic. Choose a place that you know about and would like to visit.

Organize your ideas. Make a chart. Write your opening sentence. List supporting reasons. Star the best reason.

Opening Sentence	Supporting Reasons
I think we should spend part of July in Cape Cod.	Relax as a family* Friend goes there Bay and ocean Wide, clean beaches Hotels and campgrounds

Write a good beginning. State your main reason for writing the letter in the first sentence.

Develop and elaborate ideas. Use the reasons from your chart. Use persuasive words and phrases.

Write a strong ending. Write a convincing ending.

Check your work. Make any corrections.

See how the letter below addresses the prompt.

Dear Mom and Dad:

1   I think we should spend part of July in Cape Cod, Massachusetts. My best friend Ella

2   stays there every summer. Ella says that the Cape has great hotels and safe campgrounds.

3   We can swim in the bay and the ocean. Ella showed me pictures of the wide, clean beaches. Most important, on Cape Cod we   4 could enjoy ourselves as a family. I hope that   5 you will decide on Cape Cod for this year's safe and enjoyable family vacation.

     Your daughter,

     Tracy

1. The letter begins with the reason for writing.

2. Language is persuasive.

3. Reasons are clear and well-stated.

4. The most important reason comes last.

5. This ending makes a strong statement.

TEST TIP

Writing a Summary

You may be asked to write a summary about information you find in a chart. You will need to put together this information in paragraph form. Your summary should include the important facts from the chart. In addition, you can pull these facts together and make observations about them. Unlike information in a chart, your summary should reflect your voice and style.

Writing a Summary

A **test** may ask you to write a summary from a graph, time line, or chart. You will need to read the information carefully and use it in your own sentences. Follow the tips below.

Organize your ideas. You will need to decide how to present the facts. Think about which facts you want to use first and which you will save until the end.

Write a good beginning. Get your reader's attention. Think of an opening sentence that presents the main idea.

Fact Sheet About the White House

Purpose
- Home for President and family

When it was built
- Begun in 1792, lived in by President Adams in 1800
- Burned by British in War of 1812, rebuilt by 1817

Building features
- Main building with curved porch
- West wing offices for President and staff, east wing for military aides

What tourists see
- Five rooms on first floor: State Dining Room, Red Room, Blue Room, Green Room, East Room

---

Develop and elaborate ideas. Include facts from your fact sheet that support your main idea.

Write a strong ending. Write sentences that pull the information together.

Check your work. Add any missing information.

See how the summary below uses the information.

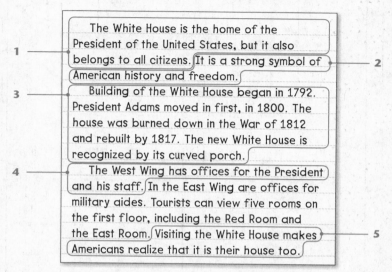

1 → The White House is the home of the President of the United States, but it also belongs to all citizens.

2 → It is a strong symbol of American history and freedom.

3 → Building of the White House began in 1792. President Adams moved in first, in 1800. The house was burned down in the War of 1812 and rebuilt by 1817. The new White House is recognized by its curved porch.

4 → The West Wing has offices for the President and his staff. In the East Wing are offices for military aides. Tourists can view five rooms on the first floor, including the Red Room and the East Room.

5 → Visiting the White House makes Americans realize that it is their house too.

1. The opening sentence states the main idea.
2. The next sentence express the writer's feelings.
3. The history is explained in order.
4. Use a new paragraph when the topic changes.
5. The ending connects to the writer's main idea.

Taking Tests **243**

Grammar Patrol

Grammar Patrol

adjective   An adjective describes a noun or a pronoun.

> Ponds are *active* places.
> *Several* chipmunks run through the *wet* grass.

Adjectives have two different forms that are used to make comparisons.

- Use the *–er* form of an adjective to compare two persons, places, or things.

> Frogs have *smoother* skin than toads.

- Use the *–est* form of an adjective to compare three or more persons, places, or things.

> Snails are the *slowest* pond creatures.

- The words *more* and *most* are often used with adjectives of two or more syllables to make comparisons.

> The ducks were *more comical* than usual.
> The goose is the *most common* bird here.

- Some adjectives show comparison in a special way. The correct forms of *good*, *bad*, *much*, and *little* are shown below.

good weather	*better* weather	*best* weather
bad storm	*worse* storm	*worst* storm
much snow	*more* snow	*most* snow
little fog	*less* fog	*least* fog

article   The words, *a*, *an*, and *the* are a special kind of adjective. They are called articles. *The* is used with both singular and plural nouns. *A* and *an* are used only with singular nouns.

> *The* animals at *the* pond are very busy.
> *A* friend and I spent *an* afternoon there.

- Use *a* before a word that begins with a consonant sound.

> *a* beaver   *a* pleasant afternoon

- Use *an* before a word that begins with a vowel sound.

> *an* owl   *an* underwater plant

adverb   A word that describes a verb is an adverb.

- Some adverbs ask the question "How?"

    The fox hides *slyly* behind the bushes. (how?)

- Some adverbs answer the question "Where?"

    Aesop wrote fables *here*. (where?)

- Other adverbs answer the question "When?"

    Often a fable tells about one event. (when?)

Adverbs can be used to compare actions.

- Use the *–er* form or *more* to compare two actions. Most adverbs that end in *–ly* use *more*.

    The ant worked *harder* than the cricket.
    The tortoise moved *more steadily* than the hare.

- Use the *–est* form or *most* to compare three or more actions. Most adverbs that end in *–ly* use *most*.

    The ant worked *hardest* of all the insects.
    The tortoise moved *most steadily* of all.

The word *not* is an adverb. It means "no." Do not use two words that mean "no" in the same sentence.

    Wrong: It *wouldn't never* matter to me.
    Right: It *wouldn't* ever matter to me.
    Right: It would *never* matter to me.

contraction   A contraction is a shortened form of two words. An apostrophe replaces a letter or letters.

- Some contractions join a pronoun and a verb.

    I have never been in a dairy shed before.
    I've never been in a dairy shed before.

- Some contractions are formed from a verb and the word *not*.

    I *cannot* believe you *did not* bring your banjo.
    I *can't* believe you *didn't* bring your banjo.

noun   A noun names a person, place, or thing.

The *settlers* came to *America* on a *ship*.
(person)   (place)   (thing)

A **singular noun** names one person, place, or thing.

The *settler* kept the *cow* in the *barn*.

A **plural noun** names more than one person, place, or thing.

The *settlers* kept their *cows* in their *barns*.

- Add -*s* to form the plural of most nouns.

  colonist*s*   river*s*   pea*s*   chicken*s*

- Add -*es* to form the plural of nouns that end in *ch*, *sh*, *s*, *ss*, *x*, or *z*.

  bench*es*   bush*es*   bus*es*   box*es*

- If a noun ends in a consonant and *y*, change *y* to *i* and add -*es* to form the plural.

  Singular: library   city   cherry
  Plural: librar*ies*   cit*ies*   cherr*ies*

- Some plurals are formed by changing the spelling of the singular noun.

  Singular: man   child   foot   mouse
  Plural: m*e*n   child*ren*   f*ee*t   m*ice*

- A few nouns have the same singular and plural forms.

  Singular: elk   moose   deer   sheep
  Plural: elk   moose   deer   sheep

A **common noun** names any person, place, or thing.

A *colonist* founded the *town*.

A **proper noun** names a particular person, place, or thing.
William Penn founded *Philadelphia*.

A **possessive noun** shows ownership.

- To form the possessive of a singular noun, add an apostrophe and s ('s) to the singular noun.

    Ben Franklin's many talents amazed people.

- To form the possessive of a plural noun ending in s, add an apostrophe (s').

    shoemakers' hammers   *blacksmiths'* forges

- To form the possessive of a plural noun that does not end in s, add an apostrophe and s ('s).

    men's hats   *mice's* tails   two *deer's* tracks

preposition   A preposition is a word that shows how a noun or pronoun is related to other words in the same sentence.

    We sing *in* the car.

A preposition begins a group of words called a **prepositional phrase**. At the end of the phrase is a noun or pronoun called the **object of the preposition**.

    Preposition: The dog buried its bone *in* the yard.
    Prepositional phrase: *in the yard*
    Object of the proposition: *yard*

pronoun   A pronoun takes the place of a noun or nouns.

    Nouns: *Linda* writes *poems*.
    Pronouns: *She* enjoys writing *them*.

The pronouns *I*, *you*, *she*, *he*, *it*, *we*, and *they* are **subject pronouns**. Use these pronouns to replace nouns that are the subjects of sentences.

    Robert Frost had been a teacher and a farmer.
    He wrote many poems about nature.

The pronouns *me, you, him, her, it, us,* and *them* are **object pronouns**. You can use these pronouns to replace nouns in the predicate of a sentence.

Paul read *poems* to *Jill*.
Paul read *them* to *her*.

The pronouns *my, your, his, her, its, our,* and *their* are **possessive pronouns**. A possessive pronoun shows ownership. Possessive pronouns can replace nouns.

That *writer's* home is in the mountains.
Her poems usually involve nature.

sentence   A sentence is a group of words that expresses a complete thought.

People of all ages enjoy hobbies.

A **declarative sentence** makes a statement. It ends with a period (.).

Hobbies are important in people's lives.

An **interrogative sentence** asks a question. It ends with a question mark (?).

What is your hobby?

An **imperative sentence** gives a command or makes a request. It usually ends with a period (.).

Please get your kite ready.   *Come to our party.*

An **exclamatory sentence** expresses strong feeling. It ends with an exclamation mark (!).

That kite will crash!   *How happy I am!*

A **simple sentence** has one subject and one predicate. It expresses one complete thought.

Kites come in many different shapes.

A **compound sentence** contains two simple sentences joined by the word *and*, *but*, or *or*. Use a comma in a compound sentence before the word *and*, *but*, or *or*.

The day was cool, and *clouds drifted across the sun.*

subject and predicate The subject is the part of the sentence that names someone or something. The predicate tells what the subject is or does. Both the subject and the predicate may be one word or many words.

Currents/move ocean water around the world.
The most common mineral/is salt.
Ocean water/moves.
Sea water/flows in vast streams.

The **simple subject** is the main word in the complete subject.

The five biggest *oceans* are really one huge ocean.

A sentence may have more than one simple subject. The word *and* may be used to join simple subjects, making a **compound subject**. The simple subjects share the same predicate.

Spiny *crabs* and colorful *fish* scurry along the underwater reef.

The **simple predicate** is the main word or words in the complete predicate.

Ocean waters *flow* in vast streams.

A sentence may have more than one simple predicate. The word *and* may be used to join simple predicates, making a **compound predicate**. The simple predicates share the same subject.

Some worms *live* and *feed* in the ocean.

verb A verb is a word that shows action or being.

Nina *paints* in art class. (action)
That picture *is* beautiful. (being)

An **action verb** shows action. It tells what the subject of a sentence does.

> The art teacher *welcomed* the students.

A verb can be more than one word. The **main verb** is the most important verb. A **helping verb** works with the main verb.

> Many people have *admired* Picasso's paintings. (main verb)
> His name *is* known all over the world. (helping verb)

A **linking verb** shows being. It tells what the subject is or was.

> Grandma Moses *was* a famous artist.

When the correct subject and verb are used together, we say they agree. The form of the linking verb *be* that is used depends on the subject of the sentence. Study the following chart.

Using the Forms of *be*

Use *am* and *was*	with *I*
Use *is* and *was*	with *she, he, it,* and singular nouns
Use *are* and *were*	with *we, you, they,* and plural nouns

The **tense** of a verb shows the time of the action.

A verb in the **present tense** shows action that happens now.

> Eli *forms* the tiles.

A verb in the present tense must agree with the subject of the sentence.

- With *he, she, it,* or a singular noun, add *-s* or *-es* to the verb.

  > The student learn*s*.   My cousin teach*es*.   He walk*s*.

- If a verb ends in *ch, sh, s, ss, x,* or *z*, add *-es*. Notice the word *teaches* above.

- With *I, you, we, they,* or a plural noun, do not add *-s* or *-es*.

  > The students learn.   My cousins teach.   They walk.

A verb in the **future tense** shows action that will happen. The future tense is formed with the helping verb *will*.

> Ann *will create* a vase.

A verb in the **past tense** shows action that already happened.

Lee *washed* pots.

The past tenses of irregular verbs are not formed by adding *-ed*.
Some irregular verbs are shown in the following chart.

Verb	Past	Past with *have*, *has*, or *had*
begin	began	begun
bring	brought	brought
come	came	come
do	did	done
eat	ate	eaten
fall	fell	fallen
find	found	found
fly	flew	flown
give	gave	given
go	went	gone
grow	grew	grown
ride	rode	ridden
run	ran	run
see	saw	seen
take	took	taken
throw	threw	thrown
write	wrote	written

The spelling of some verbs changes when *-es* or *-ed* is added.

- If a verb ends in a consonant and *y*, change the *y* to *i* before adding *-es* or *-ed*.

   study   stud*ies*   stud*ied*

- If a verb ends in one vowel and one consonant, double the final consonant before adding *-ed*.

   trap   tra*pped*   stir   sti*rred*

Capitalization

first word of a sentence   Every sentence begins with a capital letter.

> *People* enjoy having special projects.

proper noun   Each important word in a proper noun begins with a capital letter.

- Capitalize each word in the name of a person or pet.
> *Patrice Gomez* owns a cat named *Duke.*

- Capitalize an initial in a name. Put a period after the initial.
> William *L.* Chen is a doctor in our neighborhood.

- Capitalize a title before a name. If the title is an *abbreviation* (a shortened form of a word), put a period after it.
> *President* Jefferson   *Dr.* Jonas Salk

- Capitalize every important word in the names of particular places or things.
> *Statue of Liberty*   *Ellis Island*   *New York Harbor*

- Capitalize names of days, months, holidays, and special days.
> *Tuesday*   *April*   *Fourth of July*

pronoun *I*   The pronoun *I* is always capitalized.

> May *I* go skating this afternoon?

letter   Capitalize the first word of the greeting and the first word of the closing of a letter.

> *Dear* Mother,   *Dear* Sir: *Sincerely* yours,

title of books, movies, songs, and other works   Capitalize the first word, the last word, and all of the important words in the title of works.

> The Secret Life of Harold the Bird Watcher
> "The Star-Spangled Banner"

quotation Begin the first word in a quotation with a capital letter.

> The Hare asked, "*How* about a race?"

Punctuation

period Declarative sentences and imperative sentences end with a period (.).

> *I stood on the corner.*   *Wait for the signal.*

- Put a period after an initial in a name.

> J. P. Jones   Abigail S. Adams

- Put a period after an abbreviation (a shortened form of a word).

> *Mr.*   *Mrs.*   *Ms.*   *Dr.*

question mark An interrogative sentence ends with a question mark (?).

> *Do you have more than one hobby?*

exclamation mark An exclamatory sentence ends with an exclamation mark (!).

> *That kite will crash!*

comma A comma (,) is a signal that tells a reader to pause.

- Use a comma after *yes*, *no*, or *well* at the beginning of a sentence.

> *Yes*, I saw the display of Eskimo art.
> *Well*, my favorites were the bears made of silver.

- Use a comma to set off the name of the person spoken to.

> *Your painting is very beautiful, Roberta.*

- Use a comma to separate words in a series. A series is made up of three or more items. No comma is used after the last word in the series. The last comma goes before the word *and*.

> *The artists carve, smooth, and polish their work.*

- Use a comma to separate the city from the state.

  I grew up in *Tulsa, Oklahoma*.

- Use a comma to separate the day and the year.

  Pablo was born on *February 7, 2000*.

- Use a comma after the greeting of a friendly letter. Use a comma after the closing of a friendly or a business letter.

  Dear Kim,   *Your friend,*   *Yours truly,*

- Use a comma before the word *and*, *but*, or *or* in a compound sentence.

  The merchants crossed central Asia, and they reached China.

quotation marks   A quotation is the exact words someone speaks. Quotation marks (" ") show where a speaker's exact words begin and end.

- Use quotation marks before and after a quotation. Begin the first word in a quotation with a capital letter. When the quotation comes last, use a comma to separate the speaker from the quotation.

  The Tortoise said, "I'm not going to lose this race."

- When the quotation comes first, use a comma, a question mark, or an exclamation mark to separate the quotation from the speaker. The end mark of a quotation always comes just before the second quotation mark. Put a period at the end of the sentence.

  Statement: "Let's do something else," replied the Tortoise.
  Question: "Are you afraid you'll lose?" teased the Hare.
  Exclamation: "I'm not afraid!" snapped the Tortoise.

- Enclose the titles of stories, songs, poems, and articles in quotation marks.

  Story: "The Use of Force"
  Song: "Of Thee I Sing"
  Poem: "Dear March, Come In!"
  Article: "Let's Make Music"

Underline the titles of newspapers, magazines, books, plays, and movies.

In materials you read, these titles are printed in italics.

Newspaper: <u>Denver Post</u>

Magazine: <u>Popular Mechanics</u>

Book: <u>A Wind in the Door</u>

Play: <u>Man of La Mancha</u>

Movie: <u>Invaders from Mars</u>

apostrophe Use an apostrophe (') to show where a letter or letters have been left out in a *contraction* (a shortened form of two words).

we'd (we + had)   *wasn't* (was + not)

- Use an apostrophe to form the possessive of a noun.

man's   *James's*   *men's*   *workers'*

colon Use a colon (:) after the greeting in a business letter.

Dear Mr. Kurtz: *Dear Sir or Madam:*

Frequently Misspelled Words

a lot
afraid
again
almost
already
always
another
are
athlete
basketball
beautiful
because
before
believe
brother
brought
buy
caught
chocolate
Christmas
clothes
control
could
cousin
Dad's
decided
didn't
different
disappear
doesn't
don't
enough
especially
everybody
everyone

everything
except
excited
family
favorite
February
field
finally
first
found
friend
getting
government
grabbed
happened
heard
hero
his
hospital
house
I
I'm
instead
into
it's
knew
know
knowledge
let's
library
little
maybe
might
minute
Mom

morning
myself
of
off
once
one
opened
our
outside
people
piece
presents
pretty
probably
radio
really
right
said
scared
school
separate
should
since
sincerely
something
sometimes
special
started
stopped
successful
sure
surprised
swimming
that's
their

then
there
they
they're
thought
through
to
too
took
tries
truly
TV
two
until
upon
usually
vacation
very
want
was
watch
weird
we're
were
what
when
where
which
who
whole
with
would
you're

D'Nealian™ Alphabet

a b c d e f g h i
j k l m n o p q r s t
u v w x y z

A B C D E F G
H I J K L M N O
P Q R S T U V
W X Y Z . , ' ?

1 2 3 4 5 6
7 8 9 10

Manuscript Alphabet

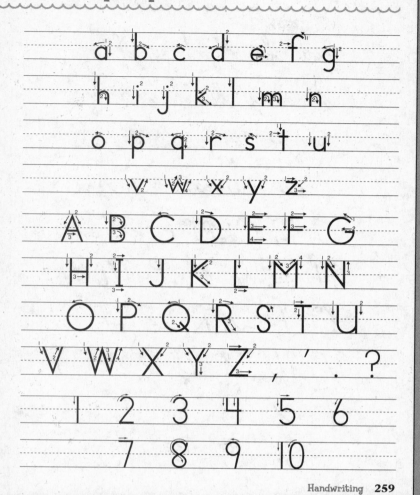

a b c d e f g
h i j k l m n
o p q r s t u
v w x y z
A B C D E F G
H I J K L M N
O P Q R S T U
V W X Y Z , ' . ?
1 2 3 4 5 6
7 8 9 10

Cursive Alphabet

a b c d e f g
h i j k l m n
o p q r s t u
v w x y z
A B C D E F G
H I J K L M N
O P Q R S T U
V W X Y Z . , ' ?
1 2 3 4 5 6
7 8 9 10

Index

V

Verb phrases. *See* Verbs.
Verbs, 110–113, 250–252
    action, 110–113
    agreement, 122–125
    future tense, 128–131
    helping, 116–119
    irregular, 134–137
    is, am, are, was, were, 110–113
    linking, 110–113
    main, 116–119
    past tense, 128–131
    phrases, 116–119
    present tense, 128–131
Voice. *See* Writing.

W

Word choice. *See* Writing.
Writer's craft. *See topics under* Writing. *See also main entries.*
Writing
    answer the 5 Ws and How, 132
    commands and exclamations, 72
    compare/contrast words, 138
    conventions, 22–25
    details, 2, 114, 162, 210
    describe goal, 163
        setting, 151
    elaborating, 222
    eliminate wordiness, 90
    focus/ideas, 2–5
    get reader's attention, 156
    good paragraphs, 229
    include necessary information, 84
    know audience, 198
    main idea, 2–3
    models, 4–5, 8–9, 12–13, 16–17, 20–21, 24–25, 27–30, 32–35, 37–40, 42–45, 233, 235, 237, 239, 241, 243
    ad, 187
    answer a question, 193
    character description, 55
    compare/contrast essay, 236–237
    editorial, 175
    e-mail, 73
    feature story, 103
    friendly letter, 127
    how-to report, 234–235
    informational paragraph, 217

DAILY FIX-IT

1

1. The apple pies was for super. *(were; supper)*

2. Can you're sister bake pies. *(your; pies?)*

3. Soon there was more traffic in the town *(traffic; town.)*

4. Does any one need new shoes *(anyone; shoes?)*

5. A log cabin kept the family warm *(family; warm.)*

6. The rodes was muddy in winter. *(roads; were)*

7. The settlers bilt a school and stores *(built; stores.)*

8. They gived all the streats names. *(gave; streets)*

9. What hapened to the cowboy. *(happened; cowboy?)*

10. He rode his Horse thrugh town. *(horse; through)*

DAILY FIX-IT

2

1. What do peple need. *(people; need?)*

2. The puppys needs a pen. *(puppies; need)*

3. The carpets is beautiful? *(are beautiful.)*

4. The woman needs supplys for the carpet *(supplies; carpet.)*

5. did the boy get his wishs? *(Did; wishes)*

6. He lerned sumthing from a wise man. *(learned; something)*

7. Now the man bring carpets too sell. *(brings; to)*

8. A carpenter make things out of would. *(makes; wood)*

9. The man brung the goats hair to the spinner. *(brought; goat's)*

10. everyone was hapy at the end. *(Everyone; happy)*

DAILY FIX-IT

3

1. What will you by with your money. *(buy; money?)*

2. Your piggy bank is heavyer than mine. *(heavier; mine.)*

3. my brother worried about saving his money. *(My; worried)*

4. Did jon's uncle give him money for his birthday. *(Jon's; birthday?)*

5. How much does it cost to go swiming at the pool. *(swimming; pool?)*

6. Tim saveing his money. *(is saving)*

7. What hapened to the dollar in my drawer. *(happened; drawer.)*

8. Dan spended it at the fare. *(spent; fair)*

9. These plantes dont cost much. *(plants; don't)*

10. We can give a flour to Mom for her birth day. *(flower; birthday)*

DAILY FIX-IT 6

1. Does penguins live in alaska? (*Do; Alaska*)

2. The feemale bird look for food. (*female; looks*)

3. Babys cant get their own food. (*Babies; can't*)

4. It is sillent on the ice of antarctica. (*silent; Antarctica*)

5. A father Penguin cares for a egg. (*penguin; an*)

6. The father wont leave even thogh he is hungry. (*won't; though*)

7. The birds slide on the ice and they play in the snow (*ice; snow.*)

8. Isnt the baby's coat soft. (*Isn't; soft?*)

9. Can birds build they're nests on ice. (*their; ice?*)

10. The mother fish for food and the father watches the egg. (*fishes; food.*)

Unit 2   Penguin Chick

Daily Fix-It   **6**

© Pearson Education

DAILY FIX-IT 5

1. Are you prowd of your new bike. (*proud; bike?*)

2. We sold peachs and they sold beans. (*peaches.*)

3. He saved his money and it was a large amount (*money,; amount.*)

4. The boys new bicycle costs alot. (*boy's; a lot*)

5. Dad teached him to ride a bike in an our. (*taught; hour*)

6. Can he ride it good now. (*well; now?*)

7. I tried to cary a box on my bike, But it was too heavy. (*carry; but*)

8. Cant you put it on your bike. (*Can't; bike?*)

9. Tom made a choyce and he was happy with it. (*choice.*)

10. Toyes and games is expensive. (*Toys; are*)

Unit 1   My Rows and Piles of Coins

Daily Fix-It   **5**

© Pearson Education

DAILY FIX-IT 4

1. Hannah dreemed she had one hundred dollar. (*dreamed; dollars*)

2. Nick and I took our pennys to the bank (*pennies; bank.*)

3. What a beautiful Sundy it is. (*Sunday; is!*)

4. dad agreed to cash the check for me. (*Dad; agreed*)

5. Beth is worried about losing her money (*worried; money.*)

6. Was that Beths quarter? (*Beth's quarter?*)

7. Have you seen this kind of nickle. (*nickel?*)

8. The boys is colecting coins. (*are; collecting*)

9. Display you're photos in this window (*your; window.*)

10. Does Jen and Jeff enjoy their work. (*Do; work?*)

Unit 1   If You Made a Million

Daily Fix-It   **4**

© Pearson Education

DAILY FIX-IT

1. White benchs sat in the middel of the garden.
(benches; middle)
2. Many colorful rose grow their. (roses; there)
3. Can we eat our lunchs in the field. (lunches; field?)
4. The workers is puling weeds. (are; pulling)
5. Most farmers don't work in citys but some gardeners do.
(cities,)
6. What pritty plants those are. (pretty; are!)
7. There are many pumpkin farmes in california.
(farms; California)
8. The boy and his uncel picks tomatoes. (uncle; pick)
9. Are there pickels on the sandwich. (pickles; sandwich?)
10. How hungry the workers is. (are!)

Unit 2   A Day's Work

Daily Fix-It   **7**

© Pearson Education

DAILY FIX-IT

1. Those children has a big collection of butter flies.
(have; butterflies)
2. Kim collects shells and Maya collects earings.
(shells,; earrings)
3. My friend jody has boxs all over her room. (Jody; boxes)
4. How can you do home work in this room.
(homework; room?)
5. Many people collects pennys and other coins.
(collect; pennies)
6. Tim displaied his collection in springfield.
(displayed; Springfield)
7. On saturday, Kate shoped for a doll for her collection.
(Saturday; shopped)
8. Jay has more then a thowsand stamps. (than; thousand)
9. Julie collected some pretty leafs at the Park. (leaves; park)
10. She droped them in the middel of her room.
(dropped; middle)

Unit 2   Prudy's Problem and How She Solved It

Daily Fix-It   **8**

© Pearson Education

DAILY FIX-IT

1. Hares family gave Bear two or thee crops. (Hare's; three)
2. Hare used his strenth in the field and Bear rested.
(strength; field,)
3. Is that Mr. Bears field. (Bear's; field?)
4. They planted strawberrys on tuesday.
(strawberries; Tuesday)
5. That farmers crops are on the wagen. (farmer's; wagon)
6. Does that streat go to the market. (street; market?)
7. Bear sqweezed the tomato and juice splashed out.
(squeezed; tomato,)
8. What great blueberrys these are. (blueberries; are!)
9. Mrs. hare raked leafs in the yard. (Hare; leaves)
10. She put them in boxs and she took them to the dump.
(boxes,)

Unit 2   Tops & Bottoms

Daily Fix-It   **9**

© Pearson Education

DAILY FIX-IT

1. The Inglish settlers had the first thanksgiving.
   (English; Thanksgiving)

2. The childrens toys were made of would. *(children's; wood)*

3. The colonys had cold wether. *(colonies; weather)*

4. The two boys's cloths were not warm enough.
   (boys'; clothes)

5. The children's school have only one room.
   (has (or had) only)

6. The first Americans's fashons were very different from
   those of today. *(Americans'; fashions)*

7. His fathers' house was prettyer than his house.
   (father's; prettier)

8. The family was surprised by november's sun shine.
   (November's; sunshine)

9. Is Autumn colorful in England. *(autumn; England?)*

10. Both the trees's leaves has fallen. *(trees'; have)*

Unit 2 William's House   Daily Fix-It **10**

© Pearson Education

DAILY FIX-IT

1. Wasnt that a colorful garden. *(Wasn't; garden?)*

2. The tullips was red and yellow. *(tulips; were)*

3. The window boxs is full of wildflowers. *(boxes; are)*

4. Theyll bloom in Summer.   *(They'll; summer)*

5. There was a rain shouer last night, so I havent watered
   the garden today. *(shower; haven't)*

6. Whens the sun comeing out? *(When's; coming)*

7. The Smiths's garden seem like a jungle. *(Smiths'; seems)*

8. What wonderful plants youll see. *(you'll; see!)*

9. The foxs didnt get into the garden. *(foxes; didn't)*

10. Those yelow flowers will bloom in september.
    (yellow; September)

Unit 3 The Gardener   Daily Fix-It **11**

© Pearson Education

DAILY FIX-IT

1. All the village, man were hunting on monday.
   (men; Monday)

2. Theyd seen deers and foxes in the forest. *(They'd; deer)*

3. Do you recal the golden eagles in the forest. *(recall; forest?)*

4. They was sitting on a pine Tree. *(were; tree)*

5. The hunters spoted a brown bare among the trees.
   (spotted; bear)

6. They went after the animal but it dissapeared into
   the woods. *(animal,; disappeared)*

7. Two woman unlode wood, and then they build a fire.
   (women; unload)

8. The fire will kept every one in the village warm.
   (keep; everyone)

9. The two men is making a boat out of branchs.
   (are; branches)

10. It will flowt on a long voiage. *(float; voyage)*

Unit 3 Pushing Up the Sky   Daily Fix-It **12**

© Pearson Education

DAILY FIX-IT

1. The fireflies lands on my jaket. *(land; jacket)*

2. The many firefly's's lights look like stars on a Summer night. *(fireflies'; summer)*

3. Lardge moths flies around the porch at night. *(Large; fly)*

4. They look a litle like butterflys. *(little; butterflies)*

5. Wasnt that a spider on the floor. *(Wasn't; floor?)*

6. Dew make the plant's wet in the morning. *(makes; plants)*

7. Many animals prowls on the edje of the forest at night. *(prowl; edge)*

8. The two trees shadows hide the mouses and foxes. *(trees'; mice)*

9. The birds nests are full of eggs in april. *(birds'; April)*

10. What is that oranje bird. *(orange; bird?)*

Unit 3   Night Letters

Daily Fix-It **13**

© Pearson Education

DAILY FIX-IT

1. Beautyful blue whales lives in the cold ocean waters. *(Beautiful; live)*

2. Theyre the bigest animals in the world. *(They're; biggest)*

3. Sled dogs was helpfull in the cold climate. *(were; helpful)*

4. The dogs's owner spoke to them quitely. *(dogs'; quietly)*

5. Kelly hopped she would see whales on her trip to hawaii. *(hoped; Hawaii)*

6. Last year they visit friends near the Pacific ocean. *(visited; Ocean)*

7. Yesterday the whales will appear on the beech. *(appeared; beach)*

8. Some will returned to the water safly. *(return; safely)*

9. Cant whales hear sounds underwater. *(Can't; underwater?)*

10. A whale blow water from it's spout. *(blows; its)*

Unit 3   A Symphony of Whales

Daily Fix-It **14**

© Pearson Education

DAILY FIX-IT

1. Did you now there is a big volcano in washington? *(know; Washington)*

2. I seen a picture of its steam and ashs. *(saw; ashes)*

3. Mr. Patricks class was assined a report on Mount St. Helens. *(Patrick's; assigned)*

4. Sharon and Juan has began their reports. *(have; begun)*

5. Thomas seen a mountain in Hawaii, and it was a volcano. *(saw; mountain)*

6. Last year he and his Family walks on hard lava. *(family; walked)*

7. Joe and Mr. stevens will climbed to the top of the volcano. *(Stevens; climb)*

8. They finaly heard about their two friend's hike on the volcano. *(finally; friends')*

9. The side of Mount St. helens had come off in 1980? *(Helens; 1980.)*

10. Many families homes was lost. *(families'; were)*

Unit 3   Volcanoes: Nature's Incredible Fireworks

Daily Fix-It **15**

© Pearson Education

Daily Fix-Its   **TR5**

DAILY FIX-IT

1. He flyed safly. *(flew; safely)*

2. The world look diferent from up in the sky. *(looks; different)*

3. The boy flew high in the sky, and they got in troubel for it. *(he; trouble)*

4. Did the boy learn a lessen. *(lesson?)*

5. Childen doesn't have wings, but birds do. *(Children; don't)*

6. Peopel move around with their feets. *(People; feet)*

7. Do the boys classmates disslike him? *(boy's; dislike)*

8. The kids think he is strang, but he like him. *(strange, but they)*

9. The girl worried about the boy but he was all right. *(worried; boy,)*

10. What a helpfull girl she was. *(helpful; was!)*

DAILY FIX-IT

1. Some of the worst weather in the world is in antarctica. *(world; Antarctica)*

2. The days is freezing there even in summer. *(are; freezing)*

3. Terry and me read about Mount everest. *(I; Everest)*

4. Its the highest mountain on the erth. *(It's; earth)*

5. Mr. Jackson showed Tracy and I a picture of cammels in the desert. *(me; camels)*

6. Sand were blowing in the dessert like a snowstorm. *(was; desert)*

7. Is Africas river the longest in the world. *(Africa's; world?)*

8. Many unusuall animals lives there. *(unusual; live)*

9. The clime up the mountain was too hard for Joe and she. *(climb; her)*

10. She slipped and she hurt hurself. *(slipped,; herself)*

DAILY FIX-IT

1. Colin and him find rocks in many places out doors. *(he; outdoors)*

2. The rocks in my poket has gold flecks. *(pocket; have)*

3. The strangeest rocks are her's. *(strangest; hers)*

4. Didnt she find them in the Middwest? *(Didn't; Midwest)*

5. That black rock of theirs's is unknown to me. *(theirs; unknown)*

6. The yellow rock was found in the camp ground by Juan and he. *(campground; him)*

7. Hers green rock was finded in South America. *(Her; found)*

8. Rob and them displayed the rocks in Ms. Shaws' room. *(they; Shaw's)*

9. The small rock is mine and the big one is your. *(mine.; yours)*

10. Can we put them both in the disply case. *(display; case?)*

DAILY FIX-IT

21

1. The little girl wore a beautifull dress from japan.
   (beautiful; Japan)

2. She was prowd of the dress that her grandmother gived her. *(proud; gave)*

3. The girls sisters told her not to wear a unusual costume.
   (girl's; an)

4. She didnt listen to her two sisters advice. *(didn't; sisters')*

5. The classes weared costumes and clothes from other countrys. *(wore; countries)*

6. James and him dressed like cowboys in a rodio. *(he; rodeo)*

7. Now Cara and Linda has a idea for a party. *(have; an)*

8. Childrens will bring food from diffrent countries.
   (Children; different)

9. Polly will creat a salad from spain. *(create; Spain)*

10. The students will enjoy they're meal from around the werld. *(their; world)*

DAILY FIX-IT

20

1. An eagle sudenly appeared on the Ridge. *(suddenly; ridge)*

2. The eagles flight took us by surprise. *(eagle's; surprise)*

3. The bald eagle live high on top the cliff. *(lives; top of)*

4. It seems like the bigest bird in the wirld. *(biggest; world)*

5. Jamal has saw a movie bout eagles. *(seen; about)*

6. They builds nests with sticks and leafs. *(build; leaves)*

7. The eagle is diveing into the Pond. *(diving; pond)*

8. The childdren were interested of the eagle's dives.
   (children; interested in)

9. Tamara and me couldnt find Dad's coin with an eagle's picture. *(I couldn't)*

10. Its worth a lot of mony. *(It's; money)*

DAILY FIX-IT

19

1. Isnt Brian the best swimer on the team? *(Isn't; swimmer)*

2. He gos to the pool for a work out every morning.
   (goes; workout)

3. The swimmer jump into the pool with a spelash.
   (jumps or jumped; splash)

4. A tuter will helped her with some strokes. *(tutor; help)*

5. Didnt you learn the backstroke. *(Didn't; backstroke?)*

6. He do the backstroke in races but the crawl is faster.
   (does; races,)

7. Hurry, or you'll miss you're swimming leson.
   (your; lesson)

8. Julia and her left really erly. *(she; early)*

9. Beths race is next, and her coatch is talking to her.
   (Beth's; coach)

10. The winer will go to the finals in new york.
    (winner; New York)

DAILY FIX-IT

22

1. Juans family came from Puerto Rico to weeks ago.
(*Juan's; two*)

2. Which is the biggest city, San Juan or New york?
(*bigger; York*)

3. The family had went to Africa and had enjoyed being turists. (*gone; tourists*)

4. It was the most greatest trip they had ever took.
(*the greatest; taken*)

5. Mom will right a letter to her nefew in China.
(*write; nephew*)

6. Isnt he a great violen player? (*Isn't; violin*)

7. Lee new english before she moved to America.
(*knew; English*)

8. Dan and her helped their parents with new werds.
(*she; words*)

9. Of all of the familys, the Gomezes had the easier time finding a home. (*families; easiest*)

10. They was helpfull to others who came from Cuba.
(*were; helpful*)

Unit 5   How My Family Lives in America   Daily Fix-It

DAILY FIX-IT

23

1. Jangmi moved happy into her knew home. (*happily; new*)

2. Her familys' house has a big laun. (*family's; lawn*)

3. The family landed safe in they're new country.
(*safely; their*)

4. Her parents and her were afraid she would disslike the new place. (*she; dislike*)

5. Jangmi and she has allmost finished unpacking the pretty things for her room. (*have; almost*)

6. She has did it very cheerful. (*has done; cheerfully*)

7. The Korean girls' had an American dish with sawsages.
(*girls; sausages*)

8. American foods is cooked different than Korean foods.
(*are; differently*)

9. Was the voiage from Asia hard for Mom and she?
(*voyage; her*)

10. It wasnt the easyest trip for them. (*wasn't; easiest*)

Unit 5   Good -Bye, 382 Shin Dang Dong   Daily Fix-It

DAILY FIX-IT

24

1. Marias mom tought her to bake bread. (*Maria's; taught*)

2. Her flower was sifted more sooner than mine.
(*flour; sifted sooner*)

3. Blake and her put wallnuts in the banana bread.
(*she; walnuts*)

4. You aught to drink a glass of Milk. (*ought; milk*)

5. The students is having blue berry muffins for a snack.
(*are; blueberry*)

6. I can finnish mine fastest than you. (*finish; faster*)

7. Charles had went to school more earlier than Ms. Lawrence. (*gone; school earlier*)

8. He braught a big bassket of bagels. (*brought; basket*)

9. Matt creeated a knew recipe for muffins. (*created; new*)

10. The muffins has strawberrys inside. (*have strawberries*)

Unit 5   Jalapeño Bagels   Daily Fix-It

DAILY FIX-IT

25

1. Jeffs uncle lives in a city neighborhood.
   (Jeff's; neighborhood)
2. His sister and him visits Uncle Jim every summer.
   (he; visit)
3. It was a rainey day, and we played baseball anyway.
   (rainy; but)
4. I played in the outfield, and catched a fly ball.
   (outfield and; caught)
5. My mom spent her child hood in New York city.
   (childhood; City)
6. She say it is busiest there than in North Carolina.
   (says; busier)
7. Her and me lived with our familys in New York City.
   (She and I; families)
8. On Sunday, childrn feed the ducks and gooses in Central Park. *(children; geese)*
9. There is much trafic in the city, there is not much in the country. *(traffic; city, but)*
10. Arent the city sights interesting to James and she?
    (Aren't; her)

DAILY FIX-IT

26

1. The classes visits the Washington Monument on tuesday.
   (visit; Tuesday)
2. is the Statue of Liberty or the Washington Monument biggest? *(Is; bigger)*
3. Maria and her daugter came to the United States in november. *(daughter; November)*
4. The Statue of Liberty greeted Maria and she. *(greeted; her)*
5. Didnt you climb to the top of the statue on Toosday?
   (Didn't; Tuesday)
6. You cant go to the top anymore but you can go inside the base. *(can't; anymore, but)*
7. Fue people has saw the Statue of Liberty until 1886.
   (Few; had seen)
8. The statues torch shines over every one. *(statue's; everyone)*
9. When the Statue of Liberty was finally presented, president Grover Cleveland gave a speech. *(finally; President)*
10. Mr. and mrs. Adams watched fireworks expload in the harbor. *(Mrs.; explode)*

DAILY FIX-IT

27

1. Did Mr Kang's pet fly all the way from China.
   (Mr.; China?)
2. Most birds cant' traval across the ocean. *(can't travel)*
3. I allways look at the birds in the cage in dr. Robinson's office. *(always; Dr.)*
4. Ms. Sanchez and him clean the cage dayly. *(he; daily)*
5. This bird has bright feathers and it sings a cheerfull song. *(feathers, and; cheerful)*
6. It's musick makes me feel happy. *(Its; music)*
7. The women was affraid the bird would fly away.
   (were; afraid)
8. The bird dissappeared on Feb 2. *(disappeared; Feb.)*
9. The old man feel selfesh because the bird wants its freedom. *(feels; selfish)*
10. Can the bird live out side in the Winter safely?
    (outside; winter)

DAILY FIX-IT

1. Carlos and Maria created a mural about they're cullture.
(their; culture)

2. The class helped Carlos and she with the desine.
(her; design)

3. The classes paints the mural on a large wall of the shcool. (paint; school)

4. We didnt know what great artests we had. (didn't; artists)

5. The class's mural feachures a celebration, and is painted in bright colors. (features; celebration and)

6. The mural is the most biggest piece of art in the neighbor hood. (the biggest; neighborhood)

7. Carlos begun a sculpchure to go with the mural.
(began; sculpture)

8. He is making it out of clay and he will finish it next tuesday. (clay, and; Tuesday)

9. The mural was a success and the class will paint unother soon. (success, and; another)

10. What subjec will they choose for the next mural.
(subject; mural?)

DAILY FIX-IT

1. Dr Allen studys insects in his lab. (Dr.; studies)

2. He carefuly looks at ants, bees and butterflies.
(carefully; bees,)

3. Ants are remarkabel insects but sometimes they are pests. (remarkable; insects,)

4. They will go after the littlest crums in you're kitchen.
(crumbs; your)

5. We learned about ants's strenth, and it is amazing.
(ants'; strength)

6. Did you know an ant can lift something ten times heavyer than its body. (heavier; body?)

7. The Masons and Marks went to a lake cabin for a vacasion on March 16 2005. (vacation; 16,)

8. The families was unprapared for the ants and other insects there. (were; unprepared)

9. Tommy found a anthill out side his house. (an; outside)

10. He staring at the tiny creetures for hours.
(was staring; creatures)

DAILY FIX-IT

1. Tina and me enjoy the naturel world in the desert.
(I; natural)

2. Tina said "I thouht I saw a snake." (said,; thought)

3. Doesnt the warm sun in the desert feel pleasent?
(Doesn't; pleasant)

4. The desert animels rests during the day. (animals; rest)

5. Roadrunners are birds and they usual live in the desert.
(birds,; usually)

6. Joe said, "Roadrunners are abel to run 15 miles per hour". (able; hour.")

7. Tina said, "I wonder if there are wolfs in the desert.
(wolves; desert.")

8. Coyotes live in the desert and they are members of the dog family to. (desert,; too)

9. Coyotes, wolves and foxs are all members of the dog family. (wolves,; foxes)

10. Chris and him hear coyotes howling in the desert in july.
(he; July)

Differentiated Instruction and Extra Practice

LESSON 1 **Sentences**

Write *S* if the group of words is a sentence. Write *F* if the group of words is a fragment.

1. The woman is happy. S
2. Driving down a country road. F
3. A break from work for everyone. F
4. The stores open early. S
5. On Friday and Saturday mornings. F

LESSON 2 **Subjects and Predicates**

Write each sentence. Underline the complete subject. Circle the complete predicate.

1. <u>The garden</u> has many kinds of trees.
2. <u>Everyone in my family</u> works in the garden.
3. <u>Many children</u> visit the library on Saturday.
4. <u>My favorite books</u> tell about faraway places.
5. <u>The people in the book club</u> read nonfiction books.

LESSON 3 **Statements and Questions**

Write *statement* if the sentence tells something. Write *question* if the sentence asks something.

1. How do I save money? question
2. I do chores for the neighbors. statement
3. My allowance goes into my bank account. statement
4. What do you do? question
5. I do not have a plan yet. statement

LESSON 4 **Commands and Exclamations**

Write *command* if the sentence is a command or *exclamation* if the sentence is an exclamation.

1. Please hand me that coin. command
2. The new nickel is so shiny! exclamation
3. Look on the other side. command
4. What an interesting picture that is! exclamation
5. Read the words around the edge. command

LESSON 5 **Compound Sentences**

Write *S* if the sentence is a simple sentence. Write *C* if the sentence is a compound sentence.

1. The family plants crops in the fields. S
2. Some years are good, but other years are not. C
3. The corn and the beans grew well this year. S
4. Last summer was hot, and it did not rain enough. C
5. They must love farming, or they would not do it. C

LESSON 6   Common and Proper Nouns

Write *C* if the underlined noun is a common noun. Write *P* if the underlined noun is a proper noun.

1. <u>Antarctica</u> is covered with ice and snow.   P
2. <u>Winter</u> lasts from May through August.   C
3. December to <u>February</u> is summer.   P
4. Roald Amundsen was a Norwegian <u>explorer</u>.   C
5. He reached the <u>South Pole</u> on December 14, 1911.   P

LESSON 7   Singular and Plural Nouns

Write *S* if the underlined noun is singular. Write *P* if the underlined noun is plural.

1. Once there were many small <u>farms</u> in our country.   P
2. Farmers and their <u>families</u> grew their own food.   P
3. We get our food from a <u>store</u>.   S
4. A <u>farmer</u> traveled in a wagon.   S
5. Today people travel in cars and <u>buses</u>.   P

LESSON 8   Irregular Plural Nouns

Write *S* if the underlined noun is singular. Write *P* if the underlined noun is plural.

1. The <u>children</u> have a pet parade.   P
2. Tim brings three white <u>mice</u>.   P
3. A pet <u>goose</u> wears a straw hat.   S
4. That dog has boots on its <u>feet</u>.   P
5. One girl walked with a <u>sheep</u>.   S

LESSON 9   Singular Possessive Nouns

Write the singular possessive form of the underlined noun in each sentence.

1. Gus visits his <u>grandmother</u> farm.   grandmother's
2. He cleans out the <u>horse</u> stall.   horse's
3. Gus brings in the <u>hen</u> eggs.   hen's
4. He drops the <u>cow</u> hay over the fence.   cow's
5. <u>Gus</u> grandmother thanks him for his help.   Gus's

LESSON 10   Plural Possessive Nouns

Write the possessive form of the underlined plural noun in each sentence.

1. The families journey ended in Plymouth, Massachusetts.   families'
2. The men agreement was called the Mayflower Compact.   men's
3. They did not ask for the women signatures.   women's
4. The colonists plan was a simple one.   colonists'
5. All male residents votes counted the same.   residents'

LESSON 11 Action and Linking Verbs

Write the verb in each sentence. Write *A* after an action verb. Write *L* after a linking verb.

1. Uncle Josh is a gardener. L
2. Each winter he buys many kinds of seeds. A
3. The seeds are in small cups of soil. L
4. By spring the seeds grow into tiny plants. A
5. Uncle Josh puts the plants in his garden. A

LESSON 12 Main and Helping Verbs

Look at the underlined verb in each sentence. Write *M* if it is a main verb. Write *H* if it is a helping verb.

1. Many people are visiting Mesa Verde. M
2. The Anasazi had built it long ago. H
3. The park ranger has told us about them. M
4. We will climb to the top of that building. H
5. I am looking at the beautiful view. H

LESSON 13 Subject-Verb Agreement

Choose the verb in ( ) that agrees with the subject. Write the sentence.

1. The boys (is, are) camping in the woods.
2. The night (is, are) dark and noisy.
3. Cicadas (chirps, chirp) in the trees.
4. A mosquito (whines, whine) loudly.
5. Sam and Ed (slaps, slap) at it.

LESSON 14 Present, Past, and Future Tenses

Tell the tense of the underlined verb in each sentence. Write *present, past,* or *future.*

1. Tough skin covers the whale's body. present
2. Water will slip easily over its skin. future
3. The whale raised its tail above the water. past
4. Now it will dive down deep. future
5. Fish hurried away from the whale. past

LESSON 15 Irregular Verbs

Write the correct form of the irregular verb in ( ) to complete each sentence.

1. A man (saw, seen) smoke above the volcano.
2. He has (run, ran) to the village.
3. People (went, gone) away quickly.
4. They have (took, taken) the road west.
5. Most had (find, found) shelter in the next village.

LESSON 16   Singular and Plural Pronouns

Write *S* if the underlined pronoun is singular or *P* if it is plural.

1. Becky and I studied the Wright brothers. **S**
2. Orville and Wilbur built gliders and flew them on the beach. **P**
3. They learned many things from the gliders. **P**
4. They made a new engine, and it worked well. **S**
5. We admire their years of hard work. **P**

LESSON 17   Subject and Object Pronouns

Write *SP* if the underlined pronoun is a subject pronoun. Write *OP* if it is an object pronoun.

1. My sister and I visited Hawaii Volcanoes National Park. **SP**
2. The volcanoes thrilled Jenny and me. **OP**
3. I took a picture of her on the black rocks. **OP**
4. A ranger showed us a lava flow at night. **OP**
5. It glowed and hissed on its way to the sea. **SP**

LESSON 18   Possessive Pronouns

Write the possessive pronoun in each sentence.

1. Dan looks for rocks on his hikes.
2. Sharon looks for plants on hers.
3. They only take pictures on their hikes.
4. We frame and hang our pictures.
5. What do you do with yours?

LESSON 19   Contractions

Write the contraction in each sentence. Then write the words that make up the contraction.

1. You're reading about Natalie Coughlin, my favorite athlete. **You are**
2. I hadn't heard of Janet Evans, who competed in 1988. **had not**
3. Wasn't John Nabor a well-known swimmer? **Was not**
4. Michael Phelps is young, and he's already had a great career. **he has**
5. Many swimmers have won medals, and they won't be forgotten. **will not**

LESSON 20   Prepositions

Write the prepositional phrase in each sentence. Underline the preposition.

1. A hummingbird came to our window.
2. It hovered above the feeder.
3. Inside the bottle was red sugar water.
4. The bird sucks the water through its long beak.
5. Sometimes it perches on a twig.

LESSON 21   Adjectives and Articles

Write the adjectives, including the articles, in each sentence.
The number in ( ) tells you how many are in the sentence.

1. <u>The</u> <u>happy</u> fans waved <u>small</u> <u>red</u> flags. (4)
2. <u>Three</u> men held up <u>an</u> <u>enormous</u> banner. (3)
3. <u>A</u> boy waited for <u>a</u> <u>favorite</u> player. (3)
4. <u>The</u> <u>noisy</u> crowd cheered for <u>the</u> <u>best</u> batter. (4)
5. <u>The</u> <u>two</u> teams played <u>an</u> <u>extra</u> inning. (4)

LESSON 22   Adjectives That Compare

Write the adjective that compares in each sentence.

1. Hong Kong has the <u>busiest</u> market I have ever seen.
2. It is <u>bigger</u> than the market in Beijing.
3. Winters in China are <u>colder</u> than in Thailand.
4. Of the three countries, Japan had the <u>nicest</u> trains.
5. The temples in Bangkok are <u>fancier</u> than those in Tokyo.

LESSON 23   Adverbs

Write the adverb in each sentence. Then write whether the adverb tells *when, where,* or *how.*

1. <u>Today</u> George moved to a new town. when
2. He misses his old friends <u>badly</u>. how
3. George sits on the steps <u>outside</u>. where
4. Children are playing in a park <u>nearby</u>. where
5. <u>Soon</u> George will have new friends. when

LESSON 24   Adverbs That Compare

Write the adverb that compares in each sentence.

1. Sean picks vegetables <u>more carefully</u> than Dana.
2. Chris picks vegetables <u>slowest</u> of all.
3. Dana chops vegetables <u>faster</u> than Chris.
4. Of the three cooks, Sean chops <u>most quickly</u>.
5. Dana uses vegetables <u>most creatively</u> of any cook in the city.

LESSON 25   Conjunctions

Write the conjunction in each sentence.

1. New York has many interesting neighborhoods, <u>and</u> one of them is Harlem.
2. Harlem is not a wealthy area, <u>but</u> it is a lively one.
3. Do you know any Harlem writers <u>or</u> musicians?
4. Langston Hughes <u>and</u> Duke Ellington are two examples.
5. Did Hughes write books, <u>or</u> did he mostly write poems?

LESSON 26 **Capital Letters**

Write correctly the words in each sentence that should have capital letters. If a sentence has no capitalization mistakes, write *C*.

1. Last week mrs. liu and dr. diaz had a meeting.
2. They planned a parade for memorial day.
3. It is always on the last monday in may.
4. My aunt and uncle always ride in an old car. C
5. I laugh at aunt sylvia's goggles and big hat.

LESSON 27 **Abbreviations**

Write each abbreviation. Be sure to capitalize letters and use periods correctly. If a phrase is correct, write *C*.

1. C.L.berry
2. jan.31
3. dr.Susan Reiner
4. Wed., June 7 C
5. Mrs.m.e.Morgan
6. fri,.sept .13
7. Miss D. W. Caras C
8. sun., dec. 28
9. mr.Henry G.Levine
10. Apr. 10 C

LESSON 28 **Combining Sentences**

Combine each pair of short sentences into a compound sentence. Use a comma and the conjunction in ( ).

1. The cave painters drew animals. They did not draw plants. (but)
2. Were animals more important? Did they just like animals better? (or)
3. Some artists paint the same subject. Others paint different subjects. (and)
4. Mel draws only trees. Annie draws only cats. (and)
5. I draw trees and cats. I also draw many other things. (but)

Lesson 28:
1. The cave painters drew animals, but they did not draw plants.
2. Were animals more important, or did they just like animals better?
3. Some artists paint the same subject, and others paint different subjects.
4. Mel draws only trees, and Annie draws only cats.
5. I draw trees and cats, but I also draw many other things.

LESSON 29 **Commas**

Write *C* if commas are used correctly in each line.
Write *NC* if commas are not used correctly.

1. Dear Dion   NC
2. My bag is packed and I have my ticket to Logan, Utah.   NC
3. Don't forget to bring your boots hat and pack.   NC
4. See you on Friday May 2007! NC
5. Your cousin,   C
   Chantal

LESSON 30 **Quotations**

Write *C* if a sentence is correct. If it is not correct, make the corrections that are needed.

1. "Glass is good for cooking and baking,"Mary said.
2. Avril noted,"Cups, bowls, and plates can be made of glass."
3. "We drink from glasses made of glass!" Shane pointed out. C
4. Cole asked, "Can you make glass knives, forks, and spoons?"
5."That wouldn't be a good idea!"laughed Emma.

Strategies and Activities
for Developing Writing Traits

Focus/Ideas

Big to Small On the board, write a general topic, such as Food. Have students think of smaller, more specific topics related to the general topic. Write their topics and discuss why they are more suitable for student writing assignments.

Food Snack Foods Homemade Snacks How to Make Trail Mix
Food Vegetables Carrots The Rabbit Who Loved Carrots
Food Chinese Food Moo Shu The Best Moo Shu in Town

Main Idea and Details Make copies of short nonfiction articles from encyclopedias or textbooks. Give the copies to pairs of students. Have them circle the main idea sentence and underline the detail sentences. Let pairs present their articles to the group and explain their markings. Alternatively, black out or cut off the main idea sentences. Ask students to write main idea sentences that go with the detail sentences. Have them compare their main idea sentences to the original sentences.

Organization

Graphic Organizers Remind students to use a graphic organizer to organize their details before they begin writing.

- *Venn diagram for a compare/contrast essay.* Write the traits that are unique to each thing in each outer circle. Write the traits the two things have in common in the center section.

- *Story chart for a story.* List the characters, setting, problem, events in order, and solution.

- *Persuasion chart for a persuasive letter or essay.* State your opinion or goal, list your reasons in order from least to most important, and think of a good conclusion.

- *Word web for a description.* In the center circle, write the subject you are describing. In the outer circles, write details about your subject.

Strong Openers Point out to students that the first sentence of their writing is important; it should grab readers' attention and make them want to read on. Here are some good ways to begin:

- Ask a question. *Why was it so quiet in the house?*
- Tell a surprising fact. *Porcupines always have four babies.*
- Talk to the reader. *Your room is your private place.*
- Use a quotation. *"Time is money," Benjamin Franklin said.*

Read aloud stories and articles that have strong openers. Ask students how the openers grab their attention.

Voice

Listen for Voice Read aloud passages from works with different and clearly identifiable voices, such as a math textbook, a humorous poem, and a Grimms' fairy tale. Ask students to identify the voice in each work. If necessary, prompt with questions: *Is the voice serious? funny? scary?* Have students match each work with the adjective that best describes its voice.

Add Voice Write several plain sentences on the board. Ask students to add personality to the sentences by adding adjectives, adverbs, and prepositional phrases. Have volunteers read aloud their elaborated sentences.

A tiger slept.
In the cage on the left, a large Siberian tiger slept peacefully with its head on its paws.

Create a Voice Assign each student a different animal, such as cat, monkey, cow, zebra, duck, lion, rabbit, and hippo. Ask students to imagine that they are this animal and they can talk. What would they sound like? What kind of personality would they have? Have students write a paragraph using the voice they have created for their animal. Let them read their paragraphs aloud to the group.

Word Choice

Show, Don't Tell Remind students that when they write, they should show rather than tell readers how they feel. On the board, write these sentences that tell and ask students to rewrite them using vivid descriptions and details that show.

I was afraid.	*Goosebumps rose on my arms, and I shivered from my head to my toes.*
I was happy.	*My grin was so huge that you could see it a mile away.*
I was hungry.	*My stomach growled loudly, and my legs wobbled in opposite directions.*

Use Clear Words Explain to students that using clear words means using exact nouns, strong verbs, and vivid adjectives. These kinds of words will help make their writing clearer, easier, and more interesting to read. Give students the following sentences and have them replace the underlined nouns, verbs, and adjectives with stronger, more vivid words.

Put the pretty pillow into the thing.
Toss the yellow silk pillow into the basket.

The girl got a nice dress at the place.
Maddie bought a black velvet dress at Design Depot.

Combine Sentences Too many short sentences in a row makes writing sound choppy. It will sound smoother if students combine some of the sentences using the conjunctions *and, but,* and *or.* Sentences can be combined *only* if they are about the same topic.

> I got out the forks. Tonight's dinner was meat loaf. *(No)*
>
> I got out the forks. Jaime brought the plates. *(Yes)*
>
> I got out the forks, and Jaime brought the plates.

Short and Long Point out that just as students should avoid writing too many short, choppy sentences, they should also avoid writing long, stringy sentences. Combine several sentences from a familiar story using the word *and* and write the composite sentence on the board. Ask students to help you rewrite this long, stringy sentence.

Conventions

Why Conventions? Show students that conventions are rules that help make their writing clear. Write the following sentence on the board and discuss different ways to punctuate it:

> Juan Carlos Mary Claire and Nadia brought bread pudding fruit salad and ice to Seth's house.
>
> *Juan, Carlos, Mary, Claire, and Nadia brought bread, pudding, fruit, salad, and ice to Seth's house.*
>
> *Juan Carlos, Mary Claire, and Nadia brought bread pudding, fruit salad, and ice to Seth's house.*

Read aloud the sentences and have students discuss how changing the punctuation changes the meaning of the sentence.

Proof It Remind students to always proofread, or check their work for capitalization, punctuation, grammar, and usage errors. Here are some proofreading strategies they can use:

- Read their work aloud.
- Keep a dictionary handy to check their spelling of words.
- Have a partner check their work.
- Read their work several times and look for one kind of error each time.

Tech Tips If students use computers to write or edit their work, suggest that they follow these tips:

- Don't rely only on a computer spell check. It can't catch all spelling errors. Proofread carefully and use a dictionary.
- Use the Print Preview or Page Layout feature to see how your writing will look before you print it out.
- Don't guess how to use a computer feature. Use the Help menu or ask a friend for help.

Prompts

Narrative Writing

You are playing outside when, whoosh, a strange-looking spaceship lands in the street. As you stare at it, a hatch pops open and out comes . . . . Write a story about what happens.

Key Features
Story

- Has a beginning, middle, and end
- Focuses on one incident or event
- Uses time-order words to show the sequence of events
- Has characters, plot, and a setting

Descriptive Writing

Describe your favorite room in your home. Tell what it looks, sounds, smells, and feels like. Give vivid details. Make readers feel as if they are standing in the room.

Key Features
Description

- Creates word pictures for readers
- Can be organized in space order, such as top-to-bottom
- Uses vivid words that appeal to senses

Persuasive Writing

You think you are old enough to have a later bedtime. Write a letter to your parents. Persuade them to agree with you. Give at least three good reasons. Save the best reason for last.

Key Features
Persuasive Essay

- Is written in correct letter format
- Uses persuasive words such as *must* or *best*
- Uses reasons, facts, and examples to make a point
- Often organizes facts in order of importance

What jobs do you do at home? Choose one job, such as setting the table, making your bed, or caring for a pet. Write a report that tells the steps for doing this job.

Key Features
How-to Report

- Explains a task fully
- Uses words like first to show the order of the steps
- Provides necessary information and details
- Has clear sentences to guide readers

Think of two people you know well, such as family members, relatives, or friends. Write an essay comparing and contrasting at least three things about these two people.

Key Features
Compare/Contrast Essay

- Compares and contrasts two things
- Uses transition words and details to show likenesses and differences
- Follows a pattern of organization
- Has a clear topic sentence

Narrative Writing Rubric

Rubric	6	5	4	3	2	1
Focus/Ideas	Excellent, focused narrative; many details	Good, focused narrative; sufficient details	Focused narrative; adequate details	Fairly focused narrative; several details	Often unfocused narrative; needs more details	Narrative with no development, focus, or details
Organization/ Paragraphs	Clear sequence of events with time-order words	Mostly clear sequence with some time-order words	Generally clear sequence with one or two time-order words	Fairly clear sequence with some lapses	Confused sequence of events	Incoherent or nonexistent sequence
Voice	Sincere, engaging, and unique voice	Generally sincere and engaging	Pleasant voice but not compelling or unique	Sincere but not engaging or original	No clear, original voice	Uninvolved or indifferent voice
Word Choice	Many vivid descriptive words that show instead of tell	Some vivid words that show instead of tell	Several vivid words that show instead of tell	Tries to use one or two vivid words that show instead of tell	Few vivid words that show instead of tell	No attempt to show instead of tell
Sentences	Clear and varied sentences	Mostly clear sentences with some variety	Generally clear sentences; tries for variety	Some sentences unclear; needs more variety	Many sentences unclear; little or no variety	Incoherent or short, choppy sentences
Conventions	Few, if any, errors	Several minor errors	Some errors	Several major errors	Many errors	Numerous errors

Rubric	5	4	3	2	1
Focus/Ideas	Excellent, focused narrative; many details	Good, focused narrative; sufficient details	Focused narrative; adequate details	Often unfocused narrative; needs more details	Narrative with no development, focus, or details
Organization/ Paragraphs	Clear sequence of events with time-order words	Mostly clear sequence with some time-order words	Generally clear sequence with one or two time-order words	Confused sequence of events	Incoherent or nonexistent sequence
Voice	Sincere, engaging, and unique voice	Generally sincere and engaging	Pleasant voice but not compelling or unique	No clear, original voice	Uninvolved or indifferent voice
Word Choice	Many vivid descriptive words that show instead of tell	Some vivid words that show instead of tell	Several vivid words that show instead of tell	Few vivid words that show instead of tell	No attempt to show instead of tell
Sentences	Clear, varied sentences	Mostly clear sentences with some variety	Generally clear sentences with some variety	Some sentences unclear; little or no variety	Incoherent or short, choppy sentences
Conventions	Few, if any, errors	Several minor errors	Some errors	Many errors	Numerous errors

Rubric	4	3	2	1
Focus/Ideas	Excellent, focused narrative; many details	Good, focused narrative; sufficient details	Often unfocused narrative; needs more details	Narrative with no development, focus, or details
Organization/ Paragraphs	Clear sequence of events with time-order words	Reasonably clear sequence with one or two lapses	Confused sequence of events	Incoherent or nonexistent sequence
Voice	Sincere, engaging, and unique voice	Generally sincere and engaging	No clear, original voice	Uninvolved or indifferent voice
Word Choice	Many vivid descriptive words that show instead of tell	Some vivid words that show instead of tell	Few vivid words that show instead of tell	No attempt to show instead of tell
Sentences	Clear, varied sentences	Generally clear sentences with some variety	Some sentences unclear; little or no variety	Incoherent or short, choppy sentences
Conventions	Few, if any, errors	Several minor errors	Many errors	Numerous errors

Descriptive Writing Rubric

Rubric	6	5	4	3	2	1
Focus/Ideas	Excellent, focused description; many strong, vivid details	Good, focused description; some good, vivid details	Description focused; some good details	Description generally focused; some details	Description not always focused; needs more vivid details	Description not focused; no vivid details
Organization/ Paragraphs	Topic introduced at beginning; details in sequence	Topic introduced at beginning; details mostly in sequence	Topic stated; details generally in order	Topic not stated at beginning; some details out of order	Topic not introduced at beginning; details confused	Topic not introduced; no order to details
Voice	Clearly shows feelings about topic	Shows some feelings about topic	Shows interest in topic	Tries to show interest in topic	Shows few or no feelings about topic	Not involved with topic
Word Choice	Many vivid sensory words and strong verbs	Some vivid sensory words and strong verbs	Several sensory words or strong verbs	One or two sensory words or strong verbs	Few sensory words or strong verbs	No sensory words or strong verbs
Sentences	Smooth sentences; different kinds	Most sentences smooth; some different kinds	Sentences generally smooth; some variety	Several stringy or choppy sentences; little variety	Many stringy or choppy sentences	Confusing, incomplete, or choppy sentences
Conventions	Few or no errors	No serious errors	Some errors	Some serious errors	Many errors	Many serious errors

Rubric	5	4	3	2	1
Focus/Ideas	Excellent, focused description; many strong, vivid details	Good, focused description; some good, vivid details	Description focused; some good details	Description not always focused; needs more vivid details	Description not focused; no vivid details
Organization/ Paragraphs	Topic introduced at beginning; details in sequence	Topic introduced at beginning; details mostly in sequence	Topic stated; details generally in order	Topic not introduced at beginning; details confused	Topic not introduced; no order to details
Voice	Clearly shows feelings about topic	Shows some feelings about topic	Shows interest in topic	Shows few or no feelings about topic	Not involved with topic
Word Choice	Many vivid sensory words and strong verbs	Some vivid sensory words and strong verbs	Several sensory words or strong verbs	Few sensory words or strong verbs	No sensory words or strong verbs
Sentences	Smooth sentences; different kinds	Most sentences smooth; some different kinds	Sentences generally smooth; some variety	Many stringy or choppy sentences	Confusing, incomplete, or choppy sentences
Conventions	Few or no errors	No serious errors	Some errors	Many errors	Many serious errors

Rubric	4	3	2	1
Focus/Ideas	Excellent, focused description; many strong, vivid details	Good, focused description; some good, vivid details	Description not always focused; needs more vivid details	Description not focused; no vivid details
Organization/ Paragraphs	Topic introduced at beginning; details in sequence	Topic introduced at beginning; details mostly in sequence	Topic not introduced at beginning; details confused	Topic not introduced; no order to details
Voice	Clearly shows feelings about topic	Shows some feelings about topic	Shows few or no feelings about topic	Not involved with topic
Word Choice	Many vivid sensory words and strong verbs	Some vivid sensory words and strong verbs	Few sensory words or strong verbs	No sensory words or strong verbs
Sentences	Smooth sentences; different kinds	Most sentences smooth; some different kinds	Many stringy or choppy sentences	Confusing, incomplete, or choppy sentences
Conventions	Few or no errors	No serious errors	Many errors	Many serious errors

Persuasive Writing Rubric

Rubric	6	5	4	3	2	1
Focus/Ideas	Well-focused argument with clear, well-developed details	Focused argument with clear details	Generally focused argument; details with some support	Argument with few lapses in focus; details attempted	Argument lacking focus; unclear details	Argument with no focus; no clear details
Organization/ Paragraphs	Excellent organization and supporting reasons	Good organization and supporting reasons	Adequate organization and supporting reasons	Some organization and support attempted	Not very organized; few supporting reasons	No organization or supporting reasons
Voice	Convincing, compelling voice	Clear, usually convincing voice	Pleasant but not compelling voice	Sincere but not fully engaged writer	Unconvincing voice	No distinct voice
Word Choice	Uses strong persuasive words well	Uses many persuasive words	Some persuasive words	Words with little persuasive power	Few persuasive words	No persuasive words
Sentences	Correct sentences; varied lengths	Correct, usually varied sentences	Correct sentences; some variety	Overly simple sentences; no variety	Some sentences incorrect	Incorrect sentences; run-ons
Conventions	Few, if any, errors	Several minor errors	Few serious errors	Some errors that confuse	Many errors	Numerous errors

Rubric	5	4	3	2	1
Focus/Ideas	Well-focused argument with clear, well-developed details	Generally focused argument with clear details	Argument with few lapses in focus; generally clear details	Argument lacking focus; unclear details	Argument with no focus; no clear details
Organization/ Paragraphs	Excellent organization and supporting reasons	Good organization and supporting reasons	Adequate organization and supporting reasons	Not very organized; few supporting reasons	No organization or supporting reasons
Voice	Convincing, compelling voice	Clear, usually convincing voice	Pleasant but not compelling voice	Unconvincing voice	No distinct voice
Word Choice	Uses strong persuasive words well	Uses many persuasive words	Some persuasive words	Few persuasive words	No persuasive words
Sentences	Correct sentences; varied lengths	Correct, usually varied sentences	Correct sentences with some variety	Some sentences incorrect	Incorrect sentences; run-ons
Conventions	Few, if any, errors	Several minor errors	Few confusing errors	Many errors	Numerous errors

Rubric	4	3	2	1
Focus/Ideas	Well-focused argument with clear, well-developed details	Generally focused argument with clear details	Argument lacking focus; unclear details	Argument with no focus; no clear details
Organization/ Paragraphs	Excellent organization and supporting reasons	Good organization and supporting reasons	Not very organized; few supporting reasons	No organization or supporting reasons
Voice	Convincing, compelling voice	Clear, usually convincing voice	Unconvincing voice	No distinct voice
Word Choice	Uses strong persuasive words well	Uses many persuasive words	Few persuasive words	No persuasive words
Sentences	Correct sentences; varied lengths	Correct, usually varied sentences	Some sentences incorrect	Incorrect sentences; run-ons
Conventions	Few, if any, errors	Several minor errors	Many errors	Numerous errors

Expository Writing Rubric

Rubric	6	5	4	3	2	1
Focus/Ideas	Exposition with strong focus on topic	Exposition with good focus on topic	Exposition generally focused	Exposition sometimes unfocused	Exposition with weak focus	Exposition with no focus
Organization/ Paragraphs	Strong topic sentences; many supporting details	Good topic sentences; enough supporting details	Adequate topic sentences; some supporting details	Some weak topic sentences; needs more supporting details	Missing some topic sentences and details	No topic sentences; few supporting details
Voice	Strongly interested, informed voice	Interested, informed voice	Voice generally interested, informed	Voice somewhat interested	Vaguely interested voice	Uninterested or uninformed voice
Word Choice	Many vivid, precise words used effectively	Vivid, precise words used well	Some vivid, precise words	One or two vivid, precise words	Few vivid, precise words	No vivid, precise words
Sentences	Clear and varied sentences	Mostly clear sentences; good variety	Generally clear sentences; some variety	Sentences not always clear; needs more variety	Some unclear sentences	Incoherent sentences; no variety
Conventions	Few, if any, errors	Several minor errors	Some errors	A few errors	Several errors	Numerous errors

Rubric	5	4	3	2	1
Focus/Ideas	Exposition with strong focus on topic	Exposition with good focus on topic	Exposition generally focused	Exposition with weak focus	Exposition with no focus
Organization/ Paragraphs	Strong topic sentences; many supporting details	Good topic sentences; enough supporting details	Adequate topic sentences; some supporting details	Missing some topic sentences and details	No topic sentences; few supporting details
Voice	Strongly interested, informed voice	Interested, informed voice	Voice generally interested, informed	Vaguely interested voice	Uninterested or uninformed voice
Word Choice	Many vivid, precise words used effectively	Vivid, precise words used well	Some vivid, precise words	Few vivid, precise words	No vivid, precise words
Sentences	Clear, varied sentences	Mostly clear sentences; good variety	Generally clear sentences; some variety	Some unclear sentences; little variety	Incoherent sentences; no variety
Conventions	Few, if any, errors	Several minor errors	Some errors	Several errors	Numerous errors

Rubric	4	3	2	1
Focus/Ideas	Exposition with strong focus on topic	Exposition generally focused on topic	Exposition that needs sharper focus	Exposition with no focus
Organization/ Paragraphs	Strong topic sentences; many supporting details	Good topic sentences; some supporting details	Missing some topic sentences and details	No topic sentences; few supporting details
Voice	Strongly interested, informed voice	Interested, informed voice	Vaguely interested voice	Uninterested or uninformed voice
Word Choice	Many vivid, precise words	Some vivid, precise words	Few vivid, precise words	No vivid, precise words
Sentences	Clear, varied sentences	Mostly clear sentences; some variety	Some unclear sentences; little variety	Incoherent sentences; no variety
Conventions	Few, if any, errors	Several minor errors	Several errors	Numerous errors

Self-Evaluation Guide

Name _____

Name of Writing Product _____

Directions Review your final draft. Then rate yourself on a scale from 4 to 1 (4 is the highest) on each writing trait. After you fill out the chart, answer the questions.

Writing Traits	4	3	2	1
Focus/Ideas				
Organization/Paragraphs				
Voice				
Word Choice				
Sentences				
Conventions				

1. What is the best part of this piece of writing? Why do you think so?

   _____

   _____

   _____

   _____

2. Write one thing you would change about this piece of writing if you had the chance to write it again.

   _____

   _____

   _____

   _____

Self-Evaluation Guide

Name _____

Name of Writing Product _____

Directions Review your final draft. Then rate yourself on each writing feature. After you fill out the chart, answer the questions.

Features

	4	3	2	1
Focus				
Organization				
Support and Elaboration				
Style				

	2	1	0
Conventions			

1. What is the strongest part? Why do you think it is good?

_____

_____

_____

_____

_____

2. What would you change about this piece of writing if you had the chance to write it again? Elaborate on one change you would make.

_____

_____

_____

_____

_____

Title

Characters

Problem

Beginning _____

_____

_____

Middle _____

_____

_____

End _____

_____

_____

Solution

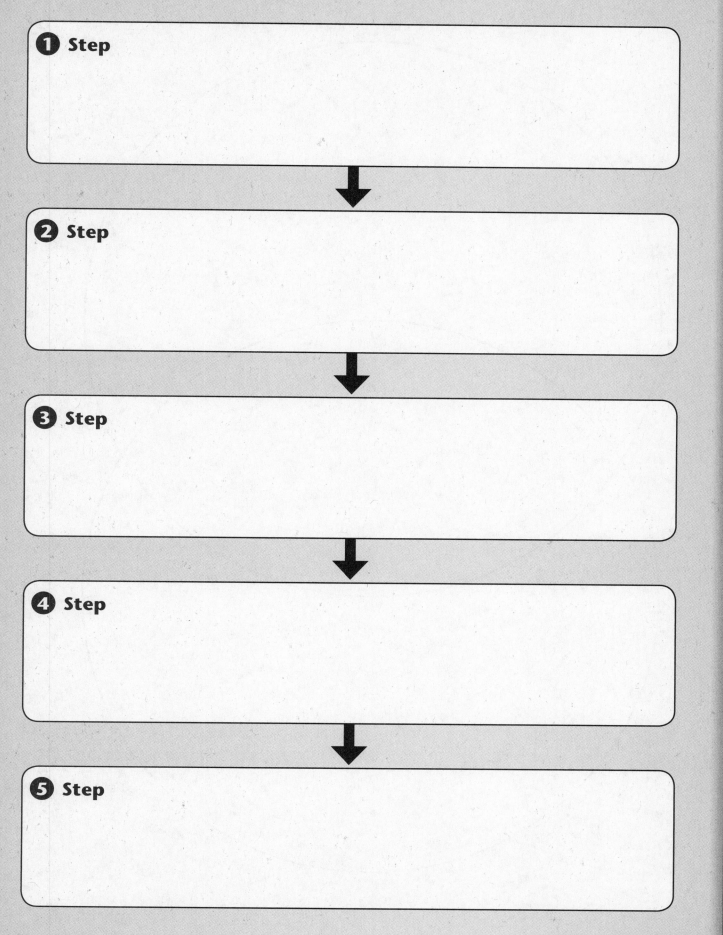

1 Step

2 Step

3 Step

4 Step

5 Step

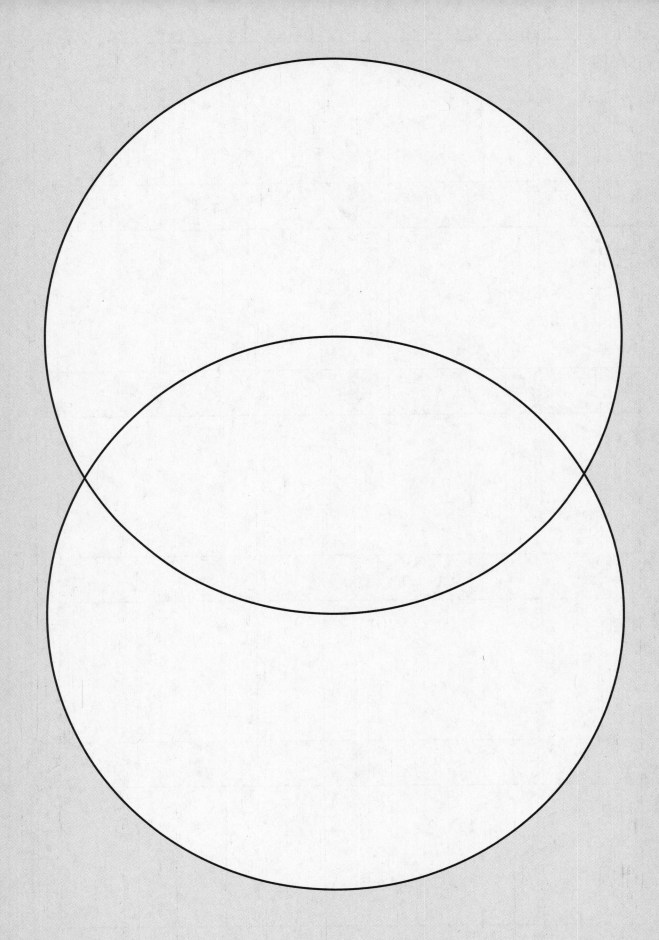

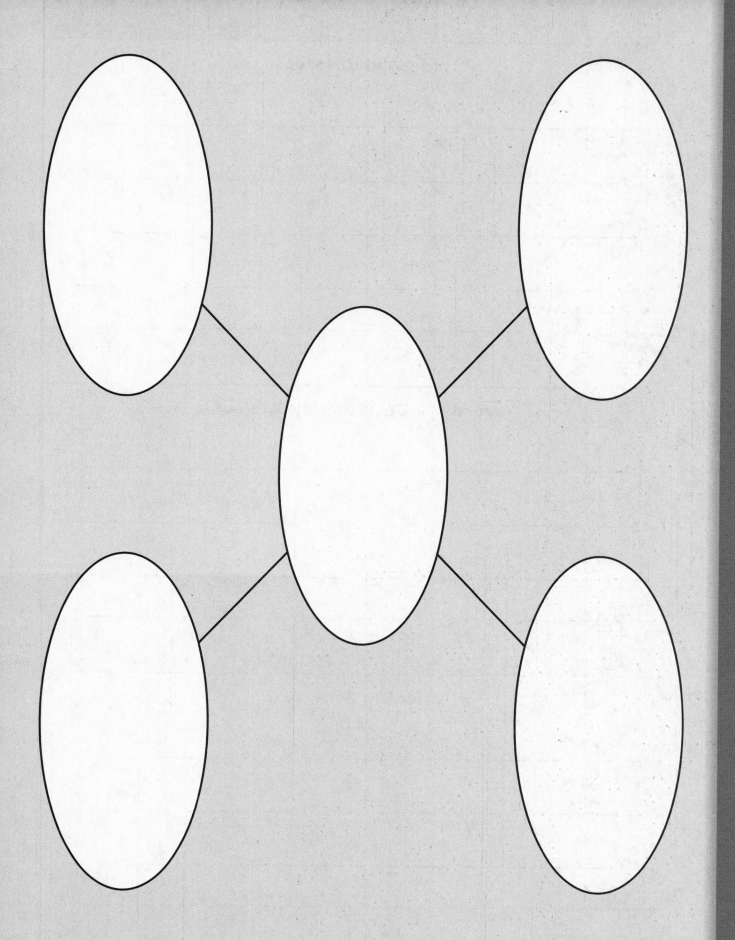

Ideas and Notes

_____

_____

_____

_____

Words to Describe My Subject

_____   _____

_____   _____

_____   _____

Opening Sentence

_____

_____

_____

Answer Key

Page 3 Possible answer
Exercise C

I love playing outdoors in winter. I sled down the hill with my friends. We make snowpeople in our yards. We build a snow fort too. We can do these things only when it is cold and snowy, so winter is my favorite time of year.

Page 7 Possible answer
Exercise C

My family and I went to the art museum. First, we took the train into the city. Then we stood in line to buy tickets. We looked at paintings and sculptures. Then we had a snack in the museum restaurant. Finally, we took the train back home.

Page 11 Possible answer
Exercise C

If your brothers and sisters drive you nuts, here are some tips for getting along with them. First, never go in your sister's room. Then she will never get mad about things you borrowed and forgot to return. Second, always let your little brother sit in the front seat of the car. Then he can't pull your hair from the backseat.

Page 19 Possible answers
Exercise B

5. Above the mountains, a big orange moon glowed brightly.

6. In the forest, a gentle wind rustled the leaves.

7. Just before sunrise, a bird began singing.

8. Once again a new day was beginning.

Exercise C

Mr. Ramirez and his little dog, Shorty, are best friends. Each day they walk to the park together. They are never apart. Shorty even goes to the library with his owner!

Page 23 Possible answers

Exercise B

   6. Last summer Melinda went to Hawaii.

   7. Did she write you a postcard?

   8. The blue ocean and white sand make the islands beautiful.

   9. Rainforests, beaches, and mountains attract many tourists.

   10. Don't you want to visit our 50th state?

Exercise C

   I collect seashells. I began collecting them last year when my family went to the beach in South Carolina. I have shells of many sizes, shapes, and colors.

Page 54 Possible answer

Last Exercise

   Being a gold miner would have been awesome! I bet I could have found plenty of gold and had fun doing it. I would have been one of the first people at the gold rush in California, so I would have gotten tons of gold before others came to take it.

Page 78 Answers

Exercise 1

   1. I jumped out of bed.

   2. The lake shimmered like glass.

   3. The kids chattered and cheered.

   4. Canoes were packed with tents and food.

Exercise 2

   Everywhere I look, I see green. I can hardly walk without running into lush flowers, plants, and tree limbs. The air feels warm and damp and smells like a hothouse full of flowers. Playful screams from birds and monkeys fill the humid air.

Page 81 Answers

Exercise B

Common Nouns:
1. birds
2. birds, winter
3. home, ocean
4. destination
5. sea, source, food

Proper Nouns:
Antarctica
South Pole

South America

Page 84 Possible answers

1. Penguins no longer fly. Now they have flippers and webbed feet that make them strong swimmers.

2. Whales, seals, and birds live in the Antarctic Ocean and along the coast of Antarctica. Many of them eat squid and other fish from the ocean.

3. Antarctica is unusual because it is almost totally covered and surrounded by ice and snow.

Page 99 Possible answers

Exercise C

11. The horse's colt ran away.
12. A cow's moo was heard throughout the farm.
13. The barn's roof was leaking.
14. A worker's coat hung on the peg.
15. The field's wildflowers had attracted the little horse.
16. The tractor's tires got stuck in the mud.
17. The hen's chicks pecked at the ground.
18. The house's windows face east.

Page 105 Possible answers

Exercise C

13. In Florida, roofs' materials must hold up in hurricanes.

14. The cities' houses were tall and narrow.

15. The lawns' landscaping was green and lush.

16. Neighborhoods' differences make them interesting.

17. Families' sizes can determine the kinds of houses they live in.

18. The children's wishes included a big backyard and rooms of their own.

Page 108 Possible answer

My cat Sam pounces on his toy mouse. He hisses and growls when he sees the cat next door. He gobbles his food.

Page 141 Answers

Exercise C

10. The government sold planes from World War I. They were made of wood and cloth.

11. Charles Lindbergh flew nonstop across the Atlantic Ocean. He was the first to do this alone.

12. Amelia Earhart flew across the Atlantic Ocean nonstop. She flew in a plane called *Friendship*.

Page 156 Possible answers

1. The first sentence creates a vivid image. The next two sentences create suspense by making readers ask questions such as *Who is* we? *Where are they? Why have they gone there?*

2. As huge waves of foamy water washed over my head, I tried to recall how I had gotten myself into this mess.

3. A Grizzly Experience

4. A loud *knock, knock, knock* sounded five feet above my head. Meanwhile, the bushes near the fence crackled and rustled as if a wild animal was barging into the yard.

Page 192 Possible answer

Exercise 2

It is important to eat a good breakfast. First, eating breakfast helps you wake up in the morning. Also, you have an empty stomach after not eating since last night. Most important, a nourishing breakfast gives you energy for working and playing all morning long.

Page 219 Possible answers

Exercise C

11. My favorite hobbies are reading, collecting rocks, and playing soccer.

12. I turned 6 on May 7, 2003.

13. I was born in Nairobi, Kenya.

14. I like math, and I also like science.

15. I like ants outdoors, but I don't like them in the house.

Page 222 Possible answer

Last Exercise

Many ants are black or brown, and some ants are rusty red like autumn leaves. Ants may be the size of a pinhead, or they may be more than an inch long.